EASY ACTION

The Original Alice Cooper Band

Martin Popoff

EASY ACTION

The Original Alice Cooper Band

Martin Popoff

WYMER
PUBLISHING
Bedford, England

First published in 2018 as part of Welcome To My Nightmare: 50 Years of Alice Cooper
Wymer Publishing
Bedford, England www.wymerpublishing.co.uk
Tel: 01234 326691
Wymer Publishing is a trading name of Wymer (UK) Ltd

Copyright © Wymer Publishing / Martin Popoff 2022

ISBN: 978-1-912782-09-7
(also available in eBook)

Edited by Stephen Francis

The Author hereby asserts his rights to be identified
as the author of this work in accordance with sections
77 to 78 of the Copyright, Designs & Patents Act 1988.

All rights reserved. No part of this publication may be
reproduced or transmitted in any form or by any means,
electronic or mechanical, including photocopying, or any
information storage and retrieval system, without written
permission from the publisher.

This publication is sold subject to the condition that it shall not,
by way of trade or otherwise, be lent, re-sold, hired out or
otherwise circulated without the publishers prior consent in any
form of binding or cover other than that in which it is published
and without a similar condition including this condition
being imposed on the subsequent purchaser.

Every effort has been made to trace the copyright holders of the
photographs in this book but some were unreachable. We would
be grateful if the photographers concerned would contact us.

Typeset by Andy Bishop / 1016 Sarpsborg
Printed by CMP, Dorset, England.

A catalogue record for this book is available from the British Library.

Cover design: Andy Bishop / 1016 Sarpsborg
Front cover image © Pictorial Press Ltd / Alamy Stock Photo

Contents

Preface	7
1940 – 1959	11
1960 – 1964	15
1965 – 1969	21
1970	63
1971	83
1972	107
1973	139
1974	197
Discography	215
Sources	220
About the Author	221
Martin Popoff – A Complete Bibliography	223

Preface

Welcome one and all to *Easy Action: The Original Alice Cooper Band*, a book that amounts to a detailed timeline and oral history of a band called Alice Cooper that existed from 1968 until 1974, hard stop.

Now, before we go any further, let me explain. What you now hold in your hands is the first of a two-volume project that represents an expanded version of my previous book *Welcome to My Nightmare: Fifty Years of Alice Cooper*, cracked in two. The second volume, forthcoming, will be called *Feed My Frankenstein: Alice Cooper, the Solo Years*.

The having and then calving of that monster of a book has been an exercise that has been particularly satisfying, because it seems that rock 'n' roll fans old and new alike regularly need reminding that there once was a band called Alice Cooper, consisting of Neal Smith on drums, Dennis Dunaway on bass, Glenn Buxton and Michael Bruce on guitars and Alice Cooper on vocals. Alice was legally just ol' Vincent Damon Furnier, but then right away he had this stage name that awkwardly doubled with that of the name of the band. Once solo, he would legally change his name to Alice Cooper and the vision would become clearer, from the outside and *From the Inside*. So yes, beginning with *Welcome to My Nightmare* in 1975, that's where we get Alice as a solo artist, carving for himself a distinguished career with many albums and tours, but making a hard break with the original band, save for bits of writing and recording and playing live much later, in fact relatively recently.

To reiterate, it's good for me and my own soul and good for the history books as well that I was able to bust the old book in two, and that the word counts with respect to where to make the break worked out quite nicely toward the fashioning of two tomes of sensible length.

In fact what's funny is how the current volume ends in 1974 and the second one covers nearly 40 years, and that both are roughly the same size. In that light, *Easy Action* demonstrates just how much intense activity the original Alice Cooper group got up to in a short space of time. In fact, I consider these guys the best exemplar of that often blathered trope that bands in the '70s "were contracted to put out two records a year." In fact it's quite rare that we saw that sort of output, but Alice Cooper came pretty darn close. And even when it wasn't technically two records a year, what you're going to find in the reading of this book is that the band was incredibly busy between records, getting up to way more than just tours, but rather feeding one of the most accomplished publicity machines of the era.

What complicates matters further is that this was a really successful band in the early '70s, meaning that whatever the guys were up to, it was hectic and frenzied, with the boys worked to near exhaustion by Shep and Joe who constantly were demanding more, more and more. In fact the workload would catch up with the guys. In particular Glen Buxton and Alice himself would turn into drunk, mental wrecks by the time of the tired last record of the run, *Muscle of Love*. There was a difference though: Alice could still function while Glen couldn't, but give it a few years, and Alice would wind up perilously near death, thinned to a skeleton because of crack cocaine—in 1983, booze was the least of his problems.

But to be sure, the story told in *Easy Action* is a fascinating and mostly cheery one, with a rich history beginning in the mid-1960s and into the glam cauldron that was Los Angeles at the turn of the decade and then over to hard-hitting Detroit where the guys would toughen up and subsequently have no problem competing with the likes of MC5, The Stooges and the Amboy Dukes.

It's really hard to believe as I write this, that most of the plot and narrative of this book happens within a whirlwind of three to four years. Again, if it wasn't successful, it would've been a different story, but the record sales, ticket sales—and perhaps more importantly, the notoriety and everlasting legend—that these guys created across the likes of *Love It to Death*, *Killer*, *School's Out* and *Billion Dollar Babies* set Alice up for life. Essentially what happened was that the brand so dramatically outsized the band that the success of *Welcome to My Nightmare* was almost assured. And then Alice and his new band, aided and abetted by the steady stewardship of manager Shep Gordon and the enthusiasm of producer Bob Ezrin, turned in a critically acclaimed record and an elaborate, exciting tour to go with it. This of course sealed the deal, with Alice never looking back, changing it up regularly, but benefiting for evermore from the brand made strong by the original Alice Cooper band.

Again, that's why the idea of having a book dedicated to the accomplishments of those five guys as a team is so satisfying for me as a documenter of this music—to this day, at any given Alice Cooper show, as the night progresses toward the end and the encores, it's the songs written and recorded in the early '70s that are yanked from the bag of tricks to drive fans crazy.

Just a quick note on process, for those of you who aren't familiar with my timeline technique (which I've used probably more than 20 times now) when I didn't know a specific date for an entry, that entry goes at the front, in sort of two different ways. As an example, 1973 goes before January 1973 or October 1973. Second, October 10, 1973, or October 28, 1973, goes before October 1973. You might see the use of the seasons as well, or late or early in the year. This is designed so that I could pop those entries into closer and more faithful chronological order. Things like the span of time representing a tour or tour leg, those entries are naturally put at the date of the first concert.

Otherwise there are brief introductory comments to start off each decade, and at the end I've provided a simple discography of the studio albums, including one outlier, the *Greatest Hits* album. I also tinkered with the timeline a little bit at the end of 1974, selecting a few entries but leaving others out, in the construction of the break between this book and the second volume, *Feed My Frankenstein*. The reason for this is to situate the stuff relating to the *Greatest Hits* album and the *Good to See You Again, Alice Cooper* video in the current volume, given that they pertain to the original Alice Cooper group and not the solo years.

Another characteristic of this busting of the old book into two is that you're going to find that in the second book, there will be substantial material related to the members of the Alice Cooper group that are not about the person Alice Cooper, most notably quite a bit of detail on the band called Billion Dollar Babies and their album *Battle Axe*. What's kind of cool is that the subtitle of that second book, *Alice Cooper, the Solo Years*, works quite well with this concept, in that you can look at it as what it *mostly* is, i.e., the story of what the guy Alice Cooper got up to from late 1974 through to 2022. But indeed, if you take the term Alice Cooper to refer to the name of the band, it still works, given that the second book is really the story of what all the guys got up to with respect to their solo careers and other bands. It's just that, as history would have it, 85.79% of the word count of *Feed My Frankenstein* is all about Ol' Black Eyes, because he is a force of nature that cannot be contained.

Happily, I can report that this is not the case with *Easy Action*, because the other thing you'll realize by the end of this exercise is that the original Alice Cooper group is about as close to the idea of a band operating as a tight-knit family that you'll ever witness in the history of rock 'n' roll. This is the story of a gang groomed in high school, galvanized by a single and unwavering mission. Happily again, I can report that judging by the mania that was the *Billion Dollar Babies* record and attendant near apocalyptic tour cycle, one would have to assess that for Alice, Michael, Glen, Dennis and Neal, this was a fulsome case of mission accomplished.

Martin Popoff
Martinpopoff.com, martinp@inforamp.net

1940 – 1959

Given that we are just starting this journey and you've just heard from me at length, I'm not going to say much here, in this first intro by major year grouping. Suffice to say Alice finds himself bumping and scraping his way through a childhood that serves as a microcosm for his future life as busy as any human being's ever, bar none, redundancy intended.

His colourful parents, salt of the earth, nonetheless live on the edge of getting by and they move around for the sake of Alice's health. He and his sisters soak in American culture, participate in the world and generally have a childhood stuffed with American apple pie but also a modicum of drama. All of this will serve Alice well as he throws himself into American cultural life while simultaneously throwing American cultural life into his life's work.

December 14, 1942. Richard Allen "Dick" Wagner is born, in Oelwein, Iowa.

December 9, 1946. Dennis Dunaway is born in Cottage Grove, Oregon.

September 23, 1947. Neal Smith is born in Akron, Ohio.

November 10, 1947. Glen Buxton is born in Akron, Ohio.

February 4, 1948. Vincent "Alice Cooper" Damon Furnier (middle name being a nod to writer Damon Runyon) is born at the Saratoga Community Hospital (a.k.a. "the butcher shop") in northeast Detroit, Michigan, to parents Ether and Ella Mae. The Furniers would soon move to Los Angeles to try help with Vincent's infantile asthma, shortly after which they would be back in east Detroit, a multi-cultural area of Italians, Poles and Irish, where Alice's dad was "an honest used car salesman."

March 25, 1949. Producer-to-be Robert Alan "Bob" Ezrin is born, in Toronto, Canada.

1951. The Furniers move to Phoenix, again, the idea being that the dry heat would be good for Vincent. Alice was regularly using an inhaler for his blocked bronchial tubes. Alice's father also had battled asthma. The Dunaways also leave Oregon and move to Phoenix.

1953. The Furniers move back to Detroit again for a few years. When he wasn't playing baseball or going to the movies, Alice would gather up a few friends and would play-act as Davy Crockett, who was all the rage in the mid-'50s. Abbott and Costello, Dean Martin and Jerry Lewis were also favourites, as well as a scary radio show called *Lights Out*.

Alice on his deep roots in horror:
When I was a kid, when I was seven years old, eight years old in Detroit, my parents would drop me off at the movies every Saturday and it was The Creature from the Black Lagoon, It Came from Outer Space, *and* The Thing. *They dropped me off at the movies in the morning and they'd pick us up when the sun was going down. There was nothing cooler than horror movies on Saturday, and that just stayed with me. When* The Twilight Zone *came out I went... if you really look at* The Twilight Zone, *it was a 30-minute story with a bizarre little ironic ending in it, and I started thinking why couldn't that be a song? Why couldn't a song do that?*

September 14, 1955. Little Richard records "Tutti Frutti," which features a fairly extreme vocal, although the song is piano-centric. Little Richard's first album wouldn't arrive until 1957. Elvis includes his version of "Tutti Frutti" on his January 31, 1956 self-titled debut album.

1956. Screamin' Jay Hawkins issues "I Put a Spell on You." Soon after, Alan Freed paid Hawkins $300 to emerge from a coffin on stage and thereafter the act incorporated horror or "shock rock" tropes like rubber snakes and his trademark smoking skull, prompting the tag "the black Vincent Price." Hawkins therefore is very much an antecedent to Alice Cooper and even King Diamond and Marilyn Manson.

Neal Smith:
Talk about outrageous costumes. I mean, he came right out of the

voodoo world almost. He had the snakes and all the Cajun stuff going on. He had great rhythms and tremendous stage presence. I mean, I hate to say it, being the owner of Kachina on the Killer *album, but he was the first one that I know of that has a snake onstage. He would wear a snake on the stage. For what he did back in the day, he was probably as outrageous in his time as Alice Cooper was and still is in that style of music. Definitely one of the pioneers.*

Author Gavin Baddeley:
Screamin' Jay Hawkins is a very significant figure in a number of respects. I mean he's been called the goth father, the forefather of goth, because he's the first guy who introduced us this really macabre element to all his stage shows. Obviously you can always go further back, but he's the first high-profile guy who starts coming out of coffins with a skull called Henry and singing about cannibalism and voodoo and so forth.

He's also been identified as the forefather of shock rock, and I think there's a large element of truth there. It's easy to underestimate how shocking some of this stuff was in the 1950s. The song which he's best known for, "I Put a Spell on You," originally was supposed to be a much more soft and seductive number and they just couldn't get it right. And so in the end they ended up getting absolutely plastered while recording this and rolling about on the floor singing this song, which had now turned into this really sinister black magic evocation. Well that's one interpretation and it's the one I favour. And again the story goes that when he recorded it, he actually had to listen to the record again in order to re-learn the song because he couldn't remember what in the hell he'd done.

But also the other factor, which is happily less relevant now, is that he was a black performer. And so alongside "I Put a Spell on You" with the voodoo elements, which again some people might refer to as racist—I'm not sure they were—he's also singing a song about the Mau Mau. The Mau Mau were this quasi-mystical revolutionary movement in Kenya active in the 1950s, secret society, who in trying to throw off the British colonial yolk committed quite a lot of atrocities. So a guy singing about this stuff would, you know, push a few buttons among frightened white Americans, and certainly frightened white British people.

Screamin' Jay Hawkins never really received the material benefits from his career that he probably should have, but he has influenced a hell of a lot of artists. I mean, "I Put a Spell on You" has been covered by so many bands, including Marilyn Manson. Everybody remembers the skull in the coffin, but there's also things like "Constipation Blues." And later in his career he took to wheeling a toilet out onstage, which is certainly an indication of being willing to go the extra mile to grab people's attention.

September 9, 1956. Elvis Presley appears for the first time on *The Ed Sullivan Show.*

Alice Cooper:
I was seven, eight years old when I first saw Elvis on *Ed Sullivan*, and I went oh, that's cool. Of course I dug Elvis. I was at that age where rock 'n' roll was just starting. Little Richard, great. Little Richard was unbelievable. Chuck Berry, still the best lyricist to this day. Anybody that would make up a word like botheration; if he didn't have a word, he would just make one up. Don't give me no botheration. I said oh, you can do that.

All those guys were very theatrical. More theatrical than bands today, even, which is a little confusing to me. It seems like in the '70s when we started, there was an Elton John that was Elton John. He was a character unto himself. Bowie was a character unto himself. Alice was a character. And now it seems like bands want to blend in rather than stand out, so it's very bizarre. So yeah those bands did influence us, but not as much as the Beatles.

Spring 1958. The Furniers move for a short time to Los Angeles. Even though Alice's grandfather, Thurman, was an evangelist, his parents are not yet full embracers of the Christian faith, although in LA, they start going to church. Alice's father, Ether, would get work in LA at the Jet Propulsion Laboratory, brought into the fold by Alice's flamboyant "Rat Packer" Uncle Lefty Ronson. Alice's other uncle on his dad's side owned a pool hall in Detroit, plus boxed and played a little guitar.

1960 - 1964

Summing up ruthlessly, one might say that the two most important events in shaping Alice — and in one case, literally scarring him — are his near-death experience of almost dying from burst insides and the emergence of The Beatles, on the radio and on *Ed Sullivan*.

Along with that, young wise-cracking Vincent Furnier, meets his future band mates, and before this period of high school years is out, they've put on a show as a fake band and then at the very end of 1964, as a real band. Both ends of that duality bear some significance, given that what will become the Alice Cooper group is both a theatrical thing and a musical thing.

February 1961. The Buxtons leave the rust belt and move to Phoenix. Coincidentally, this month also represents the opening in the local JC building of Jack Curtis' VIP club, where the future Alice Cooper band boys would hone their act. With a capacity of about 400, Curtis tended to pack 700 kids in the place.

April 1961. Alice's father Ether Furnier is ordained as a minister.

May 1961. The Furniers move from LA back to Phoenix, Alice's father taking a job with Goodyear Aerospace where he continues to work with top secret military technology. Soon he will put this career path behind him and become a pastor, working with the local Apache community. Alice's life revolved around baseball and church, which he attended three days a week.

July 4, 1961. Young Vincent Furnier almost dies when it's discovered that his appendix had burst, sealed over, and seeped poison into his system gradually, gravely infecting most of his organs. After throwing up green for two days he's admitted to hospital with acute peritonitis. Doctors, who didn't think Alice would survive, immediately drain three quarts of infected fluid from him while they quickly consider how to save his failing organs.

Cooper would be in hospital for three months, amusing himself every evening by watching the six o'clock dust storm out of his south-facing window, as well as commandeering the first TV remote control he'd ever encountered. Already a light 80 pounds going in, Alice eventually emerges from hospital for more convalescence at 68 pounds and losing his hair as well. Sports was out of the question, driving Alice nuts, as he ate a regular regimen of steak and beats to get iron back into his blood. A year later, doctors open Alice up again and remove his appendix.

August 25, 1962. Bobby "Boris" Pickett & The Crypt-Kickers merges horror and (lite) rock with perennial Halloween favourite "Monster Mash." Two weeks later it is banned by the BBC as offensive.

September 1962. Vincent, 14 years old, enrols at Cortez High School where he excelled at long-distance running. Meanwhile, the Buxtons move house, resulting in Glen enrolling in Cortez as well. Alice is getting well enough to try his hand at long-distance running, which he and Dennis do together to great success, writing song parodies together as they trot through the desert.

Dennis Dunaway:
Glen was just a natural born rebel. The very first time I went over to his house he was sleeping late because it wasn't a school morning and I thought, "Man, its afternoon and he's still asleep." His mom just pointed to his room. So I go in and I open the door and it's all dark except for this one little orange light and there's just a foot sticking out from under the blanket. This was in Arizona so you hardly ever saw a dark room during the day, but he had tin foil on his windows and stuff. He had been partying the night before and that's kind of how it always was.

March 22, 1963. Beatles' first album, *Please Please Me* is issued, featuring the likes of "Twist and Shout" and "I Saw Her Standing There."

September 16, 1963. The Beatles "She Loves You" is issued as a single in the US. Alice remembers this as the first Beatles song he had ever heard, on the radio while up a ladder painting the house with his mother. The Furniers had just bought their first house in a new development where the houses were an astronomical $10,000 but $9000 if you painted it yourself. Soon from the radio came "I Saw Her Standing There" and more Beatles as they painted. Alice calls up Dennis the next day after seeing a picture of the Beatles in the paper and the two discuss.

Alice Cooper:
When the Beatles happened I was 15; the Rolling Stones, how great is that? The Kinks. We're starting to see hair now coming down to the shoulders and I was just at that age going, "Absolutely, that's exactly what I want to do."

Michael Bruce:
I walked into high school one day, and they were playing "She Loves You" and I was mesmerized. I hadn't heard anything about the Beatles and I heard them playing that record. I had been taking a little piano and I had been playing a little acoustic guitar as a folk singer, and when I heard that, I just decided, that's what I'm gonna do (laughs). So I went out and got an electric guitar and started; you know, locked myself away, basically inside my place every night and learned all the Beatles songs I could. And I kind of learned how to write from listening to them as well.

January 11, 1964. The Whiskey A Go Go opens in West Hollywood, at 8901 Sunset Strip.

February 9, 1964. The Beatles perform on CBS' *The Ed Sullivan Show*, playing five songs. The monumental rock 'n' roll event may not have directly invented heavy metal, but it sure inspired scores of future hard rock musicians—and musicians of many ilk, among the shows estimated 73 million viewers—to pick up a guitar and play.

Spring 1964. Vincent Furnier, Dennis Dunaway, Glen Buxton, along with school chums John Speer and John Tatum, perform as The Earwigs at the Letterman Talent Show at their school, Cortez High School in Phoenix, Arizona. The band simply mimed to the Beatles, but they are bitten hard by the rock 'n' roll bug. As Alice says, nobody talked about baseball anymore; it was all about the Beatles. John Speer quickly started learning how to play drums, Dennis picked up the bass, and Alice, inspired by "Love Me Do," learned harmonica.

The Earwigs circa 1965

May 11, 1964. The Beach Boys issue "I Get Around" as a single. To this day it's Alice Cooper's favourite song.

Summer 1964. Dennis works on his grandfather's farm near Creswell, Oregon to raise enough money to buy his first bass guitar.

Early October 1964. The Earwigs perform their first shows with real instruments, at lunch hour at Cortez High School.

October 23, 1964. The band play their first real gig, the Pit and the Pendulum dance at the guys' high school, Cortez.

Dennis Dunaway:
The very first gig that the band did, before we became Alice Cooper, we played in 1964, a Halloween dance at Cortez High School, and at that gig we had giant spider webs on the stage that we made out of clothesline and we had a coffin that we made out of cardboard that we painted and everything, because Alice and I were in art class together. And we had a ghoul that came out with makeup who came out of the coffin between songs, and then he would do some shtick while we were deciding what song we were going to do next.

    Because I guess we knew about theatrics but we didn't know about a song list then (laughs). And we had a working—a small—but still working guillotine that a friend of ours from high school, his father was a carpenter and we got him to build that for us. So we had all of those elements already in '64. And by the time we got to Zappa and stuff, we had a million of those kinds of ideas. We just didn't have any money to do it, to do any of our ideas at that point. But shocking the audience came along before the name Alice Cooper. Alice Cooper was just the crème de la crème of our ideas of getting attention.

    Our influences had a lot more to do with art. Alice and I were big enthusiasts of the Dada art movement and the surrealists, and a lot of it came from how those artists did their happenings. You know, Salvador Dali was known for having these events where he would get all these people together and then he would do something crazy, and that had more to do with it than any bands, I think, except maybe The Who, because they smashed their guitars and we thought that was exciting. So that was of course when we saw the vision of bringing theatrics to rock 'n' roll.

    People talk about Screamin' Jay Hawkins or Screaming Lord Sutch. I mean, it does seem like an obvious influence, and I really don't like it when bands deny their obvious influences. So I'm not doing that, but we really didn't. We weren't aware of Lord Sutch at all, and Screamin' Jay Hawkins was just a very vague thing. I mean, we had heard his name, but it wasn't like we said, 'Oh yeah, this guy is creepy; let's do that' (laughs). Ours came more from just, actually, it came from the Halloween dance in '64. So we did a Halloween dance and we thought this is great and it just stuck. I mean, to this day Alice still uses those exact same elements in his show. So it was just because it was Halloween and then every day was Halloween. That particular show was on Halloween, but after that, we enjoyed doing that so much that it kept coming back.

1965 - 1969

During this period, rock grows from adolescence to bed-headed teenager-dom. Acid hits the scene and we get the likes of Cream, The Doors, The Grateful Dead and Pink Floyd, and then on a heavier tip, Blue Cheer and Led Zeppelin. The Spiders do their largest period of grind and woodshedding, '65, '66, and become The Nazz in '67. By March of 1968, the band is renamed Alice Cooper, with Neal Smith rounding out the original lineup when he moves in with the guys at one of a few different band houses in this period, December of 1967.

Things quickly heat up, with notorious gigs about town resulting in an almost adversarial relationship with the rock establishment, led by Bill Graham and the psych bands from LA and San Francisco who find the band's use of props offensive. But the hippie generation is about to get dark, the perfect environment in which a band like Alice Cooper might translate, connect, flourish. The Manson murders happen in August of 1969 and the Altamont concert results in violence and one death, into September of '69, with the Rolling Stones framed as evil, Mick as an out-of-touch shaman and the Hells Angels suddenly less glamourous.

Over in Detroit, Dick Wagner puts out a record with his band The Frost, The Stooges debut with a self-titled, MC5 proposes a slashing and burning live album in *Kick Out the Jams*, and Creem magazine is born, all of this happening in 1969.

In Alice Cooper world, the band audition for Frank Zappa in July of 1968, quickly pick up a couple of on-the-make managers in Shep Gordon and Joe Greenberg and by November are recording their debut album. Into 1969, Frank has his new label going, Straight Records, along with his first act for it, a band he essentially humours, just like The GTOs, Wild Man Fischer and on some level, his own Mothers of Invention.

Alice Cooper begin touring across North America and into Canada as their debut album, *Pretties for You*, emerges. The album is pretty much a late-fer-dinner slice of psychedelic rock, but there's something different about the look of the band—arguably, they are the first rock stars, if of an easily dismissed ilk, because the music doesn't quite back the bravado, the long hair, the flashy clothes, the visual assault of five of these in front of your eyes. Again, with the hippie generation growing cranky, strung-out and violent, it all makes sense, even if L.A.'s furry freaks would gather enough indignation to—as the story frames it—kick Alice Cooper to the curb, where they would gather up their meagre possessions for a move to Detroit.

February 9, 1965. The Earwigs play at the Washington Grad School Talent show.

April 30, 1965. The Earwigs place first at the Sears combo Contest at Chris-Town Mall, in hometown, Phoenix, Arizona.

May 1, 1965. The *Phoenix Gazette* runs a piece on Neal Smith and the Laser Beats. Into the fall, the combo win a battle of the bands. Neal is about to graduate from Camelback High School, which he discusses in the *School's Out* song, "Alma Matter," credited solely to Neal.

Neal Smith:
Ever since the British Invasion I wanted to be in a band. And I started playing drums when I was 12 years old, and it was well after that that the British Invasion happened, and I was just totally knocked out by what was going on. At that time there was shock value with the Rolling Stones compared to like the Beach Boys. Beach Boys were one of these clean-cut bands, American boys, and all of a sudden these rowdies from the UK come over and just make total chaos everywhere. And so I wanted to be part of something like that. I went to a Rolling Stones concert in Phoenix, Arizona, in the mid '60s, and I just couldn't believe the girls around me were screaming and going so crazy. I'm going, well the music's good, I like this band, but I don't get why these girls are doing that, but I like it. I'd like to be part of something like that some day. That was my motivation.

June 13, 1965. The Yardbirds first studio album, a US compilation called *For Your Love*, is released.

Alice Cooper:
We were always Yardbirds-oriented; we were always Who-oriented. And to me that was hard, hard rock. I mean, we just didn't like medium rock.

We liked the Yardbirds because they had out-of-control guitars and they had feedback as part of their leads, and I went, that's good stuff right there and you had Keith Moon kind of drums, and everything was driving. So that was the beginnings of it.

Neal Smith:
We were a product of the British invasion of the mid-'60s. Arizona was a test center for a lot of the British invasion music that came over, before it was released in other parts of the country. So we heard tons of that music and were really aware and bombarded by a lot of bands, including all the bands that didn't make it. There were bands that played in Arizona like The Undertakers, which were a great English band, which never really made it, and The Yardbirds and The Zombies or some of the other great bands from that era that had commercial success. They were like the Stones or The Who, but they still had commercial success with their music and we were lucky to be kind of baptized in fire by that sort of environment musically.

Mid 1965. The Earwigs play their first shows at clubs around hometown Phoenix.

Alice Cooper on the deep bonds within the band:
We went to high school together. We were on the track team together. We were in journalism class together. We went to college together. We went through the Vietnam draft together. We did all that. I accidentally shot Neal when we were out shooting rabbits while we were drunk. There's so much history between us. We starved together, then all of a sudden we went from being the most hated band in LA to the number one band in England. So, how does that happen? We were at the right place with the right stuff.

September 1965. The Spiders issue, on Mascott, their first single, "Hitch Hike" (Marvin Gaye)/"Why Don't You Love Me" (The Blackwells). The band is an ambitious bunch of grounded, regular guys looking for a way to wake people up. The competent garage rock sides are produced by Jack Curtis, working at Audio Recorders of Arizona. Early on, The Spiders carve an identity by being the local band that specialized in The Rolling Stones, ceding Beatle territory to others, such as The Pendletons and The Vibratos. As well, cropping up were Sunnyslope and The Excels, who became The Tubes.

Dennis Dunaway on the band's disparate multimedia influences:
Big influences came from the fact that Alice and I were in art class together in high school. I mean Alice was like 16, 15 and I was 16 when we met. And we were in art class together, we ran long distance, cross country on the same team. We were in English and eventually journalism together. But art had a lot to do with our concepts. Salvador Dali, Dada, and television had a lot to do with it.

There was a local television show in Phoenix, Arizona called Wallace and Ladmo, *which was on for years and years. And when we were little it was called* It's Wallace? *and it was directed toward kids. But as he got older and as his audience grew up, he started getting more and more clever with double entendre. And so college students would tune into the show, and little kids would still laugh at the same joke for a completely different reason.*

But the great influence we got from that, everybody in the Alice Cooper group, like everybody in Phoenix, grew up with Wallace and Ladmo. *But the great thing is whenever their skits would bomb, it was almost better than when it worked because that was the humour of it. And that was an element of our shows—we weren't afraid to bomb. So we would bring out maybe ten props and try them, and if something bombed it didn't matter because there were ten other or nine other props that night. And so we actually got a lot of confidence from that show. And of course there was the horror films and gangster films, Cagney and Bogart—Glen Buxton was heavily into those—Three Stooges, things that sort of fuelled our immaturity throughout our career.*

September 4, 1965. Having transitioned from The Earwigs to The Spiders, the band play a landmark early gig, at Jaycees, the VIP Club, supporting The Yardbirds. By this point, the band had moved on from their Rolling Stones phase and were playing, Alice claims, a dozen Yardbirds songs, which indeed makes up a bunch of the band's set on this night.

Dennis Dunaway:
We opened for the Yardbirds and we all of a sudden decided that the theme of that particular set would be silverware and forks from the cafeteria, or the restaurant at the VIP. So we came out, we had plastic forks stuck in our hair. Glen brought out a tray of forks and spoons and he played slide with a spoon, which he always did from that night forward. Even on songs like "Black Juju," Glen is playing slide with a

spoon. But anyway, he used the spoons onstage and Jeff Beck loved that idea so much that when the Yardbirds went on, Jeff Beck had come over and taken the tray of silverware and he used it when he played. He held his Telecaster up and did triplets, and let gravity bring it down. And then he was throwing spoons and letting them ricochet off the strings.

But that was one set. And then another set, there was a big cast iron old bathtub with the feet on the bottom. I mean this thing weighed a ton. And we decided that Alice would be in front of it pointing like George Washington crossing the Delaware. And so we heave-ho'd this thing up to the stage and Alice climbed onstage and we did our set, he got back in, we heave-ho'd it back to the back room.

It was just always stuff like that. And then eventually we started building props. We built very early on a strobe effect. You used to be able to go to army and navy stores and get these ammunitions canisters that were metal. So we got one of those that had a light in it and cut a hole in the end and put a motor in it so we had this spinning disc with slits cut out of it, and that would do a rolling effect. It was very soothing compared to the erratic effect of the electronic strobes.

One of the things that was bad but we thought was good—bad in the club owner's mind—it would catch on fire every night because it got so hot inside the thing. All this smoke would come out and we thought that was cool, but the club owner was always like... we drove him crazy, this guy Jack Curtis at the VIP Club, who was really the first guy who really believed in the band. But he couldn't fire us over anything because we were packing the place. They were coming to see what we were going to do next.

December 4, 1965. The Spiders and Neal Smith's band, The Laser Beats, play together on the same bill, on Teen-Age Day at the Phoenix Art Museum.

February 1966. The Spiders play three hometown shows in Phoenix, at three different venues, supporting The Byrds.

Dennis Dunaway on keeping people guessing:
We played at this local club in Phoenix, Arizona which was the hottest club going, and we managed to become the house band there. But the ongoing thing that we could see was that they would have a house band for a couple of weeks and they would spit out that week's flavour of gum and get somebody else.

And so I had the idea of, well, let's keep the band changing so much that it doesn't get old. Within two weeks we'd be like a new band. So we started doing theatrics every weekend. We did eight sets a weekend, and we would do something new each weekend, and then that escalated to something each night, and then that got escalated to something each set. So we would go out in the parking lot between sets and find an old tire and bring it up and roll it across the stage or we would come out with toilet paper all over and throw toilet paper into the audience. Just stuff like that. And so we had to keep outdoing ourselves.

Summer 1966. Michael Bruce joins The Spiders, replacing John Tatum.

Michael Bruce:
It's funny, when I went down and auditioned for The Spiders, they were the house band at the VIP Lounge, for a guy named Jack Curtis down on Seventh Street. The Jaycees ran it; it was a place for teens to go on the weekend, Friday, Saturday night, try to keep them out of trouble, steer them away from drugs and all that. And The Spiders, we jokingly called them The Rolling Clones, because that's all they did. But I mean, I really liked the Rolling Stones too—when Brian Jones was in the band still. Between the Buttons, I used to listen to that every day.

Late August 1966. The Spiders venture to Copper State Recording Studios in Tucson to record their second single. While in town, the band plays a gig supporting The Yardbirds.

Dennis Dunaway:
I think back in the early days before we did Pretties for You. *We were quite a good southwest regional garage band. I think we could have knocked out a hit or two like The Music Machine or those bands, and we could have had big success that way, and we could have done it at a time when we really could have used the money. But we chose the artistic direction. We had this driven vision, and that was more important than putting food on the table at the time.*

September 1966. The Spiders issue, on Santa Cruz Records out of Tucson, their second single, the fuzz-rockin' "Don't Blow Your Mind"/"No Price Tag." Both songs are originals, the A-side, at 2:35, credited to Dennis and Alice, the B-side, at 2:06, to Glen and Alice. Meanwhile, Alice signs up for art courses at Glendale Community College.

Dennis Dunaway:
My biggest influences were painters like Dali, Magritte, Ernst and Miro. I've always been an artist and the band was another way of expressing art. It didn't matter what instrument I played. I ended up with bass because everyone else chose their instrument before I did. So in order to learn how to use that tool for expression, I sat down with Glen Buxton and a phonograph and he helped me learn blues patterns from Bill Wyman via Rolling Stones recordings. I learned a lot from McCartney too, but more through listening to his parts rather than playing them. But hearing Paul Samwell-Smith of the Yardbirds made me realize the bass can go anywhere you take it and that concept set me free to pursue my own direction.

Alice Cooper on his brief time at Glendale Community College:
I became a creative writer; I was a journalist. That was one of my... I was a journalism major and an art major also. You put those two things together and you start realizing that the press is your buddy, it's not your enemy. I used to tell the press, look, the more things I do the more it's going to sell your papers, right? I'm your best friend.

January 4, 1967. The Doors issue their self-titled debut album. Jim Morrison and the band would be an influence on the Alice Cooper group, as well as be friends of the band in the late '60s, when they both plied their trade in and around southern California. The Doors never took Alice Cooper on tour, but they did indeed play a few shows together. Robby Krieger remembers one show at a hockey rink (with plywood over the ice surface) in Las Vegas where the band's chickens escaped and they had to jump into the crowd to corral them. The bills with Alice came to be because Doors manager Bill Siddons liked the band. Robbie became one of Alice's early golfing buddies, playing with him in the early '70s at Valencia. Krieger says he was a pretty bad golfer at that time, still drinking a lot, but of course got much better later on. They still play a couple times a year.

Dennis Dunaway:
You're talking about Hollywood in the '60s, so, like everyone in that exciting scene, we ran into tons of bands and actors. Jim Morrison was the only person that ever got away with blocking the view of the television in our house. Anyone else would have gotten yelled at by Glen, Alice and Neal. People that knew us would step quickly around the television. Jim sat on top of it.

March 17, 1967. The Jimi Hendrix Experience's "Purple Haze" is issued as a UK single; recorded January 11 and February 3, at De Lane Lea and Olympic Studios in London, UK.

Late March 1967. The Spiders play their first out-of-state shows, venturing to Los Angeles and Concord, CA.

Spring 1967. Alice quits college as the band starts to take off.

Michael Bruce:
We used to take peyote and drive to this mountain. There was a park there with picnic tables, and there was only one that had electricity. So we'd plug in our amps and we'd take some peyote and just jam all night. Just crazy experimental stuff. And I remember one morning, we saw this thing glowing from behind the mountain, and as it came up, we thought it was the mothership. And as it got higher and higher, the heat from the desert was making it shimmer, you know? And it actually turned out to be, I think, Venus, one of the closest times it was near the Earth. But we were so stoned we thought it was a UFO.

May 12, 1967. Jimi Hendrix Experience's debut *Are You Experienced* is released in the UK. The bar is raised in terms of both guitar pyrotechnics and pyrotechnics.

Mid-1967. The Nazz, or just Nazz, issue a single pairing "Wonder Who's Loving Her Now?" with "Lay Down and Die, Goodbye," both originals. The band is now setting up shop in LA, but the single is recorded at Viv Recording Studios in Phoenix.

August 5, 1967. Pink Floyd's debut album, *The Piper at the Gates of Dawn* is issued.

Neal Smith:
Not a lot of people talk about Charlie Carnell, our light guy. The light show was very flashy. We were influenced by the first time we saw Pink Floyd with Syd Barrett, in Santa Monica at the Cheetah Club, and there were some very cool things they did with lights. So we did a spin of our interpretation of that. The shiny clothes became a format, a background, for the lights to land on. That's what we were thinking. On Pretties for You, *1969, Dennis has a full silver suit on. The clothes were an intricate part of it.*

Michael Bruce:
I loved *Piper at the Gates of Dawn. We met those guys. I was fascinated by their whole trip, the stage show and the lights and whatnot, and we started getting into a little of that ourselves with our band. When Pink Floyd came here, their roadie Les Braden, he stayed in America. He worked with Pink Floyd and he stayed as an illegal immigrant and lived with us and became our roadie/mentor and it worked out just great. And we got to meet Eric Clapton and Jack Bruce — we went up to Jack's room and he played us the song "Wheels of Fire." And we got to hang out with Hendrix, and this was all because this roadie, right?*

August 22 – 27, 1967. The band, now called The Nazz (named for Yardbirds song "The Nazz Are Blue") perform over six nights at the Cheetah Club, in Venice, California. Regular shows continue at that venue through the end of the year.

Late Summer 1967. Neal Smith moves to LA, staying at The Nazz's band house in Santa Monica.

November 5, 1967. Pink Floyd perform two shows at The Cheetah Club, between gigs in San Francisco. They stay at The Nazz band house.

December 1967. Neal Smith replaces John Speer as drummer for The Nazz.

Neal Smith on being the last member of the classic Alice Cooper lineup:
I went to Camelback and everyone else went to Cortez. The other drummer they had was a good friend of mine, and he was a different style of drummer. I was always very much a showman. I always wanted to be the biggest, baddest and the best. Even more than that, I wanted us to be the coolest musicians on the planet. I think ultimately the group Alice Cooper was the hippest band of the era. Nobody was cooler than us.
    I probably fit in with Glen, Dennis and Michael musically better than the other drummer. He was very good, but he had a different philosophy. I have a philosophy about making it, but it was to be a little more experimental with the music and a little more album-oriented music, but still to have the hits. The first time we started going out into the desert we would have a couple of beers and a couple of joints and

just have fun. Alice—he was Vince at the time—was not even there. The other drummer was still in the band and I was just going out to play with some friends. It was nothing more, nor nothing less than that.

Dennis and I were oil and vinegar. We were totally different. When we play together we just know where each of us is going and it is amazing. He makes a change and I make a change and it just flows together. We are on the same wavelength when we are just jamming freestyle on music. I think we are one of the most underrated rhythm sections in rock 'n' roll. The chemistry just gelled better once I was there. I really understood what they were doing.

Early 1968. The Nazz get kicked out of their LA band house and retreat to Phoenix. All five members escape the military draft, Neal most dramatically, after accidentally getting shot in the ankle by Alice. Also in '68, the VIP club ends its seven-year run.

Dennis Dunaway on the band literally fighting their way to acceptance:
Alice and I both went to the draft board and we just dressed the way we always dressed. We dressed crazy all the time, on the street and onstage. And I had a white satin shirt on that had white tassels all over it. And of course people didn't know what to think of that. It didn't even look like something a woman would be properly attired in. The combination of everybody together added up to something where hardly anybody wore anything that anybody had seen someone wear before.

Like Glen Buxton with all of his safety pins holding his pants together was quite a statement, even though it was really a necessity in those days because we didn't have money for food. We spent it all on beer. I mean I had like powder blue boots, I had satin green pants, I had a copper sequin shirt and then my hair was down to my waist. Nobody's hair was as long as ours either. So the ongoing joke with us and Jimi Hendrix—we used to run into him at the Landmark Hotel in Hollywood—was we would make fun of how he dressed, and of course we were dressed at least as crazy as he was.

Back, sure, back then it was shocking, especially where we started out in Phoenix, Arizona. It was tough. A lot of cowboys around, a lot of people that liked to get in fights, and we were the perfect target for everyone. Normally, before we came along, they fought amongst themselves, but when we came along everybody agreed that we were the target.

It was a threat to a lot of people who didn't know what to think of our sexuality. Even though we were heterosexual we didn't look like it at all. So therefore a lot of violent threats came our way and humiliating comments. You couldn't go anywhere. So that actually drew the band into a tighter bonding because we hardly went anywhere unless it was a pack, where all five of us went everywhere together. But the consolation was girls were attracted to it. We didn't anticipate that but we certainly were happy about it.

Elvis got in a lot of fights. He was in the south and he liked to wear pink shirts. Elvis always had that kind of corny element of fighting in all his movies, but that was real. He was down in the south and he was the target that the Alice Cooper group was. I mean when you're in the south, even if you don't dress crazy, even if you tried to conform by cowboy standards, they would find something wrong. "I don't like the way your hat is tilted—what are you going to do about it?"

Confrontation thrived down there. The weekend wasn't successful unless you could go back to work on Monday and talk about a fight you were in. And that's what Elvis came up through. I loved Elvis, I love doo-wop. I'm the age where I was around when all that was happening. Elvis platters were coming out and my babysitters were bopping around the house, and it was quite exciting.

January 1968. Blue Cheer's debut, *Vincebus Eruptum* is released. A shockingly heavy album for its day, it is considered by many to be the first heavy metal album of all time. Here, we will assign it much weight, but deny it that title due to lack of skilfulness, lack of modern metallic flourishes, and assumed lack of visceral heavy metal intention.

February 1968. Dick Wagner's early, heavy band, The Frost, play their first show at the Grande Ballroom.

March 11, 1968. The Nazz relocate to Los Angeles after a couple months back in Phoenix.

Neal Smith:
When we moved to Los Angeles, there were like 20 or 30,000 bands in those days. It was like geez, what do we have to do? First of all, there was already a band called The Nazz, so we had to change the name. So we changed to Alice Cooper and that was a little bit different, and we were always thinking about being memorable more than anything else. We didn't care if people hated us or liked us. We just wanted them

to remember the name Alice Cooper. And the more we sunk into debt and the more we sort of hit a ceiling as far as the amount of money we made, we just got frustrated and we started doing more crazier things.

March 16, 1968. The freshly renamed Alice Cooper play the Earl Warren Showgrounds, in Santa Barbara, California. Also on the bill (somewhat as co-headliners) are Blue Cheer and The Nitty Gritty Dirt Band. The band literally change their name after the typically psychedelic poster advertising the show is printed. They are introduced from the stage as Alice Cooper. A story is floated that Neal dropped acid consulted a Ouija board on who Alice Cooper was and the answer came back, "13th century witch." Never happened, says Alice, who, in his scotching of the myth, says the Ouija session story was attributed to show booker Dick Phillips and his sister. However, the idea was soon played up on press releases, resulting in a gig where a pile of witches showed up to a gig to basically worship with—or worship—Alice, which spooked the band.

Dennis Dunaway:
We were in a blizzard of new band name ideas. But when Vince suggested Alice Cooper, everyone paused. But our image was already triggering lots of threats so we weren't sure if we could survive with that name. And so the blizzard of names continued. But with suggestion after suggestion, the Alice Cooper name kept gaining strength in comparison. When I got home that night, I told my parents that our new name was Alice Cooper, and when I saw the look on their faces, I was sold. So the next night when the band got together, Vince had my added enthusiasm. And everyone agreed on one condition, that Alice Cooper would be the name of our group to be shared equally. And years later, at the band's farm in Pontiac, Michigan, we even signed contracts to legalize that agreement.

Alice Cooper on the new band name:
It was the perfect name for us. We could have been The Husky Baby Sandwich or The Scabs but I said why give it away? Why should we have a scary name? I said we should have a name of the old lady that lives down the street that's the sweetest old lady that knits every day. But you're pretty sure there's bodies buried in the basement. I could have said Betty Smith or anything but I happened to say Alice Cooper. I said a little old lady named Alice Cooper that maybe makes children into pies when nobody knows it. And I thought that's a great name. And then I thought Lizzie Borden, Baby Jane, Alice Cooper. It had a rhythm to it. It had a scary

little sound to it. And people weren't expecting us. When they heard Alice Cooper they thought it was going to be a blonde folk singer, and they got us, you know? I said that's the perfect name. The idea was, let's not be obvious. I said let's make Alice Cooper—which is a perfectly sweet, little old lady—let's make that the scariest name in America.

Neal Smith:
Alice Cooper. What does that mean? It was wide open. It was untamed territory. We could create whatever Alice Cooper was. We could make it a monster, we could make it a lamb, whatever. I liked it myself because it was like The Who. It was a name that was never used before—just a woman's name for a band. And the shock value that we talked about at the time was these five crazy long-haired guys with makeup, shiny clothes and playing loud, weird music and Zappa loved us, was that we'd get onstage and that's Alice Cooper. When they thought a character like Mary Travis from Peter, Paul and Mary would be on a little stool with acoustic guitar and long, blonde hair singing about puffing some dragons or something like that. So when people came to see us, that wasn't what they were expecting.

April 1968. Alice Cooper move into their new band house in Topanga Canyon. Matching the extremity of the band's music and vision, the guys went beyond regular bunk beds to triple-decker.

April 12, 1968. The band is in a car accident en route from Phoenix to LA. As the story goes, Alice signs the police report, "Alice Cooper." In Alice's (likely fanciful) recollection of the event, a lady cuts them off as they are driving at five in the morning, on a Good Friday (Cooper is correct about that—April 12, 1968 was a Friday), the van flips over three times, skids on its roof, and everybody is thrown out of the vehicle. Alice's dad had set them up with the vehicle, got it insured, a brand-new yellow van that cost $3000. Nobody is hurt, but because they are all scraped up they have to get tetanus shots. Alice cites the fact that they emerged without so much as a broken bone, despite their vehicle being totalled, as the second miracle in his life, the first being his recovering from peritonitis, which he frames as God "putting his mark on him."

April 20, 1968. The band—Dennis Dunaway, Fabian Buxton, Neal S. Myth, Alice Cooper and Mike Bruce—are featured in a Phoenix alternative paper called *A Closer Look*.

Dennis Dunaway on the band's influences:
Musically? The Yardbirds, the Doors and the Stooges. Neal liked Sandy Nelson, Gene Krupa and Keith Moon. Michael liked the Beatles. Glen liked Chet Atkins, Les Paul and Jeff Beck. Alice liked Burt Bacharach and Leonard Bernstein. We all liked Bernstein and Gene Barry's James Bond soundtracks. I liked avant garde electronic music. Frank Zappa was thrilled to hear that I loved doo-wop and electronic music and he spent a whole afternoon digging stuff out of his record closet and playing it just for me.

May 23, 1968. An important homecoming show finds Alice Cooper supporting Iron Butterfly at the Phoenix Memorial Hall.

June 27, 1968. Alice Cooper support the label boss, Frank Zappa, at Wrigley Stadium in LA.. The two parties would turn out to be a good match for each other, because although Alice Cooper and Frank Zappa were, from the artistic perspective, freaks, Frank and at least Alice, the person, were not doing drugs, while all around them almost everybody was. Plus with the rest of the Alice Cooper band, it stopped at pot and acid and in general, the guys were very dependable and hard working.

July 12, 1968. Alice Cooper audition for Frank Zappa at his 1914-built log cabin on Lookout Mountain and Laurel, in Laurel Canyon, across the street from Harry Houdini's castle. Zappa signs the band. The band meet the GTOs, with Pamela Des Barres taking a shine to Neal and Alice getting together with Miss Christine, who does some of the band's early makeup and helps with feminine clothing choices. As a speed freak, Miss Christine was always working and working fast, sewing clothes, coming up with combinations of wraps and feather boas, sometimes sewing outfits directly onto Alice. Much of the wardrobe work she did with Alice would take place at the Landmark Hotel.

Alice Cooper:
We thought at first everybody's going to love this. Then we started realizing that a lot of bands—I won't mention any names—but a lot of jam bands that were really big from San Francisco really hated us, because what they saw in us was the fact that people loved it. And now they were going to have to not wear their Levis and their sandals. Now they were going to have to do a show. Now they were going to have to actually work at it.

Because we were bringing a show in. It was like Broadway, only demented Broadway, and it was pure rock and it was louder than them. So it scared everybody to death. The press hated us for that. They said if you guys have to do all that, that means you're not good players. We went through that—until Frank Zappa picked us up. And everybody respects Frank Zappa as being the best guy, the smartest, most intelligent guy in the business. Well Frank Zappa was the only guy that would sign us.

Michael Bruce:
Alice was hitchhiking around, and he got to know the GTOs and Miss Christine invited him to the log cabin. And she eventually got us the rehearsal and said, "Have the band come over at six." So we were so excited, that we couldn't possibly imagine he meant six PM. We got over there in the wee hours, set up our stuff, and were playing at six o'clock, the music that you hear on Pretties for You.

So all of a sudden I see—there's the staircase, because this was down in his basement, this guy walking down—he's got his hair tied back, drinking a cup of coffee, and he goes, "What the fuck is going on here?!" And we said, "We're the Alice Cooper band. You wanted us to be over at six." He goes, "I meant six in the evening!" That's what I remember. But he listened to it; we were performing all that material you hear on Pretties for You *and we could do it live. And he was impressed with the fact that we could do those arrangements over and over. And he said, yeah, I want you on the label.*

Mid-July 1968. Shep Gordon and Joe Greenberg walk into a fashion shop called Inside Outside and wind up talking to Cindy Dunaway. Shep and Joe had been spinning their wheels at the Landmark Hotel and knew they had to do something. Cindy said she had a brother with a band, Frank Zappa wants to sign them and they need a manager. Joe blurts out, "I'm a manager!" Soon after they talk to Neal on the phone and the band bring a tape down to the Landmark for them to hear. It was irrelevant what was on the tape, because the most interesting thing about them, besides how long their hair was, was that Frank Zappa was going to sign them in three days. On the band's part, they saw these guys were living at the Landmark, plus they bought the Shep's and Joe's complete like about being the west coast managers of The Lefte Bank.

In Shep's telling of the story, there's a convergence of events. Yes, they went into the store and met Cindy. But also, when they had checked into the Landmark, Shep says they were doing a little drug-dealing, and they were partying in the hotel, and Jimi Hendrix suggested if the cops asked how they were paying to live at the Landmark, tell them you're a manager. And then Lester Chambers of The Chamber Brothers, who were also at the party, said that they had this band living in their basement, Alice Cooper, that they should talk to.

And indeed, at first, Joe and Shep intended to use band management as a front to continue selling pot. Shep says there was a period there when he and Joey were paying the band $10 a week just to say they managed them, saying Alice would walk down from Topanga Canyon to the hotel to collect the money and then they'd spend it on Boone's Farms wine (this befuddles the timeline somewhat, as lore has it this all happened in a matter of a couple days). In any event very quickly, prompted by a scare where they almost got arrested, Gordon and Greenberg shifted gears from their nascent pot operation and took on this new project, Alice Cooper, even if the dealing continued low-key, along with a side job Shep had, selling copies of the *Los Angeles Free Press* underground newspaper.

To sign the contracts with the band, Shep and Joe meet with parents of the band members because they are too young to sign. Alice figures the parents were satisfied because they were Jewish and from New York, plus they looked the part. Joe figures that they saw that he and Shep were as young as the band, so they probably didn't know how to rip their sons off.

Immediately, Shep and Joe begin new jobs in the city as co-managers of Alice Cooper. A period of awkwardness ensues with Frank Zappa having first told the band their new manager is Herbie Cohen, who is running Straight/Bizarre with Frank. But the band says no, indicating that their new managers are these guys they met a few days earlier. Shep and Joe hash it out with Herbie Cohen, now newly belligerent because he's just been told he's not managing Alice Cooper. Shep in fact says that Herbie went after him with a chair, and that the GTOs had to intervene.

According to Alice, Shep and Joe are offered $30,000 but Herbie wants the publishing. They settle on $3000 with the band hanging onto their publishing (it was recommended by a lawyer named Sam Norton that when he goes in to negotiate, keep the publishing). Shep tells an incredulous band that if he was offering $30,000, they were worth ten times that. Alice Cooper didn't know what publishing was, but they were soon glad that they kept it (in telling the story, sometimes Shep specifies that they kept two-thirds of the publishing, not all of it). In a simpler telling, Joe talks about simply taking an offer of $6000 and that the band was happy. Alice says Joe and Shep celebrated the deal by buying new wheels for the band, a '54 Cadillac limousine for about $800.

Dennis Dunaway on the band's tough time getting their point across:
Our music was just way over the top, bizarre. That didn't help, but I think the biggest factor was that people came, they would hear the name, and they would come expecting to see Joan Baez or something. And then they'd come in and see what we looked like, and you know, nobody wore chrome clothing or sequins and stuff like that in those days. Except maybe Liberace (laughs). But then when they would see what the band looked like, people would start screaming insults and line up for the doorway.

As a matter of fact, the first time Frank Zappa was in the audience, and our potential managers, Joe Greenberg and Shep Gordon, had come because Zappa was going to consider having us on his record label. And the place was packed when we started, but within three songs it was emptying out so fast I looked behind us actually wondering if there was a fire or something. So because of that, I got this idea of breaking down the barrier between us and the audience. So I wrote a song called "Return of the Spiders," which the lyrics were, "Stop, look and listen." And so I thought okay, that will get people to stop (laughs). It didn't really work.

But then we decided okay, we're going to start breaking down the barrier by throwing things into the audience, so we'll make them part of the show. So they'll feel like they're part of the show and then they'll want to stay because they're in the show. And that led to me putting mirrors on my bass so the reflection would go into the room. And then that led to the giant weather balloons that we would throw into the audience that were full of smoke and money and confetti and all kinds of stuff. So that's how that developed. That was really to keep people from leaving the room, initially.

August 3-4, 1968. Alice Cooper play the Newport Pop Festival, at the Orange County Fairgrounds in Costa Mesa, California. The festival is cited as the first to draw over 100,000 people. Their set is four or five numbers. Joe and Shep had begged the promoters to put them on the bill. The promoter said that he had enough bands and "Would you please leave?" Day of show, the band turns up at security with all their gear and Joe tells the guy he's got The Joseph Cotton Blues Band with him—James Cotton Blues Band were on the bill, but Joe blanked and mentioned actor Joseph Cotten instead. They are let through. They go up on stage, set up and start playing. They are screamed off the stage by the promoter.

Also on the bill are Canned Heat, Chambers Brothers, Charles Lloyd Quartet, Country Joe and the Fish, Electric Flag, Paul Butterfield Blues band, Sonny & Cher, Steppenwolf and Tiny Tim.

September 1968. Track Records issues *The Crazy World of Arthur Brown*. Arthur's histrionic vocal style—from his falsetto to his scream to his growl—becomes an influence on and inspiration to both Bruce Dickinson and Ian Gillan. The single, "Fire" (the album's heaviest and most demonic track) issued the previous month, hits No.1 in the UK. An additional point about "Fire" is that its heaviness is partly derived from an ominous keyboard riff (courtesy of Vincent Crane), rather than electric guitar. The video for the track has Arthur pioneering the use of pyro, which shoots from a helmet on his head.

Arthur Brown on Alice Cooper:
He likes to explore images and he's very good at choosing—or having chosen for him sometimes—images that visually are very potent. And his best images are very simple. I remember doing one concert and he had the wind machine blowing and his hair was out here and things were just flying around. And it was a very moving spectacle. Some of his things are more like an illusionist conjuring stuff. He went through that phase.

I suppose that if you're looking for kinship with me, it's a delight in theater. Delight in not just standing with pleasant imagery, but exploring the unpleasant and having a sense of humour about it. Not being sort of terribly invested in the damage one can do, but more just looking at the world and taking images from it. I think he went through a period the same as I did where there was too much visual imagery and it became like a pantomime. And his musical background was obviously what he explores—different from my own—but similarly very energetic music.

Alice has been quite straight-forward in that regard, in citing influence from what I was doing, in terms of things like makeup, which we were sporting before Alice used it. And when he came over and we did some concerts in '71, he said, "Wow, that was real psycho," you know. And so I can see some of that in his performance, but I can also see the fact that he took it in his own direction. It's his own thing. And I'm very flattered that he sees a connection.

Dennis Dunaway:
We had heard about Arthur Brown, and we of course had to send away for his album. We used to send away for the British albums all the time. And I love that album, his first album, which has one side that is incredible; the other side is not as good, but we had heard of him and liked him of course, for his theatrical stuff. We were also friends of The Doors by the mid-'60s, so they had their theatrical inclinations as well, and we also knew of Pink Floyd. As a matter of fact, they stayed at our house, on their very first tour. Syd Barrett was still in the band, and they were doing something very different from us, their lighting was theatrical. Which we prided ourselves on being the very first band to take our own light show on the road with us. We had our own light show since the VIP Club in Phoenix, Arizona. We had a guy, Charlie Carnell, who was very advanced. As a matter of fact Chip Monk used to come to our rehearsals in later days, and we would see Charlie's new lighting effect that he invented in the Stones show (laughs). And Chip Monk was admitting he would do that. He would tip his hat to Charlie. It wasn't like he pretended that he made up those ideas.

Alice Cooper:
I'd never seen Arthur Brown. I had never heard of Arthur Brown. It was one of the strange things. Arthur Brown and I happened at about the same time. He was going on in England but didn't have any hits over here. We were going on over here but didn't have any hits in England, and we were wearing almost the same makeup and doing very theatrical things.

So when I saw Arthur Brown I did a double take. I have a doppelganger. And I think when he saw me it was sort of like, wow, there's somebody over there doing this thing too. He set his hat on fire, I had the boa constrictor. I really liked Arthur Brown. I think Arthur had the best voice in the business. His range was amazing, but he really only did that one thing. He did the fire trick and that was about it, whereas I thought every song should have a piece to it.

Author Gavin Baddeley:
One hit wonder is certainly unfair and unkind for such a talented figure, but Arthur Brown is remembered for "Fire." As the God of Hellfire. And if that had a political message, it was to a certain extent the same kind of political message you were getting from the Rolling Stones, touching upon the crackling energy of revolution that people felt on the streets. And if you talk about the God of Hellfire the same way as Mick Jagger

singing about sympathy for the Devil, you're giving everything an extra sort of charge of blasphemous or even Satanic energy, which means you're not just attacking the status quo and the government, but you're also implicitly provoking religious sentiments. It's a two-barreled attack.

But Arthur Brown is an example of an artist who is taking sort of proto-psychedelic sounds and giving them an aggression and energy which perhaps they lacked. The summer of love was most people's abiding memory of the late '60s, however accurate they may or may not have been, but this was the suggestion that summer of love might turn into something else. But if you wanted to get a bit carried away here, "Fire" is evocative of the burning barricades and so forth, which again you find in the Rolling Stones' "Street Fighting Man." It's the idea that somehow there's a dangerous energy out here which we can unleash, at least partially, through music.

October 1968. Alice Cooper move band house again, setting up shop with Shep Gordon along as well, at John Philip Law's house on Observation Road in the Hollywood Hills. There's an interesting story as to how Vincent Furnier became the Alice Cooper in the band called Alice Cooper. Shep says that they had met with a publicist, Pat Kingsley, who sent everyone out of the room saying, I can't deal with five guys called Alice Cooper. The idea was for Shep to pick the best talker of the bunch, and that person will be Alice Cooper. The band themselves suggested Vince.

Dennis Dunaway on the band's evolving identity:
In the early days, there was a period when we were very confident as a band, and quite solid when we worked at the VIP. Because when we started, we would do cover songs, and Alice was very confident that if we did a Rolling Stones song that he was Mick Jagger. And if we did a Paul Butterfield song, he was Paul Butterfield and played the harmonica and everything. So he had a lot of stage confidence through acting, because he was pretending he was someone else.

But when we got to LA and decided we were going to shed all of that and move onto our original image and everything, everything seemed fine at rehearsals, but when we got to a live show, Alice would spend most of the set with his back to the crowd. And then we would go back to rehearsals and things seemed normal again. And our gigs were few and far between in those days, because LA had thousands of bands looking for even an audition (laughs).

Anyway, I came up with this idea of having a character, a different character for each song. So we had a song called "Nobody Likes Me," the one where Alice is singing through the window in the door, we had a song called "Levity Ball," which was inspired by the movie Carnival of Souls, and so Alice would envision that he was a person who could see all of these ghosts dancing in his room. And Alice still uses the gestures he had for that song.

And we had a song called "Fields of Regret," our most popular song, for the people who did remain in the room in those days (laughs). We would sing out, "Fields! Fields!" People loved "Fields," because it was a dark song and Alice did this dark character. And so he would change characters, and then when we would drop the song, the character would be dropped and a new character would be invented for whatever song replaced that. But I noticed... I didn't develop the character. The band really had a lot to do with developing the character that became Alice. It was definitely a collaboration, but I was the first to recognize that that's what the audience wanted. And so I said, "We should do more songs that are that character. As a matter of fact, we should do that character all the time." And Alice is the one that of course had the talent to pull it off. Alice Cooper became the character that we decided to do all the time.

Neal Smith on the "Nobody Likes Me" door prop:
It was in a pile of junk behind our house. It was sitting down one day with a couple beers and thinking, "Nobody Likes Me"—because it's well documented we played lots of shows and people kind of walked the other way when we were playing—and so we thought, well, we wrote a song called "Nobody likes Me," and it was a forlorn kind of song. So we thought of this character just sitting at the door, the window, looking out of the home, nobody coming to my house to play with me, I'm just bored. So we fixed it up and painted it and put feet on it so you could stand it up. I remember some of the airports we went to, down would come the luggage and all of a sudden there was a door coming. You'd see these golf clubs and then some baggage and a door.

October 11, 1968. Alice Cooper play Philadelphia, with the MC5.

MC5 manager John Sinclair:
I first heard of Alice Cooper when he was on Frank Zappa's bizarre label, with Pretties for You. That was pretty far out to begin with. And then when the MC5 played a show in Philadelphia with Alice Cooper, there were about 100 people there—total flop (laughs). But we liked them

and they liked us and we said, "Man, you guys gotta come to Detroit. They would love you guys in Detroit." And it turned out to be true. Because they were bizarre and they rocked. They were a great, great band. "I'm Eighteen," "School's Out"—those are great records. But Vince is from Detroit (laughs). I think that was bred into him before he moved to Arizona with his parents. And those other guys fit right in. They were all hard rocking guys, Rockin' Reggie and those guys.

November 1968. Alice Cooper record what will be their debut album, *Pretties for You*. Completely run over, recalls Shep Gordon, Frank foisted upon the band his brother to "produce." Completely green, the guys played what they had on the first day and then it was declared, that's your album. Shep says perhaps there was a second day, but as he recalls, Frank looked at his watch and said that it was 9:15 and that he'd be back at 5:15 and that whatever is done will be the album.

Alice remembers Frank's involvement as a bit more substantial, saying the album took three days and Frank was there but moving them through the songs swiftly, as well as convincing them to just play them live, picking the best of two or three takes.

Neal Smith:
Pretties for You *was a very complicated record that we rehearsed morning, noon and night and that's all we did. I would always want to be as well-rehearsed as possible going into the studio and we took that passion and work ethic into all of our albums. It also started our affiliation with Frank Zappa. Frank wanted to change the name of the band to Alice Cookies and he wanted put every song on a single disc and in a tuna fish can. We we're like, "What the fuck are you talking about man?" We flipped. He wanted a tin with 13 discs in it. So that was our first fight with a record company. He wanted to change our name and that was never going to happen. Alice Cookies was not going to happen. Anyway, it was recorded quick and released and we had our first album.*

Michael Bruce on the Alice Cookies near debacle:
We were at a meeting over at his house. This is not the log cabin. He's now moved onto Mulholland Drive; he's got a big house up there. We walk in, and you know that Edward Beardsley painting on Pretties for You*? There's that huge painting hanging on the wall. We didn't know at the time that was going to become our album cover (laughs).*

So anyway, we're downstairs, and he goes, "About the title of the band, guys; I've got this thing." So he pulls out this, like, cookie tin. Like that crackers or sweetbreads come in. And it was about the size of a CD. And he says, "So here's what I want to do. I want to call the band Alice Cookies."

At the time they had this thing called a hip pocket record player. You slide these tiny records in and you could take them to school and carry it in your back pocket. Basically a record fit into this thing and you pushed it down and there was a phonograph needle and it played the record. So it was going to be a tin of those, and each song would be on one of these little mini vinyls, smaller that a 45. And the players were in the back of some magazine. It wasn't like you could go down to Sears and buy one or something, you know? And, well, we had a bad feeling. So we dragged our feet and moved past that hurdle.

But we did like the painting. His daughter Moon Unit had taken a crayon and scribbled on it. But that ended up being our album cover. The funny thing is, after Frank died, they went through all his estate and everything and that painting is missing. They never found it and they don't know where it went or who took it.

December 6, 7, 1968. The Mothers of Invention play the Shrine Exposition Hall in LA. Supporting are Easy Chair, the GTOs, Wildman Fischer and Alice Cooper.

January 12, 1969. Led Zeppelin's self-titled debut is released. Arena rock is born.

February 7, 1969. Amidst all manner of shows, small to large, in their adopted hometown of Los Angeles, Alice Cooper travel to Denver to play the Denver Auditorium with Iron Butterfly and the Steve Miller Band.

Author Gavin Baddeley on the evolving Alice Cooper show:
There was a certain level of opportunism about Alice Cooper, at least in the early years. They were originally a bunch of guys from Phoenix who decided they wanted to start a band. The most obvious model for this was the Beatles. So the idea was they'd be a Beatles-type band, but they sort of missed the point and called themselves the Earwigs and then the Spiders.

Then it became clear the next big thing was that all these crazy limey bands seemed to be dressing like chicks. Well, we'll give this a go as well. So there's this sort of half-hearted drag they put on. And again, it's all attention-seeking. But the shift from a band who were playing all these kind of whacked-out Beatles-influenced songs to Alice Cooper, the artist who was being guillotined onstage every night while busty nurses walked about with huge syringes, it's a series of evolutions.

February 19 – 23, 1969. Alice Cooper are booked for five nights at the Whisky, supporting Linda Ronstadt.

Early 1969. The Frost, featuring Dick Wagner, issue their debut album, *Frost Music*.

Dick Wagner:
The first album is poorly recorded or at least poorly mixed. It doesn't really have a great sound but I think the songs were pretty inventive and really showed a change in my writing, a motion forward that eventually led to all my writing with Alice Cooper, and my range of stuff with Lou Reed. I call that an experimental record. I came out of The Bossmen doing real pop, commercial, English-sounding Beatles-type stuff. I put The Frost together because I wanted a band that could really play this new music of mine and The Bossmen weren't really capable of that.

May 1969. The band move to Cincinnati, Ohio, after being "thrown out of LA." But the rental turns out to be a scam, and they are tossed out by the university students rightfully returning to take over for the school year.

April 12, 1969. Billboard magazine reports that Frank Zappa and manager Herb Cohen have formed Straight Records, and that their first act is Alice Cooper.

Michael Bruce on the formation of Straight Records:
What happened was the Freak Out! album by Frank Zappa and the Mothers became a huge hit. The hippies liked Frank for putting down the establishment. But after getting to know Frank, I realize that he was putting down hippies. You know, because he didn't drink or smoke or do drugs.
    But he made a ton of money and now he's gonna get taxed really heavily. So he decides he's going to start Straight Records and sign every weird band, like Captain Beefheart, Wild Man Fischer, GTOs, Alice Cooper band. Tim Buckley was the only really legitimate guy on the label; he was really musical.

And so they would come through one door and, "Okay, sign a contract, Herbie is your manager, see you." Boom, boom, boom. And then a couple days before we were supposed to sign with Frank, we met Shep Gordon and Joe Greenberg and we talked with them and they agreed to go represent us. Because they were saying, "Hey, you know, you guys, they're going to bury you." And they were right.

So we had this meeting at the Landmark Hotel, met Joe and Shep, and then Shep walked into Frank's place and he says, "I'm managing the band." And Frank was very upset. Because they didn't want anybody meddling with their label, you know, and their business. After being on the label for a while, I kind of find out, I mean, Herbie and his bother, Mutt Cohen, they'd get royalties and they would just sit on them, invest them, and when the bands started whining and crying about it, finally, they would give them their money. But it was like trying to pry yourself loose from Jaws or an alligator something, to get money from them. I guess we were really a pain in their sides, Herbie and Frank.

And also being on his label, we were his discovery. You'd read a review or anything about the band, it was Frank Zappa discovered us; he was a notable person at the time. So our next ambition was to get as far from the label as possible so we could do our own thing. Thanks, Frank, for discovering us—now we're going to get the hell out of here.

March 1, 1969. Creem magazine begins publication, in Detroit. The magazine is started by Barry Kramer (dead at age 37 in 1981), and Tony Reay, with financing provided by The Grande Ballroom's Russ Gibb. The magazine's ample coverage of heavy metal would last through at least 1981, with much good-natured fun made of the genre's hairy personnel. Arch-rival Circus would also cover much metal, but with less of a hipster sense of irony.

April 18, 1969. Alice Cooper play the Agrodome in Vancouver, British Columbia, supporting Frank Zappa and Canadian heroes, The Guess Who. The following night the trio play Seattle.

May 1969. Screaming Lord Sutch and his famous buddies record some pretty rocking tunes, however they wouldn't be issued until early 1970.

Author Gavin Baddeley:
Screaming Lord Sutch was always—this sounds cruel—an interesting failure. He's an example of how you can perhaps use shock to make

up for your limitations in other departments if pressed. Screaming Lord Sutch—who incidentally wasn't a Lord by any stretch of the imagination—was a compulsive attention-seeker and by his own estimation far from a brilliant singer. But he worked out that if you threw some more elements into the mix, then you could try and carve a career out of it.

But he was always lurking on the periphery. The closest he came to success was with a song called "Jack the Ripper," which in its own camp way is quite sinister. And he used to come onstage, again in a coffin, and this time dressed in Jack the Ripper garb. We don't actually know what Jack the Ripper wore because we don't know who it was, but everyone thinks he wore a top hat and a cape and obviously had a big knife, and used to chase girls dressed as Victorian prostitutes around the stage and so forth.

And another significant aspect of Screaming Lord Sutch's act is that his backing band included a who's who of significant sort of proto-heavy metal performers of the late '60s. But the tragedy with "Jack the Ripper" is it was actually banned by the BBC. There's a misconception that being banned is the automatic road to success, that you're a controversy, a success from scandal. That only works if you can still get your work out there and people buy it. With "Jack the Ripper" being banned by the BBC, it kind of canned any money he might have made out of it.

June 6 – 16, 1969. The band play venues around New York City.

June 21, 1969. Alice Cooper play the Toronto Pop Festival at Varsity Stadium in Toronto, Ontario.

June 25, 1969. Alice Cooper issue their debut album, *Pretties for You*, on Frank Zappa's label, Straight Records. The band is pictured heavily glammed-up, more so—and somewhat pre-dating—the more famous glam bands from the UK. Besides working with the GTOs and Neal's sister Cindy on their clothes, an early event that helped push the wardrobe was the purchase of, as Alice recalls, 50 pounds of old *Ice Capades* outfits bought at 25 cents a pound.

1969

Dennis Dunaway:
Those albums were exclusively limited to a small group of people with impeccable taste (laughs). We spent most of our time rehearsing and batting ideas around. We wanted to show the world something unique. So creating those crazy abstract songs was a fun process. Our day could end with a new song or it could just be a long day of improvising. But improvising is how we gained our intuitive feel for each other's playing. Ideas started with "What if..." And each and every idea was a challenge to be topped, or made crazier. And we became razor sharp at it.

I really liked "Fields of Regret" because it was dark and eerie. The middle part is a good example of how we used instruments like orchestration — bass, guitar, cymbal repeating in that order. And "Today Meuller," Toodie Mueller was/is a friend from our earliest days. She was innocent and bubbly and she got us to gigs in her Baby Blue Mustang, so we wrote a happy song about her.

"Nobody Likes Me" belonged on Pretties for You *as much as "Strawberry Fields Forever" belonged on* Sgt. Pepper. *But it somehow fell by the wayside. I wrote it to symbolize how audiences were treating the band then. Alice sang through a window in a door, "Nobody likes me, it's all my fault." And we answer, "Oh yes, we all like you, we like you a lot." But by the final verse, it's revealed that we hated him. We wore masks to sing our responses to Alice because we represented the audience. The masks were shaped like birds symbolizing how people would fly out the exits when we played.*

And you see that it says produced by Alice Cooper. The band name belongs to all of us equally. That's just one example that confirms that. Each of us have always received 20% of the royalties on every song on Pretties for You *because the credits say "Music, lyrics and arrangements by Alice Cooper" as well as that production credit like that right on the label.*

We wanted to use Salvador Dali's Geopolitical Child *for the front* cover of Pretties, *but they claimed that it would cost too much, so we used a painting that Zappa had just purchased—he probably took a tax deduction on it. For the back cover, the band did a photo session at an art gallery. We loved one particular photo but Bizarre lost it. None of us were happy with the alternate one they used.*

Alice Cooper:
Frank Zappa loved Pretties for You *because it was just so bizarre. He said, "I couldn't even teach the Mothers of Invention to play this stuff, it's so weird."* Easy Action *as well; you know, you listen to those albums, and you say this is a good psychedelic band here but no direction at all.*

Neal Smith:
We were all thrusting an image and Alice was obviously the focal point on stage. But coming out of Hollywood, we had, Dennis and I... our hair was longer than anybody in rock 'n' roll. And certainly Glen and even Mike had long hair. So there was that feminine side, but also music was very powerful. But we weren't trying to do anything except look different than any other band.

My idol growing up was Brian Jones of the Rolling Stones, and I thought he was so cool. He had longer hair than the Beatles and it was blonde. And I thought man, I want my hair even three times or four times as long as his and my clothes even more outrageous than his. And to this day, when it came to rock 'n' roll, I always was a flashy dresser.

And the band, we got into that glitter thing. And it was because we love Hollywood. My sister would go to the back lot sales at Fox and MGM and Warner Bros., when they were selling their costumes, and get us a lot of stuff back there. And that was all glitter stuff from the '30s, '40s and '50s. I mean, nobody really talks about it, but look at Pretties for You—*Dennis is all dressed in silver on that album. I can't think of too many albums in 1969 or prior to that that anybody was actually dressed like that.*

Michael Bruce on Frank Zappa not producing Pretties for You:
No, he came; he said he was sick. He was there about three days. He was just wanting to get it done and he said he was sick and he left. And his manager, Herbie Cohen, comes down--he was gonna produce the album. He ended up falling asleep on the couch. And thank God for Ian Underwood. He was the keyboard player in the Mothers, and he went on to do synthesizer in a pile of hit movies. He finished the album for us and did a great job.

July 4, 5, 1969. Alice Cooper are a last-minute addition to the Saugatuck Pop Festival, and hence do not appear on posters for the event. Included on the bill are Brownsville Station, The Bob Seger System, MC5, the Stooges and The Crazy World of Arthur Brown.

July 25, 1969. Alice Cooper play the Seattle Pop Festival. Other notable acts include The Doors, Chuck Berry, Santana, The Guess Who, The Byrds, Ten Years After and Led Zeppelin.

August 1969. The Stooges' self-titled debut is released.

Alice Cooper:
Nobody did punk better than Iggy and the Stooges. We grew up with those guys in Detroit, and the first time I saw Iggy and the Stooges, I just went, this is... I don't even... there was no such word as punk at that time. So I just called it Detroit street rock. Because it was very simple; there was nothing complicated about it and it was in-your-face, and it had some anger to it. And our rock did the same thing. We were a little more sophisticated than The Stooges, but there was always an angry clever twang going on in our music.

Dennis Dunaway:
The Stooges were the originals. That was the first band that had that punk attitude, and they had it in spades. When we came to Detroit, we were kind of a Hollywood glitz image, our band had. We were all wearing chrome and sequins. This was before David Bowie. I don't know why everybody always gives him credit for it, starting that look, but anyway, we landed in Detroit, and we see these hard rock, high-energy audiences, and all of the bands are doing that. The MC5, SRC, Ted Nugent, and even Suzi Quatro with the Pleasure Seekers, Frost, Bob Seger. It was a very, very alive, high energy, with everybody on their feet with their fists in the air. And if you came out and did a ballad, it wasn't a good idea (laughs). But we showed up and we had this whole completely different thing going on. And luckily they liked us, and we were admitted to the VIP Club there that was going on in Detroit.

The first thing that happened was Iggy started wearing silver lamé gloves, and MC5 was totally glittered out. But it was an even exchange in my opinion, because we took the high-energy edginess of the music scene and incorporated it into what we were doing, and we got darker because of it as well, because the bikers liked us a lot.

Now Iggy and the Stooges, back in those days, in the Eastown

EASY ACTION - The Original Alice Cooper Band

1969

Theater, where we played a lot and they played a lot, there was a stage that was about two-and-a-half, maybe three-feet off the floor, and Iggy would dive into the audience. But there was no such thing as a moshpit yet (laughs). The crowd would part and Iggy would hit the floor. I mean, you could even hear it over the volume of music that they did. And then Iggy would walk around and pick a fight with somebody.

And one night Alice and I were walking into the club, because we were going to play after they did. And Iggy came around, and he was looking around to start a fight with somebody. So Alice and I stopped to watch that going on, and he came around and looked at Alice, and you could see, he was ready to start a fight with Alice. And then they kind of stood there looking at each other for a few seconds, and then he just smiled and moved on.

But MC5 were doing this extreme high-energy show with a lot of political overtones. It was interesting too, because the politics of that day was the same in Canada as it was in the Detroit area. But in Canada it was more like "Imagine" and John Lennon had a big influence, and it was like, "Let's stop the war; let's make love instead of war." In Detroit it was, "Stop the fucking war!" (laughs). So it was the same message; it was just a completely different attitude behind the delivery.

So yeah, the Stooges were the originators of the punk thing, and even though Alice and Iggy had a very similar kind of thing, we followed the Stooges at the Fillmore West once and that was where you could really see the contrast of the differing characters. They were both edgy, they were both threatening, but when the Stooges did their show, it was like they nailed you to the wall on the first song and then every song after that. When we followed them, we came out, the first thing we did was shift gears and pull everything back onto our terms, rather than trying to overpower the Stooges, which nobody could do. So we shifted gears and pulled things back, and then the character, Alice's character, sucked them into this deep, dark kind of the thing.

August 2, 1969. *Pretties for You* appears at No.194 on the Billboard charts.

Iron Butterfly guitarist Mike Pinera:
I met Alice Cooper in '69 and he came over and opened for Blues Image at a club, the Experience here in LA on Sunset Blvd., and everybody was so scared of these guys. They had these long fingernails with polish and then the black makeup under the eyes, but to me, man, I just saw some cool guys. The band would see them coming and say, "Don't let them in

the dressing room. Don't let those guys in here." And I'd wait until my band was gone, then I'd bring them in and share our sandwiches and our coffee with Alice and the boys because they didn't have any food... they didn't have any money for food and they were stuck there all day until it was time to play.

August 8, 9, 1969. The Charles Manson/"Helter Skelter" murders in L.A., which represent the death of the innocent '60s, although the event is one of a handful of cultural touchstones to do so. America finds out that hippies are not all peace and love, a revelation that would also come to Black Sabbath, who will represent a new pessimism, cynicism and fatalism amongst the ranks of the very hairy.

Dennis Dunaway:
Just before '68 when the Alice Cooper group first started traveling to California, to Hollywood, we got there right at the tail end of this amazing era of the Sunset Strip. It was just, you walk down the street and it's unbelievable. Buffalo Springfield over here, the Doors over here, and the amount of people all dressed up, hippies and all kinds of people—I had never even heard the word silicone before. It was amazing. California girls.

And then it all changed with the Charles Manson thing. All of a sudden all this love and peace and everything got darker. And there was also this big crackdown in Los Angeles in particular—and I'm sure other parts of the country—where they wanted to suppress what they thought was a threat. And therefore you started seeing things like paddy wagons pull up and put everybody who was in line to go into the Whiskey A Go Go in the paddy wagons and haul them all away.

You couldn't walk down the street without being checked, and if you didn't have your ID with you... to this day my wife and I always carry our IDs because of the LAPD back in those days, because you'd be shipped out of town. Buffalo Springfield had "For What It's Worth, "There's something happening here, there's a man with a gun over there." Well that was about Pandora's Box, a popular club on the Sunset Strip where there was a big crackdown.

And therefore you had the Doors. It became the establishment was against us, a lot of bands thought, and therefore our music is going to be our way of fighting back. So lyrics started getting more political. Not ours. We weren't really politically motivated, we were more culture motivated. We just saw that the peace and love generation was burning itself out. Bill Graham is convinced that we ruined everything, our band in particular. He hated us. We weren't really angry at anything. We were just totally into perpetuating this vision that we had. It's all we cared about. All we cared about was music.

September 6, 1969. An article appears in Billboard reporting that Alice Cooper are beginning legal proceedings to break ties with Straight Records.

September 13, 1969. Alice Cooper mount a historic stand at the Rock 'n' Roll Revival festival, Toronto, Ontario. This is the site of the famous Alice Cooper chicken incident, in which a chicken thrown off the stage by Alice gets torn apart by the crowd. The false story that Alice could never live down, however, was that Alice tore apart live chickens on stage—and worse.

Dennis Dunaway:
The Toronto Rock 'n' Roll Revival footage is an insight to how we applied our artistic influences to the show. That night we used a metal folding chair with the concept that a common item can take on significance when it's featured in the spotlight with the whole band looking toward it while playing a big fanfare. Making a chair seem that important sparked curiosity and assumptions. It had to mean

something, didn't it? We also incorporated a football that night, which Alice kicked into the crowd. That kick was the cue for an explosion of musical and visual chaos. It was a rock 'n' roll revival and not many Canadians knew about us so it was completely unexpected. We were fearless about trying things in our show. It was like an evolving string of assaults to the senses. Very few people outside of the Alice Cooper group realized how fast and furiously the show evolved. People would comment about how different one night's show was from our previous night's show. And if they had returned the following night, it would be different again.

But what happened that night... see I grew up with chickens. My grandparents raised chickens when I was a little kid, and when I moved to Arizona we had chickens, and then later on in the Detroit area, Glen was doing this thing where he would tap the top of his neck with his right hand, fingers on his right hand, and it would make a sound that reminded me of chickens clucking. So I thought, just another one of these things where we would kind of, during that era, still from the VIP days, or the club in Phoenix, we would just grab things backstage and incorporate them into the show.

Well I got this idea that it would be funny to have chickens sitting on Glen's amp when he did this finger-plucking part, which was the solo he did in one of the tunes. And so I got this guy to go out and get chickens and set them on Glen's amp. And the great thing is, these chickens looked totally oblivious to what was going on onstage, which was total chaos. And they would look at Glen when he did that sound and tilt their heads like they were trying to understand what his guitar sound was saying to them.

So we loved that, and that led to Neal and I were having a pillow fight at a cheap motel. Neal and I were sharing a hotel room in Cincinnati, and we were just bored so Neal hit me with a pillow. So I hit him back and a feather came out of the pillow and floated in the air. So then we were like hitting each other as hard as we could. Actually I think we were even getting pissed-off at each other, or upset at each other, and more and more feathers came out.

So we go, wait a minute, that's it. Feathers came out of the pillow, and so I got the idea of chickens, feathers, let's rip the pillow open. And then Michael Bruce got the idea of using a fire extinguisher to blow the feathers to kingdom come. And of course once Alice and I established the idea of doing theatrics onstage, everybody joined in. Neal had an art background. Michael was the least likely to join in, but he came up with some great ideas as well. So that was one of the pretty amazing *things, I think, that you could have five personalities that were so different from each other, but all were on the same page when it came to doing the craziest theatrics we can think up.*

I had an acoustic bass amp, which was the bass amp to have in its day, and it started sounding not good any more, all muffled and everything. So I'm like what's going on here? So I took the grill cloth off and the amp was full of feathers. The CO_2 tank had blown the feathers right through the grill cloth. So every month or two I had to empty it out.

Anyway, so the chicken sound led to us using chickens. Unlike the stories that everybody has chosen to believe over the years, we said we didn't back in those days, because we had so much pressure from the Humane Society and everything, but the chickens were our pets. Glen kept them in his hotel room, he put them in his bathroom, and they even had names and everything. We used them every night.

But that particular night, Alice got this idea to toss one into the audience, which was a bad idea. But I do believe his part of the story that he really thought the chicken would fly. Because that's just how he was. He didn't grow up on a farm like I did (laughs). So he thought he would toss the chicken and it would fly away, whereas the chicken landed in the audience. And what we didn't anticipate, or intend, was the audience ripped it apart like it was a valuable souvenir.

On that particular night, there's footage of it called The Chicken Incident *by what's his name, D.A. Pennebaker, and if you watch that, if you slow down the frames, you can see Glen playing a lead guitar break, and you can see how it's come out of the pillow case, and you can see that the pillowcase has something in it besides feathers. Some of them you can see have feathers and one of them you can see doesn't. And you can actually do frame by frame, and you can see Alice take the chicken out and toss it into the audience. It was just... you know, he was supposed to take the chicken out and just set it down or let it loose on stage, so it would be walking around when we were doing this feather storm.*

So the chickens were just another element in our ever evolving props. The Rock 'n' Roll Revival wasn't the first time we had used them, but it was the last because we really didn't like what the crowd did to our pet chicken, Pecker. Following the chicken incident at that show, we continued our heavy schedule of playing every gig we could get. But we noticed that lots of people were showing up at our shows with rubber chickens. It took a few nights before we figured out what was going on.

But we intended to do something different for every show, and we had gotten comfortable with winging it. We would use anything as a prop. We would even grab things on our way to the stage—a watermelon, a bicycle, a garbage can, anything. If we used something and it bombed, fine, we had so many other things that it didn't matter. And many people were convinced that our odd choice of props had some significant underlying meaning. They would come backstage and say things like, "I know why you opened the umbrella over Glen's head while he did his solo." In reality, we were just having fun. That was the art of it. And then stories and rumours inevitably started to fly. Some make me smile and some make me see red.

Neal Smith:
My recollection of the story is that we were playing these large clubs and we would release doves, kind of like an anti-hippie statement, when we released the feathers. I mean, it made sense. It'd be feathers and some birds flying out. And I remember that our roadies couldn't find any doves for that show, but they found some live chickens. I think we were doing a version of "Animal Pajamas" or "Lay Down and Die, Goodbye." But I think it was "Animal Pajamas," which they call "Freak Out

Song" on *Science Fiction* and all the bootleg albums that you find from that era. It was actually a remake of the Spiders' first hit, "Don't Blow Your Mind." That was a local hit in Arizona, but we rewrote it as "Animal Pajamas" and did a big freak-out thing on it, and I did a drum solo, and we had guitar solos and Dennis does this amazing bass solo, and it was just a free-form thing.

It ends up with the CO_2 and the feathers flying, and also Alice had a flare gun too and it came down into the crowd, and it didn't quite burn out before it landed. Nobody ever talks about that but I actually still have the flare gun (laughs). But you know, the chicken came out, Alice throws it out, Alice throws it out into the crowd—I don't know what happened to it.

You know, the thing about that, there was a group of people that were there that were physically challenged folks that were in wheelchairs in front of the concert. John Lennon had been there, a lot of big celebrities. I mean, we were on stage with big celebrities during that show. So they had a section, which was great, so everybody was invited to the concert. And Alice says that it went in there and they stomped on the chicken and killed it.

I mean, all Alice did was throw it out into the crowd, and where it landed and what happened, I don't know. But I remember that the roadies couldn't find a dove, couldn't find any doves to release, because it was the Rock 'n' Roll Revival/peace festival, so we were going to throw the doves out and they couldn't find any. So the guys found a chicken, and the story... and I love Michael Bruce, who had this representation of it: Alice always said he was from Detroit, a city boy, he threw a chicken out and thought it would fly. And Michael says, "How many times have you ever seen a chicken fly by the window?" So I don't buy that story that Alice didn't know chickens can't fly. So he threw it out and I don't know what happened, and the worldwide press across United States and Canada was crazy.

But I don't remember that story Dennis says about them being on Glen's amp. But I remember the chickens that one night. We may have had them as just kind of a bizarre thing, but I know they were on stage. I know that the roadies put them on there; they didn't just suddenly appear. So whether we used them several nights... yeah, they maybe were on Glen's amps, because at that time Glen was still on the left-hand side of the stage before Michael was pushed over there. At any rate, we never killed a chicken—that was the thing.

Alice Cooper:
First of all our manager, Shep, was one of the guys that put the show together, and they were going to pay him. And he says, "Don't pay me. The only thing I want you to do is I want Alice to go on between John Lennon and the Doors." You know, on a Saturday night. And we were really not that well-known. We were notorious, but we weren't well-known then. So the Doors go on, and everybody goes, "Oh, it's the Doors." And Jim, we actually knew the Doors pretty well. They were friends of ours.

And they got done and then we go on. And we do our set and we do the feathered pillows and the CO2's coming out, and the next thing I realize, I look down and there's a chicken. Now I didn't bring the chicken. Nobody in my band brought a chicken. Somebody in the audience went, let me see, I got my keys, I got my wallet, I got my drugs, I got my chicken. Who brings a chicken to a show? I swear, we have no idea where the chicken came from.

There's a chicken onstage, I'm from Detroit, never been on a farm in my life. It had feathers, it was a bird, it should fly. You know? So I picked it up and I went, okay, and I tossed it lightly into the audience thinking it'll fly away or somebody will get a great souvenir. I got Alice's chicken. It went into the audience and the audience tore it to pieces. Blood everywhere. And threw what was left onstage.

Of course now the next day in the paper it was Alice Cooper kills chicken. And in the melee, everybody will swear that I ripped the chicken's throat out and ate the head and did all this stuff. It never happened. Frank Zappa called me the next day and he says, "Did you kill a chicken onstage last night?" And I went no. He said, "Well don't tell anybody; they love it." And I got my first lesson in, okay, they love it. You know, now I became much more notorious than I was before.

I realized that it was maybe the best thing that ever happened to us, the sacrifice of this poor chicken. And now the kicker to the story is this. I would never hurt an animal. I'm an animal lover. But the first five rows at the concert were all people in wheelchairs. They're the ones that killed the chicken, which makes it even more bizarre, you know? Because now the crippled people crippled the chicken in anger somehow.

And I thought that is so weird because Canada seems peaceful and loving and wonderful. Did we bring that out in them that they would kill a chicken? I mean that was even more bizarre to me. And that story then, to this day, when we play, "Are you going to kill chickens tonight?" I say, "How come nobody's hassling Colonel Sanders? He's killing billions of chickens. He's like the Hitler of chickens." One poor chicken got thrown in the audience and I'm the chicken-killer forever.

But in the end I totally get the folklore behind it. I've done much worse things than that since then, but the chicken thing seemed to be the one. That was the launch button for Alice Cooper. Now I looked on the side, there's Jim Morrison on this side and John and Yoko on this side going, yeah! They loved the performance art of this whole thing.

September 14, 1969. Alice Cooper play the Toledo Pop Festival, which includes on the bill, the MC5, the Amboy Dukes, The Frost, The Rationals and Früt.

Dick Wagner:
The first time I saw Alice Cooper was at the Toledo Pop Festival, I think, when they had the fans blowing and they threw out the chicken feathers. I'd say they were already pretty shocking by that point. And Alice got hung or electrocuted at that show; I think it was electrocuted. So I thought that was just great, very clever. Because like, my old band, The Bossmen used to do little skits and stuff, so we were attuned to the idea of theatrical rock.

Dennis Dunaway on Shep, Joe and the power of bad reviews:
Shep Gordon and Joe Greenberg—we talked Zappa into signing us and he said we needed a manager and we had three days to find one. My wife, Cindy, who was—and is—Neal's sister found Joe and Shep. They and Zappa came to see us perform at the Lenny Bruce memorial show at the Cheetah Ballroom in Venice, California. And all of these bands were playing that day, Iron Butterfly and quite a few great LA bands. And the place was packed when we started playing. And within three or four songs the place had evacuated. We're thinking, well, we just blew a record deal.

But Shep Gordon—probably more than Joe Greenberg but Joe went along with it—Shep thought this was amazing. The most amazing thing he had seen. All we had to do was harness that power. That we could drive those people out of the room that fast all screaming insults at us. So he started advertising the band that drives people out of the room. So people started coming to see us to see why people left.

And then our album **Pretties for You** did not get very good press. I think one writer said, "Songs Disney had sense enough to leave in the can," which, that was a stake right into my heart because I thought this was the greatest album in the world at the time. So you know, we're all *depressed, and Joe and Shep are like, "No, are you kidding? This is good! If he wrote something good about you guys, we wouldn't be able to use it." And we're like, oh, really? And sure enough as time went on, bad reviews... not like we had any choice. I mean we would work extremely hard on our music and then somebody would talk about that we used the snake. So it was always negative press. Even when we'd get positive press there would be something negative in it usually, or there would be another story that was completely negative, because people still didn't like us because of our image.*

October 31, 1969. The Black Magic & Rock 'n' Roll Festival, otherwise know as The Black Arts Festival, Olympia Stadium, Detroit, which includes America's most prominent occult rock act Coven. A poster for the event reads: "Witches, Devils, 6 PM – 3 AM. Tickets 5:00." Acts listed are: Arthur Brown, Dr. Tim Leary, Frost, MC5 (whited out), Ralph Adams, Mystic Peter Murkos, Amboy Dukes, Bonzo Dog Band, Stooges, Coven, Pink Floyd, Savage Grace, Kim Fowley, Alice Cooper, Sky, Teegarden & Van Winkle, Satan (Ainsley), SRC, Frut, Bob Seger, All the Lonely People and Pleasure Seekers. A second poster reads: "Mike Quatro, Russ Gibb and Mike Keener present A Black Arts Festival" with the highlighted bands being MC5, Stooges, Frost, Bonzo Dog Band, Bob Seger System, Arthur Brown, SRC, Pink Floyd. One fan has documented that the show turned out to be a rip-off, with no performance by the likes of Pink Floyd, Bonzo Dog band, Alice Cooper, The Frost, MC5, Arthur Brown or The Amboy Dukes.

December 1969. The Frost issue their second album, *Rock and Roll Music*, which, like MC5's *Kick Out the Jams*, is recorded live at the Grande Ballroom.

Dick Wagner:
The Frost was always heavier live that we were on the record so we captured a bit of the live heaviness on that album. We were kind of like the most popular band, but we were also the outliers. We were the ones doing the rock 'n' roll with melody and harmonies, very sort of sophisticated for the time. And I was fortunate enough to be one of the two guitar players in town who was really getting recognition, the other being Ted Nugent.

We did some touring but not that much. The band could've been much bigger, had we had the opportunity to really tour. But we didn't have the proper management at the time and we really didn't have an agent. I was basically doing everything. Doing all the calls for gigs. And then the band broke up because Bobby and Donnie wanted to go home and go fishing. They didn't want to go out on the road, and have to suffer going through the winning of new audiences. Because it's a task, every time you play brand-new place, especially if they don't know who you are. But The Frost had a certain magic about the band, and we pretty much scored every time we played. We made fans; people loved us. Even San Francisco, where we open for B.B. King; even that audience loved us.

December 6, 1969. The Altamont Speedway Free Festival in Northern California, headlined by the Rolling Stones, results in lots of violence, one murder, and three accidental deaths. The event-gone-wrong is considered the death of the '60s, or at least the death of '60s psychedelic rock, an idea foisted up the Manson murders as well. It is a rare large festival of the day with no heavy rock, just heavy security.

December 29, 1969. The Chicago Pop Festival at the Aragon Ballroom finds Alice Cooper on a bill with both the MC5 and Coven, not to mention John Lee Hooker and Howlin' Wolf.

1970

Alice Cooper begin 1970 by watching Black Sabbath's debut record come out. I'm joking, but it's sort of important in the wider scope of things, because with both acts being on Warner, it will become framed for the first half of the '70s that these are the two spooky and dark competing rock acts operating amongst everything else. Despite the presence of Bowie, not really doing much until 1973 as the original Alice Cooper group wanes, plus no Kiss or Blue Öyster Cult for a while, this is basically it, along with a slight blip for Arthur Brown.

In March of 1970, Alice Cooper issue their second album *Easy Action* to zero effect. But being in the right place at the right time, with the sordid Straight Records run by Frank, (not exactly a straight shooter) and the nasty Herbie Cohen, Alice gets sold off at a discount to Warner Bros. and all of a sudden they are on a major.

This happens concurrently with the move to Detroit and a trial by fire than finds the band increasing their intensity levels to match that of the harder Detroit rockers. The "chicken incident" of late 1969 still causing an uproar, the band play a fest in Cincinnati that gets them on TV.

But the most important gig turns out to be a low-key club show in September at Max's Kansas City in Manhattan, attended by Bob Ezrin, who is sent down to get Shep off of Jack Richardson's back and tell these pests once and for all, no, you are not going to be the next Guess Who. Turning the tables, Bob loves the band and takes on the project as his first rung up the ladder (eventually putting him over *The Wall*).

As they mourn the death of Jimi Hendrix, Bob and his new charges knuckle down at the band house and at a nearby studio in Chicago on what will become the hit *Love It to Death* album, debuting before the year is out with anthem for the ages, "I'm Eighteen." Alice is now a midwest band — it's not exactly rust belt at this point — soon to become an east coast band, but emphatically not an LA band. For the next three years it will be about pragmatism, hard work and not a ray of sunshine.

January 30, 31, 1970. Raucous gigs at the Eastown Theatre in Detroit finds to Alice Cooper and The Stooges on the same bill.

Dennis Dunaway on keeping up with the competition:
Well, I mean the obvious competition was killer back then. You had Hendrix and the Beatles and the Stones and the Kinks and The Who and everybody else, and those bands all, in retrospect, they all had their own unique styles. Even though there were clone bands back then, as well as there are today, back then it seemed like the aim was to become more individual. So our goal was just to stand out from everybody else. And some of our influences were those obvious ones, but we also, early on, became very geared towards incorporating art into the show.

One of the many things we did was we built this big giant wheel. We called it the Electro-lucent Mind Machine, and it was made out of plywood, and it had to be eight feet tall or whatever size the largest sheet of plywood comes in. And we cut it into a circle, then we painted it with all kinds of abstract kind of hieroglyphics. And it also had hidden things so that under a black light these words would show up that were invisible in regular light. And we had a motor on it, and we would get the thing spinning, and we had a very early strobe light, before other people did, that we had made out of an ammunitions case from the old army and navy store.

And so this really came from, like I mentioned, our interest in the Dada art movement and incorporating art into what we were doing. Because I was an artist. I was such an artist that—I still am too—but I was such an artist that when I was in grade school, there were years where nobody even knew my name. They just called me The Artist. And so to give up art to pursue music, I wasn't ready to do that. So Alice and I decided we were going to bring our art with us, and incorporate it.

February 1970. Screaming Lord Sutch, one of England's favourite underground wild men of rock 'n' roll through the '60s, finally issues his debut album, entitled *Lord Sutch and Friends*. Characters like Sutch and more so Arthur Brown represent the UK's answer to Alice.

Dennis Dunaway on the band's effect on people:
Oh yeah, skirmishes with society was an everyday occurrence with us (laughs). All we had to do was walk down the street, even in Hollywood, and the way we dressed and the length of our hair... our hair was longer than any other band at the time. And when we walked down the street, people would either get upset or they would like it. But there

was hardly ever that we would pass anybody who didn't have a strong reaction. And then of course after the chicken incident happened in Toronto, every time we showed up to play, animal rights people and the Humane Society and the fire marshals and everybody, it seemed like there would be so many people there to stop us from doing the show. The promoters always had to convince them that it was just a show.

Neal Smith on hippies, freaks and rock 'n' rollers:
We were very anti-hippie all the time, and as things progressed, we were always decadent. But we were decadent even when we were poor. And so, you know, it was Dennis' idea, when you open up the album cover on Love It to Death, the most unusual thing was Alice's eyes, and it was the whole inside of the album cover. And when you look inside the pupils, you see a picture of the band. We were doing that all the time. We just wanted to come up with things that were different. You know, people called us Dada rock in the middle and in the beginning, and they also called it third-generation rock, and they were trying to come up with a name because they just couldn't figure out what the hell we were doing.

    I guess we were considered freaks because of that early sound plus given that we were associated with Frank Zappa. But I mean, I never associated myself with anything other than rock 'n' roller, I just wanted to be rock 'n' roll. As far as my image, I consider two kind of people, there are cool people and there are not cool people, and I always thought our image was just trying to be ultra-hip all the time. The more money we had, the cooler we looked. Sitting there with a $5000 jacket on and sitting in a Rolls-Royce, I'm no fucking hippie, I'll guarantee you that. I'm wearing a diamond ring that has 18 diamonds in it.

    So like I said, we were always decadent, we were always rock 'n' roll, and it was just trying to be different. It was a rock 'n' roll interpretation. Hippies were the fans. Actually I never considered too many bands hippies. So I look at it a little bit differently. But of course back then, Zappa signed us because he thought it was freaky. It's a band called Alice Cooper and the singer's called Alice Cooper. It's a very androgynous band and we're there with the GTOs, Wild Man Fischer, Captain Beefheart, all these freaky bands, and our first couple of albums were pretty crazy. But again, I never considered us hippies or freaks.

Friday February 13, 1970. UK release date for Black Sabbath's debut, *Black Sabbath*. Sabbath, also a Warner Bros. artist, would long be linked with Alice Cooper as premiere scary hard rock bands through the first half of the '70s.

March 1970. Leicester's Black Widow issue their debut album, *Sacrifice*. Black Widow were known for being the most overtly Satanic and theatrical UK band of the time although not that heavy. Still, the band's act, where they performed a Satanic mass, would generate the kind of scared hysteria Alice would experience in his heyday.

March 27, 1970. Alice Cooper's second album *Easy Action* is released.

Dennis Dunaway on Easy Action *and the producer of the album, David Briggs:*
I don't know who hired David. He had just finished producing an album for Neil Young and Crazy Horse and that's what he should have been doing. We all got the impression that he didn't like anything about us. Despite that, he got an album out of an unprepared band. As for those songs, Alice wrote "Shoe Salesman" with an evident double entendre lyric about a dealer. Glen was pretty faithful to Alice's original acoustic guitar part on that, as well as on "Laughing at Me." But Glen raised the bar with his Chet Atkins influence.

"Beautiful Flyaway" was Michael's piano tune, which I've always loved. He reminded me of a little Mozart brat when he was recording it. Michael is singing and playing piano on "Beautiful Flyaway." David Briggs played piano on "Shoe Salesman," which was one of the welcome few times he seemed to care about the sessions.

I liked "Lay Down and Die, Goodbye" because it contained a free-form sound collage that was disturbing. I would have been happy if the whole album was like that.

"Lay Down and Die, Goodbye" includes the line, "You are the only censors; if you don't like what I am saying, you have a choice, you can turn me off." That is an excerpt of Tommy Smothers' farewell speech in response to the network pulling the plug on the controversially groundbreaking Smothers Brothers Comedy Hour. I think it was David Briggs' idea to use it.

We tried with "Lay Down And Die, Goodbye," to write a proper song, but we still weren't good enough at our craft of songwriting to be able to pre-determine how the song was going to come out. Writing a song for us would be like shooting a shotgun at a canvas and just seeing what it looked like. Briggs called the song psychedelic garbage, and he looked like he wished he could turn it off. I think his negative comments seeped into the feel of the recording.

For the cover of Easy Action, the photo of the band facing away was Neal's idea. It proved to be very effective for emphasizing our androgynous look. Especially since nobody had ever seen anything like that before. But really, Easy Action is my least favourite of all of them. For one thing, we were forced into the studio when we only had about a third of the material to do an album, because of contractual obligations. We had a lot of ideas for songs, but I don't think there are more than one or two songs on that album that we had actually written before we went into the studio, so we kind made that album up on the spot. And we didn't have anywhere to rehearse. So that's how that was slapped together. So we already had good intentions, but we just didn't have the means to pull it off, by then. Even though I do really love some of the songs, and I love the way Glen played on "Laughing at Me" and "Shoe Salesman," stuff that is a completely different style for the band. It was very Chet Atkins-influenced on Glen's behalf.

Neal Smith:
We wanted to improve our production so we got David Briggs who had worked with Neil Young. When we did "Lay Down and Die, Goodbye" he called it "psychedelic shit." So that gives you an idea about how much he was into what we were doing or understanding what we were doing.

Michael Bruce on recording Easy Action:
David Briggs, when we did Easy Action, *his idea of producing a record, he'd come in and he'd kick back in the chair, put his feet up on the console, in his cowboy boots, and he'd start rolling some big doobie and smoking it, and he'd go, "Okay, that's a take, next song!" You know, so, we were about ready to get out of the music business. I played "Beautiful Flyaway" through once, and he goes, "Okay, okay, that's good!" I had to talk him into letting me do it again.*

Spring 1970. The Alice Cooper band move to Detroit. Suddenly they are part of a harder rock stew that includes The MC5, The Stooges, the Amboy Dukes, SRC and Bob Seger.

Dennis Dunaway on the band's move to Detroit:
Well, it wasn't a definite date. We left LA, because Pretties for You *didn't take off for us and we were traveling on the road, basically just doing any gig that we could come up with. We were touring with what I called the Zorro method, because we would play in Oregon, and then we would go to Boston, and then we'd go to LA and then we'd go to Florida. Sometimes it was an M, which was just a sideways Z. But we had to just take whatever gig and then get there. So we jumped in the car.*

But Detroit had a lot of fans who liked what we were doing more than other parts of the country at the time. So we came to Detroit and here we are this glammed-up Hollywood kind of act, and then here's MC5 and the Stooges and this artistic sort of inspiring of each other. We all of a sudden saw this high-energy thing happening in Detroit that was even maybe more loyal, dare I say, than the San Francisco groups were to their bands. Well, San Francisco and Detroit had the audiences that were the most loyal to their bands; let's put it that way. But if you played in Detroit, it was fists in the air for every single person in the audience—but you'd better not play a ballad, or like Glen Buxton used to say, a girl's song.

So we drew that energy and that made our music improve. But you know, Iggy started wearing silver lame gloves and MC5 started wearing shiny fabrics in their outfits, so there was a meeting of the arts there. And it was good for us. We started playing all these festivals that Mickey Quatro mostly put on. And it would be Cradle and Catfish and Savage Grace and Mitch Ryder and the Stooges and MC5 and on and on. But mostly the same Detroit bands.

But every time it would be sold-out, packed and fists in the air. So that became our bread and butter. So we started staying at this dive hotel, the Grass Ship—I hope it's not still there. Anyway, that was kind of our home for it seemed like a year. Living out of suitcases, really. And then we got the farm in Pontiac outside of Detroit.

Alice Cooper:
We were in LA and we realized we were just a fish out of water in LA. We were this band that was not groovy, we were not into peace and love, we were not into love-ins, we were not into, "Isn't everything groovy?" We were more interested in switch blades and blondes and Ferraris. And we just didn't fit in. We were notorious because we didn't mind a little violence onstage, and that was the last thing LA was about. LA was about Buffalo Springfield. The Doors was about as close as they came to anything violent, and Jim was just kind of volatile. But we were out-and-out Clockwork Orange, pre-Clockwork Orange.

And so we didn't fit in at all. We finally said the first place that gives us a standing ovation, we're going to move to. And we got this gig at the Saugatuck Pop Festival in Michigan and that's what happened. And I'm from Detroit; that's my hometown. We did our show and the audience loved it. Just total opposite of LA. This audience was a black T-shirt, black leather jacket, greasy black hair audience who saw us and went yeah! Attitude! This band had attitude and they loved that. Then when they found out it was from Detroit, I was the missing son. I was the missing finger in that glove.

Maybe that's where that string of violence comes from in me, is it's built-in, it's in the DNA. And the sensationalism of it. You don't just sing the song, you act it out. If you're going to say "Welcome to my nightmare," give the audience a nightmare. Don't just say it. If you're going to do "Gutter Cats vs. the Jets" and it's West Side Story, do the knife fight from West Side Story.

Neal Smith:
Detroit's always in our hearts. It was Detroit and the Midwest that broke the band. Before we even brought Bob Ezrin in we were surviving by selling a few albums on Frank Zappa's label and having a part of the country that really "got" what we were doing and enjoyed it. At the

time The Stooges and the MC5 were big bands in Detroit and we moved in, we came in from out west and we set up camp there and we started playing all of the top places and playing all of the big festivals.

And I asked a couple of people in the area, "Why do you guys like us so much?"—just out of curiosity, because most people don't care—"You have some great bands here with the MC5 and The Stooges." And they said, "Well, you're doing what they're doing, but you're doing so much more!" And to me, I understood what they were saying. And so the Alice Cooper fan base was established right between Detroit, Cleveland and Toronto—that was our launching grounds.

Michael Bruce:
When we moved to Michigan, it was a whole different style back there—the music was different. A lot of people were going over the UK and bringing music back. And in the Ann Arbour area, we got a roadie there, Martin Priest, and he built a PA for us, a really kick-ass PA. And now, when we played a show, one night to the next night we could sound just as bad-ass. Consistency is what really made it happen. Because, but the props and whatnot that we used, the music always had to be the backdrop for that and it had to be spot-on. So he did a great job and that was a real factor in our early days.

Plus we were stuck out on a farm. We lived in Pontiac, and it had a dirt road and a well for water, but it did have a big horse paddock in the back, indoor, where they trained horses. It was the size of a football field. And there was a workshop at the end of it, and we could play our little hearts out. And that's where we burned a lot of midnight oil.

The house was... I think it was two bedrooms and then the bathroom, and then a small little... I think Glen was sleeping in the dining room. And I don't know where everybody else slept. If I think back, it was six or seven of us at the time, and certainly there weren't that many bedrooms, and so no, we didn't play in the house. And we were poor. We used to go to the Farmer Jack's grocery store and steal the meat from the department because we couldn't afford to buy any at the time.

Creem magazine journalist Jaan Uhelski:
They were really minimal players when they first came to town. They had a house out near where I worked. They were just unbelievably strange flowers that had taken a route in some sort of suburban oasis, and had a band house and practiced all the time and pranced around and wore amazing clothes. I mean I would see them come in masks in

the mall where I worked. This is right around the time they had Ezrin come out to produce them. But you know, they were kind of a joke. They were just not really good before this, not until probably the third album that they actually got good. They were almost unlistenable, but again their show was so great; it was like a phenomenon. I'm not sure if they were never not dark also. I mean they were always funny but the songwriting got so much better, and they started to make anthemic things. You could really see the development in them but when they first moved there, they were the proto band.

As for Alice and Iggy, they were rarely in the same place. I mean every time I interview Iggy, he says that Alice just wanted to be next to him. I think it was almost a strange hero-worship. They rarely talked; again it wasn't the same circle. They were on bills together but that's it. Alice was born in Detroit. I have a feeling that they just fell on their faces in LA and that they were a joke because of their association with Zappa. And Zappa thought they were a joke after a while, after embracing them, and was just dropping them.

They didn't have many moves left. Detroit had a reputation. He's always loved The Stooges. I think he really wanted to get back to that hardness. And they were really a hard band at that point. And I think they hadn't got their theatrical direction down yet. God bless your countrymen, Bob Ezrin, if he hadn't come in and whipped them into shape, they wouldn't be the band they are.

But they rented a farm out in the outskirts of Detroit, which was incredibly cheap rent. All of them could live there, and they brought Bob Ezrin down, and Bob moved in with them, and he really did drill them. He taught them how to write songs, he put them through their paces and made them practice all the time. It was like the military. And I remember them being really poor. I used to manage a boutique when I worked at Creem, and I remember Alice and Neal Smith coming in, and me giving them free clothes, because they were just down on their luck financially. But they were a presence. They weren't of us, they weren't Detroiters, but they played there a lot.

MC5 drummer Dennis Thompson on Alice Cooper's move back to Detroit:

The powers that be in New York, when they came to Detroit and found us, well then they hired The Stooges and The Frost, and more bands got signed as they came to Detroit and recognized the talent. Alice Cooper got signed. They were an LA band who came to Detroit to get muscled-up. Because when they first came out here and played, they were god-awful. They were a sideshow, clown carnival band. They came to Detroit and the attitude in Detroit was kick out the jams or get off the stage; you know, play and play well, play really well. And they really, really improved, really tightened-up and got some strength to their music.

MC5 guitarist Wayne Kramer:
I think Alice Cooper moved to Detroit because Detroit was the portal at the time. It was the gateway, and there was a lot going on. There was a lot of work. You could perform regularly all over the area. It was a good hub. You could shoot down to Cleveland, you could go to New York, over to Chicago. Living was inexpensive. You'd have a band house. I mean the MC5 lived in a converted dentist's office. I think our rent was $125 a month, with a rehearsal room downstairs for another $75 a month. That's pretty reasonable, even by 1968 standards. And I think Alice and the guys were intrigued with the music. They saw what was happening with the MC5. The first time I ever played with them, we were both appearing at a club in Philadelphia. And we were in our dressing room, they had their own dressing room, and they sent their roadie over. He said, "Yeah, I'm with Alice Cooper. Is MC5 wearing all your spangly clothes tonight?" "Yeah man, we're wearing our shit. Are you guys wearing..." "Oh, we're going to wear ours, too." "Okay, cool." Checking out the competition.

Amboy Dukes drummer K.J. Knight:
Alice Cooper, I'll tell you what, they went through a tough transition. When we played with them, a lot of times, man, they would be booed off the stage, and I don't think people understood or had a grasp of what they were trying to do. But after they had a couple of hit singles, and after they started playing out so often, they picked up so much popularity that it was just unbelievable. They became very successful, a huge group.

Johnny "Bee" Badanjek on Alice Cooper's move to Detroit:
They were up the road, I-75, out near where Pine Knob is or DTE, the outside venue; they rented a farmhouse, an old white farmhouse off of Brown Road, Pontiac, and he had a big barn. And they converted the barn into a rehearsal space. And they used to have these parties all the time. There'd be like 500, 700 people, everybody from Detroit go out to the farmhouse on the weekends. There'd be drinking, jamming, girls, the feeding of Alice's snake in the aquarium. That was the highlight; they'd throw a rat in there or something and girls would go screaming and

stuff, great time. But they also started getting their sound together, and then they did Love It to Death *and got popular really fast. Alice's father was a preacher and earlier they were between Detroit and Arizona so he was aware of the scene. They stayed here for a while, but then they started getting real big and they were travelling.*

I'll tell you a story. One time, when I was playing with Detroit featuring Mitch Ryder, and we were doing opening shows for Alice, and we were in Washington, DC, the old hockey arena. There were two shows, an afternoon show and a night-time show, and it was packed. Ten thousand kids. Alice is on, and he's on the part where they put him on the gallows; they're going to hang him.

And we already played our set. I'm sitting on the anvil cases with some of the biker guys who were security and we're watching this. Alice is up there, they put this clip behind him to catch the rope, and so he's hanging. He's actually got his hands tied because they've got handcuffs on his hands, right? So the clip slips and he's actually hanging. His face is turning red, and everybody on his crew is going, oh, the boss is getting into it today, this is incredible.

And I'm looking at him, me and Dirty M, and I'm going something's not right. It looks like he's going get me down, get me down, I'm really hanging. And everybody's going he's really into it! The audience is mesmerized. I'm going get him down, he's dying! And they finally realize it, and these guys run up and take him down, and Alice is done. His face is red as a tomato, his hands are still tied. He's going, "What took you guys so long?"

May 20, 1970. Four students killed by the Ohio National Guard at Kent State University in Ohio, where protests over the American invasion of Cambodia were taking place.

Neal Smith:
I think that sooner or later something like Alice Cooper would have happened. The revolutions, the Vietnamese war, the turmoil of the '60s, Kent State, this was normal TV now. You could see students killed in a university. You see all this tragedy all around you every night on the news. That didn't happen in the '50s; it was happening in the '60s and the '70s. People were bombarded by all this stuff and that's why Alice says we were almost a reflection of what was happening in society. We were in the right place at the right time and we did the right things at the right time. If it wouldn't have been us, maybe the next extension after the Doors would have been another band.

June 1, 1970. The US release date for Black Sabbath's *Black Sabbath*, prompting long and loud visits for the only band to rival Alice in the spooky rock sweepstakes.

June 13, 1970. Portions of Alice Cooper's performance at the Cincinnati Pop Festival, at Crosley Fields in Cincinnati, are broadcast on local TV.

Dennis Dunaway:
We were mostly banned by television stations who didn't want to touch us with a ten-foot pole, because of our image. That's why there's not very much footage of the original Alice Cooper group, as visual as we were, and that's perfect for an interesting show. They had this show called the Midsummer Rock Festival, which was in Cincinnati, Ohio, and what happened was, there was supposed to be a baseball game and I believe the baseball players went on strike. So a major network's sports hour, where these hours are worked out, the promoters brought in this rock festival and the television station decided they were going to broadcast it and they used sportscasters.

And there were a lot of bands on the bill, the Stooges, Traffic, Grand Funk Railroad, Mott The Hoople, on and on. And we were on there and it was televised nationally. And we decided that we were going to play a song that we had never played before, "Black Juju." We never even rehearsed it before. I discussed the arrangement in the car on the way to the show. And then we had gotten this idea, probably because we were used to stealing pillows out of hotel rooms. We decided to steal the sheets and Alice would put a sheet over each guy. Anyway, he put a sheet over each guy while we were performing this song, and his sheet, somebody in the audience got a hold of, and they pulled it out of Alice's hands.

So he threw a sheet under Neal's drums and then he climbed under there, and the cameraman climbed under there so he could see Alice, broadcast Alice, and he showed Neal, and Neal started blowing kisses to the camera. And he had this blue eyeshadow on, and we didn't know this until after the fact, but evidently a lot of the affiliated stations across this country pulled the plug on us right then and there and they said it was rare that people would pull the plug between commercials—they would usually wait till the next commercial.

And Alice getting pelted with a cake was a surprise to everyone. But when the cake hit Alice, he didn't retaliate like anyone would expect. Instead, he grabbed a gob of it and smashed it in his own face. It was the most unexpected thing that he could have done. That was our fear of failure. It made us invincible on stage. And like Alice said in his acceptance speech at the Rock and Roll Hall of Fame induction, "We won't promise that we'll never embarrass you. We're Alice Cooper—that's what we do." We used embarrassing situations on stage for dramatic effect anyway, so the cake fit right in.

So we always had things like that. Even in the early LA days. We played this show, probably because they thought, again, Alice Cooper was a folk singer or something, and we showed up. And it was a really popular talk show, a daytime talk show, and we played and they had us lip-synch our song. We really didn't want to do that but they forced us to do that, and so all we could hear was the drums. We couldn't hear the track, because they had such a little thing. Anyway, Neal was very upset about that and he was cursing. The curtain closed and he was cursing, but what we didn't know was that Neal's mic was live out into the audience. So we got banned for that (laughs).

Mid-1970. Zappa's Straight Records is sold to Warner Bros.; Alice Cooper inherits a major label deal.

Neal Smith:
Warners Bros. bought out Straight Records, which was Frank Zappa's label and there were ten bands, which I still think was one of the most amazing business deals ever done at the time. Warner Brothers bought out ten bands from Straight Records for about $50,000. This was already after we'd recorded Easy Action. *Linda Ronstadt was with a band called Stone Ponies and also James Taylor was in one of the groups that Frank Zappa had at the time. So they kinda got Alice Cooper as a bonus because they'd really wanted Linda Ronstadt and James Taylor.*

Dennis Dunaway on the underwhelming work done by Straight/Bizarre:
Bizarre was supposed to be in charge of it, but it seemed like our first two records were pretty much promoted from our managers' telephone and out of the trunk of their beat-up old Cadillac. Pretties for You *got some publicity when Woolworths refused to carry it with the girl's panties showing. So it was censored with a sticker, which caused a slight boost in sales.*

Later on the Alice Cooper group went to a Woolworths to see if they were stocking Easy Action *and they had a big poster of us in the front window. A kid was standing on the sidewalk staring at it so I got the other guys to sidestep between the kid and the poster. We waved at him* and pointed to our poster. He freaked out and begged us to wait there while he ran to get his friend. We took off.

Michael Bruce:
We were on our own on the first two albums. So, it was five minds turned loose in the studio and you got a helter skelter stampede. There's a whole lot of ideas, but not one particular one that is followed through.

August 7 – 10, 1970. At the Strawberry Fields Festival in Bowmanville, Ontario, at which Alice Cooper was on the packed bill, Shep Gordon talks to producer Jack Richardson about working with his new charges. Richardson, from the advertising field and as straight-laced a rock producer as one could imagine, declines but suggests his assistant, Bob Ezrin.

August 10, 1970. The Alice Cooper band appear as themselves in the movie *Diary of a Mad Housewife*.

Neal Smith:
There was so much to write about—about the band and about Alice, really—that the sky was the limit. We were getting mainstream press even before we'd even recorded Love It to Death, and at that point we hadn't even sold 20,000 albums with two albums, and the press was bigger than our success was. And also being in the movie *Diary of a Mad Housewife*, which was released in 1970 helped bring a buzz on the band in the underground. College stations were playing Easy Action, but we weren't ranking at mainstream at all when it came to the actual music.

Photographer Bob Gruen:
Alice Cooper, that was somebody people were scared of. Because he was a boy with a girl's name. Because he brought a sexual connotation into it that Kiss didn't have, in the sense that you were more afraid of the New York Dolls because there was a sexual connotation. With Kiss it was more about rock 'n' roll, it was about fantasy, it was about scary monsters, but it wasn't about your son turning gay, going for a gay guy. Alice Cooper, one of his early publicity pictures, he was half man, half woman, where on one side he was a scary looking guy and on the other side he had lipstick and his hair was fixed up a little more and he looked more like a girl. That was an image that frightened a lot of people, that a man could take on a female role and be open about it.

August 14, 1970. Space rockers Hawkwind issue their debut album, a self-titled that captures them not quite fully formed yet. The band would rapidly build a following as a theatrical although more so, loud and psychedelic band. Hawkwind and Alice Cooper as represented on the first two albums bear similarities in that they both proposed a post-psychedelic era psychedelia.

September 8, 1970. Alice Cooper play at Max's Kansas City in Manhattan; in the crowd is a young Bob Ezrin, who sees the band perform for the first time. Before the show, Bob attends hit Broadway show *Hair*, so he brings along the *Hair*'s Canadian lead Allan Nicholls. Emerging from the subway and following the laser beams in the street, they turn the corner and there's Max's. The brief from Jack Douglas and his partners back at Nimbus 9 is to "get rid of Alice Cooper."

Dennis Dunaway:
We were still hitting rock bottom. We were starting to lose our faith at one point, especially a particular night when we came to New York City. New York City was a tough nut to crack for us. We played several gigs there and the sound systems were bad and the acoustics were bad and the audiences were just really cold to us. They just weren't on our side at all. We were booked into Max's Kansas City. The dressing room was

full of beer cartons, of empty beer bottles, so we had to tune up on the stairs. And there were like five people in the club. Neal in particular was very upset. Who advertised this? So the band decided that it wasn't worth playing that night.

And me, I was always giving my Knute Rockne, "One for the gipper," and I would always say the smaller the crowd the bigger the rumours. And I remember going to Buxton and saying, "Well, why don't we not play and start a rumour that we did?" Anyway, that night we played but we were all upset. It was an angry, angry set. And one of the people in the audience was Bob Ezrin, who was just a kid at the time.

And he came up afterwards and he said, "Oh I loved that song, 'I'm Edgy.' It's such an edgy show and it was perfect with this song, 'I'm Edgy.'" And as it turned out, he meant "I'm Eighteen." But he says, "I'm going to get you guys a record deal," and we're like yeah right, kid. We'd buy you a drink but you're not old enough. And we ended up getting a record deal.

Alice Cooper:
He heard us at Max's Kansas City. He heard "Eighteen" and he went, "Oh, what's that song, 'I'm Edgy?'" I said, "You mean 'Eighteen?'" He said, "Yeah, that song is so dumb, it's a hit." But we would play it and he would go, "No, dumb it down." We were trying to be the Yardbirds.

Neal Smith on wanting Jack Richardson to produce the band:
Jack Richardson thought we were just a bunch of transvestite, drug-taking, beer-drinking weirdos from California. And we wanted Nimbus 9, Jack Richardson's company, to produce us. We had done two albums that artistically we were happy with, but financially and commercially, we didn't have a gold album, that's for sure. So, we wanted somebody that was doing hit records, and who was doing hit records in the late '60s but The Guess Who? They just kept having hit record after hit record, and we were like, "Who is producing these records?" So we found out it was Jack Richardson of Nimbus 9, up in Toronto.

So we did a big press to get him to come and see us live, and we were playing at Max's Kansas City in New York, and it was just a showcase for somebody from the record company to come on down and check us out. We wrote so many times, "Jack, will you come and see us?" "No." "Jack, will you come and see us?" "No!" We asked him tons of times and he didn't want to come and see us. And our managers Shep Gordon and Joe Greenberg were in his office every day up in Canada. They went up there specifically to pressure him, well "convince" him, let's put it that way, to see the band.

*So he said, "Fine. I have this new guy Bob Ezrin; I'll send him down."
And he's thinking to himself that Bob Ezrin is classically trained, he's
a technician, there's nothing about this weirdo group that he's going
to like, and he's going to see them and go running back to Toronto
with his tail between his legs. That's the story Jack Richardson told us!
So Bob comes down to see us at Max's Kansas City—and he loves the
band! He gets it. And he goes back to Jack, and he says to Jack, "There's
a new huge wave of music coming and this band is the tip of it, and
either we get on board with it or it's going to pass us by."*

September 18, 1970. The death of Jimi Hendrix, arguably the person who invented flashy heavy metal. Also on this day, Black Sabbath issue their hit second album, *Paranoid*. The '60s is in the rear-view mirror and soon, so is Alice Cooper's '60s music of the first two records.

September 19, 1970. Alice Cooper play at The Warehouse in New Orleans, Louisiana, as part of a rip-roarin' bill with The Stooges and the MC5.

Late 1970. Dick Wagner's band The Frost issue their third, last and heaviest album, *Through the Eyes of Love*.

Dick Wagner:
*The third album was the one that I produced, did a lot of the arranging
and stuff in the studio, you know, not much pre-production with it.
The album was pretty heavy actually, but it had a terrible album cover,
just terrible. That was Vanguard; whoever they had working in the art
department at that time came up with that beauty with the gas masks—
it was just stupid. We had a good laugh over that one.*

Early November 1970. Alice Cooper work with new producer Bob Ezrin, at RCA Mid-American Recording Center in Chicago on tracks that will comprise their third album. The brief however is to get a four song demo done, so Warner can green-light the band proceeding toward the full-length.

At this point, Bob is relieved that Jack Richardson hasn't fired him after coming home from New York and raving about this band he was instructed to turn down. However Jack said he wasn't about to produce them and that it was up to Bob to handle the job if he liked these guys so much.

Bob's first trip to the infamous band house was memorable to say the least. He's taken aside by one of the roadies, out to the barn where's he's handed a knife blade of dirty white powder that he has to snort as a sort of dark initiation. The drug turns out to be horse tranquilizer and Bob swears he drove back to the city and doesn't remember a minute of the trip.

Michael Bruce:
Shep had been going up to Canada and he met Jack Richardson and some of the people at Nimbus 9. And supposedly the story there was, whoever fucks up at Nimbus 9 has to produce the Alice Cooper group (laughs). They heard our first two albums and they weren't too impressed. But Bob, I guess Bob screwed up, so he went down and caught our show, and that's where he thought the song we were doing was "I'm Edgy."

So he came out to the farm. I was so excited, I rode out to the airport to meet him and talked his ear off all the way back to the farm (laughs). And we started working out there with him and it was great. We went through all the material and analysed it and added parts and took out parts. He was a classically trained pianist. His father wanted him to be a doctor but he was a rebellious kid so he became a rock 'n' roll producer. But before Bob came out, we were struggling. We had done two albums that didn't exactly set the music industry on fire. Unless they were piling them up and burning them.

Bob Ezrin on the art of hit-making:
I was in that world every day and that was my reality. But all of us just felt like Alice Cooper and this Detroit music was the true American sound and radio was catching up. When I was working with those guys and living with them in Detroit, hanging out with them and Nugent and the MC5 and Jimmy Osterberg, you know, Iggy... and I had produced Mitch Ryder right after the first Alice Cooper album. I did Mitch Ryder, also in Detroit. And so I spent a lot of time there, and from that point of view, being my first real experience in an American city, being into an American city's culture as opposed to just being a visitor, from that point of view, everything was rocking and hard. Everything was larger than life. The people were loud and brash and the bands were heavy, and to me that felt like the seed of the next revolution.

So I just thought this was where everything was, this was a true expression of where American youth was. I didn't see it as a dangerous thing to do. I thought it was absolutely natural. And maybe that was good. Maybe in our ignorance, we just stormed ahead and were doing what we did instead of worrying about what was expected of us.

Alice Cooper on Bob arriving at the farm in Pontiac and being greeted by Dennis wearing a frog's head and saying "Ribbit:"
It didn't surprise me at all to walk downstairs and find Dennis in a frog outfit. When that sort of thing happened you would just walk by him and go, "Oh, hi Dennis." It never occurred to any of the rest of us that such a thing would ever be odd to anyone else. If you knew Dennis then you were used to that sort of thing. It must have been a bit of a shock to Bob. Imagine just walking in and finding a frog. And then he would discover that everyone else in the band had very distinct personalities. Luckily, we all worked well as a unit. I consider the Love It to Death *album the first Alice Cooper album, because when we hired Ezrin to come be our producer, he changed the sound, the look, the feel—the whole thing. He was the one that defined what we actually sounded like.*

November 11, 1970. Alice Cooper issue as a single "I'm Eighteen," (at this point, just "Eighteen") backed with "Is It My Body." The single performed well, spending eight weeks on the chart and reaching No.21 on Billboard. In Canada, the single vaulted to No.7. Its success moved Warner to tentatively allow the band to record a full-length.

Alice Cooper on "I'm Eighteen:"
"Eighteen" was just a riff we used to jam to, to warm up. I remember when we first started to do "Eighteen," it was in Detroit; we used to rehearse in this dump. And everybody had a bottle of Boone's Farm Apple Wine. It was just the worst; I mean, I don't think it's ever seen anything except chemicals. It was just the worst, and we'd all have a bottle of that and that was just the chord progression (sings it), and it was a good riff for everybody to warm up and jam a little bit on, and Bob Ezrin kept hearing that and he kept saying, you know, that's really a good riff. And he would listen to us rehearse and he'd say let's make something out of that.

    And again, it's one of those things that I would like to say, it was during the war, the end of the war, and there was always that controversy of, "I'm a boy, I'm a man." I can go get killed for my country but I can't buy a beer. So "Eighteen" was that juxtaposition of being both. And then, when it sounded like a complaint, then it turns the corner. It says I'm 18, I've got angst, I don't know what I am, I don't know if I'm a boy or a man, and I like it! And that was the selling point of that. It was the fact that instead of I hate it, it was I'm 18 and I like it. And everybody related to that and said, "Yeah, I dig being screwed-up."

Dennis Dunaway:
Following the lack of acceptance for Pretties for You, *we decided to write songs in a more relatable style. We would have come much closer to achieving that on* Easy Action *if we had had a rehearsal space and another month or so. But by the time Bob saw us at Max's Kansas City, Michael had spearheaded the development of songs like "Caught in a Dream" and "I'm Eighteen." Neal had written "Hallowed Be My Name" and I had written "Black Juju" as a vehicle for the Alice character.*

1971

At this point one can safely say that Alice is in that apocryphal spot that a clutch of '70s bands experienced (and complained about with a chuckle), where they put out two albums in one year and to boot, did it while barely falling off the road. Alice is all the rage in 1971, playing bigger and bigger shows off the back of their boy-to-man hit anthem "I'm Eighteen." The rest of *Love It to Death* doesn't have near the same impact, but it paints a picture as dark as the album cover, of a band uneasily sophisticated for heavy metal, so they aren't.

First half of the year, "I'm Eighteen" reaches No.21 on the charts, the band gets big royalty checks and Jim Morrison pops a clog in Paris. Into the second half, the band find time to record what will become *Killer* while also touring Europe for the first time.

In an exaggerated version of what happened last record out, *Killer*, issued in November of this year, would be dominated by a single not quite characteristic of the rest of the album. "Under My Wheels" would be a happy glam boogie rocker, after which a deep dive into the rest of the album (save for "Be My Lover") reveals a record more nightmarish and shocking than its predecessor, which had a few things on it that were still psych in spirit. And Lord save us, what an album cover, as Neal introduces us to his snake Kachina, a trademark beyond cane and greasepaint and glam-gone-wrong that is added to the band's bulging bag of tricks.

January 26, 1971. Alice Cooper play the Fillmore North in Toronto, Canada, sharing the stage with Free and Cactus.

March 8, 1971. Alice Cooper's third album, *Love It to Death* is issued. Billboard calls the band "the first stars of future-rock." Biggest hit on the record is "I'm Eighteen," which, although essentially a morose ballad, paints the picture of the young metalhead who might be a fan of Alice, Sabbath, Deep Purple or The Doors. The initial issue is on

Straight Records but the album was quickly reissued by Warner Bros., new owners of Straight.

Warner Bros. Love It to Death *press release*:
Centuries ago, in the 17th century, astrologists and scientists became aware of a celestial and earthly turbulence which seemed to be concentrated in and around England. The island's atmosphere was charged with energy, the earth seemed to tremble; it was as if nature herself was thrashing about and the stars had come together. Its effect on the people of England was one of extreme unrest. Suspicion and fear spread from the castles of the rich to the small hamlets of the poor. During this unnatural upheaval—on February 4, 1623, in Sussex, England—Alice Cooper was born.

1623-1636: Alice Cooper, whose mother and father left the richness of their castle in England, changed their names and became simple inhabitants of Sussex, was a strange child. She seemed to be always listening to voices no one else could hear, often smiling secretly, as if she shared the world's joke. Much of her time was spent with her sister, Christine, who was three years older. Christine taught her the magic of the strange plants that grew abundantly in the forest. She taught her the ancient words of old that could make the thunder crash and the fire burn. Alice's mother and father died by fire the year of her 12th birthday. One year after the death of her parents, Alice witnessed the death of Christine, who was called witch by the village and burned at the stake. Alice, with the help of Christine, seeing a new life in another time, died by poison. Her age: 13 years—place: Sussex, England—in the year 1636.

The Journey: The road twisted and curved, the trees were shadows in the black memory of my mind. The mist was heavy as it swirled around me. I was aware of centuries past and a world of memories.

There was light ahead. Having come so far, I knew my time was near. I had traveled the roads of eternity, searching for the way back; and now I felt the energy beneath my feet, the time had come. Peering through the glass, I saw a room filled with a presence strangely comforting, a room full of waiting. There was a plaque hanging crookedly on the wall.

1948 - ?: Alice Cooper, age 20 years, a new time, a new life is back today. He is now, as he was then, the mocking voice of the past, echoed by Christine, whispering always of tomorrow. Alice, having re-entered, is now of today and has gathered around him those of yesterday.

Glen Buxton, lead guitar: A brooding figure of the past, a Black Night (sic) once feared by many, has been brought by Alice, to tell of centuries of hate and a world of fear. Dennis Dunaway, bass guitar: An artist of the courts, painting the picture of history, knowing the colours of tomorrow. Michael Bruce, rhythm guitar, vocals: A poet of the streets, writing songs of centuries, a figure in the fields of tomorrow. Neal Allen Smith, drums, vocals: A Warrior King, born of power, bred in the strongholds of the Gods. He is here now, leading Alice toward the future of yesterday.

If you can stomach any more of this kind of crap... contact Warner Bros. Records.

Alice Cooper on Love It to Death:
Love It to Death *changed a lot of thinking about what was going on in music. It was a really hard-edged, Detroit, eerie... you know, it had classical things in it, but you could tell that this band was not classically-oriented. But all of a sudden you would hear this classical piano that would come in, over top of all this horror. And that's why it's really unique. You know, at that time, I've got to be honest with you,* Love It to Death *was a really hard record to make.*

When Bob Ezrin got hold of us he said, "Look, everybody wants to love you guys, but there's nothing to hang the handle on. I mean, you guys have no handle, no musical handle." So he took us for eight months. We sat in Detroit in a barn, ten hours a day, and we learned how to play. And I developed a sound, Alice's vocal sound, Dennis developed a bass sound, Glen had a guitar sound, Neal had a drum sound. So when Love It to Death *came out, it was the first time people heard it and said, "That's Alice Cooper." It had its own sound. You know, when you heard Jim Morrison, you always knew it was Jim Morrison. When you heard Mick Jagger, that's Mick Jagger. This time they heard it and said, "That's Alice." So we had an identification there; people could identify with us now.*

But I wouldn't say we were heavy metal. You know, I think the first time I ever saw the moniker heavy metal was Rolling Stone talking about us. It was in a big Rolling Stone article, and they called us heavy metal and it had parentheses around it, so that was pretty much the first time I ever saw that term. I think really, the first heavy metal band was probably Iron Butterfly. I mean, "In-a-Gadda-Da-Vida" was heavy metal (laughs). But we always liked The Who and The Yardbirds and then I think Led Zeppelin took it to another level and then you started getting your Black Sabbaths. But we were always right in that soup. I mean, hard rock was never far from heavy metal.

Michael Bruce:
It was our third album and we felt it was a make-or-break situation. It was also our first adventure with Bob Ezrin and I knew that the way this man worked, I could tell he was putting everything he had into it. It was a lot of hard work and it paid off.

Neal Smith:
During and after Love It to Death, *we were starting to find our niche. We were all art students in college and high school, and we were also fans of the old horror movies, all the way from* Frankenstein *to* Wolfman *and not only that, but the westerns. I was a big fan of John Wayne and all the early guys, Roy Rogers and the Cisco Kid, and all those movies had hangings in them.*

But the vibe of that album had a lot to do with the culture of Detroit and us being in Detroit. Of course Motown is there, but this is like the anti-Motown. And I think drugs played a part in it too. Because when we were in California, the drugs around California were more mellow, more natural, marijuana, pot, LSD — it was more of a mellow thing. But when we went back to Detroit, there was a lot of THC, harder chemicals, and people even had the heavier stuff than that. So the harder drug culture played a part in the harder sound.

Detroit is a big industrial city, as opposed to California with the beach and the sun, where it's beautiful all the time and it's mellow and laid-back. If you're starving in California, at least you're warm. If you're starving in Detroit, Michigan in the middle of winter, you're starving but you're freezing. So it's a totally different vibe there. And it's one that inspired us to greater things. We basically wrote Love It to Death *in the Midwest. So it was a very different vibe. We were in the right place at the right time for our writing. And also for the crowds — the fans that took us into their heart before anybody else did were those crowds.*

Bob Ezrin:
I don't think that Detroit music was what was inspiring the band, particularly. The band didn't know that they needed to change. It was a combination of their strangeness and my sort of more classical and structured musical upbringing. We put all that together and it came out sounding like the new Alice. I just felt the songs were all over the place and they didn't have... there was no sort of focal point to them, and plus I didn't feel like Alice Cooper really had a sound. Or if there was a sound, it was back in the Pretties for You days and it was so outrageous that they weren't going to succeed with it.

We did want to succeed. We weren't just making music for our own indulgence. We were making stuff that everybody would hopefully love. That was the goal, to make stuff that people were going to love all over the country, and they would buy records and come to the shows and enjoy the ride with us.

So none of those other guys influenced this band musically. If anything it was the other way around. At the beginning, we were doing stuff that people were going, wow, wait a minute, that's unusual. And it was only unusual because it was just sort of basic goofy, very simply-structured stuff. It was all I could do at the time, was very simple structural stuff. But it had any integrity to it and a flow to it. The material really hung together and so it served the music well. Plus it was theatrical.

Dennis Dunaway on the move away from a full band credit to individual credits on Love It to Death:
I preferred crediting everyone. Dividing up who did what never mattered much to me. I let others decide the breakdowns because I was obsessed with thinking of the next thing we were going to do. There are a lot of songs that my name probably deserved to be on as a songwriter, but then there are others that I feel like I'm generously included. Michael once said, "It's pretty much a wash concerning my credits."

The ones credited as band songs truly all came together as band songs. I mean we pounced on every song thinking of every possibility to make it better. And we stuck to a hard rule that every idea had to be played by the band. Only then could a majority vote eliminate it. And then everyone would move forward with a positive attitude—no grudges. That wasn't easy, but it was an extremely important key to our success. Few songs came through our mill with little changed—"Caught in a Dream" and "No More Mr. Nice Guy" did)—and many changed radically several times over, like "Elected" and "Lay Down and Die, Goodbye." But most were group efforts from scratch.

"Black Juju" was mine. I remember, I plugged my bass into a small guitar amp and cranked it to a sinister distortion. Like Dave Davies "You Really Got Me" guitar sound, but with a bass. I was alone in an old motel that had a little room with a water heater. I removed the metal plate from the heater and used the glowing pilot flame as the only light in the room. I imagined the flame as an inferno, and that inspired the riffs.

A week later, I discovered a hot old attic in an off-campus dormitory in Cincinnati. I went in there with pencil and paper and my Frog bass. It was dimly lit in a spooky way and I got into an Edgar Allen Poe frame of mind. That's where I wrote the lyrics, which included the concept of Alice hypnotizing the audience with a swinging pocket watch. The band liked it as it was. Ever since we had dropped "Fields of Regret" I had been talking about giving the dark side of the Alice character another dramatic vehicle, and finally there it was.

March 19 – August 28, 1971. Alice Cooper tour intensively the US Midwest and the eastern seaboard, including the band's usual high propensity of festival dates along with a handful of Canadian dates, including a far-flung stop to play the student centre at Memorial University in St. John's, Newfoundland.

Dennis Dunaway on the band's approach to the design of the show:
Well, the idea as it struck us was black and white. That's why the front of the album is dark and the back is light. We had songs like... the white part of it would be songs like "Caught in a Dream;" it's an uplifting song—it's not a dark character song. But we also had "Black Juju," so the set was like that. It started out bright and then it got very dark, shifted gears, after about four rockers, then it shifted gears and got very moody and very dark and then it became uplifting at the end, after Alice got killed (laughs).

We had an electric chair. Yeah, I came up with the idea. We wanted to put on a morality play-type thing. And that was developing in the music. With "Dwight Fry," Alice is going crazy, and then "Black Juju" was just very dark with nothing necessarily going on as far as being a victim or whatever. But still, it was conducive to all of this all of a sudden very dark thing that was going on.

So we were thinking, well, why don't we have Alice do something

bad? And then he'll be punished for it. Like a million operas or whatever (laughs). So we're trying to think of how he should get killed, and I thought of the electric chair. And we're like, yeah, we can't even afford food; where are we going to get an electric chair? I said, I'll build it. And I did build one, which is in Canada now, in Ottawa. I saw it just recently. But I have the second one. The first one was a little bit rickety because we didn't know what we were doing yet, but then the second one we built to be sturdier for the road. And then we built two collapsible ones after that. So there were four electric chairs altogether.

But yeah, by Love It to Death, we already had these songs for the dark character that was Alice. I wrote "Black Juju" and Neal wrote "Hallowed Be Thy Name." We had several songs that were aimed at this dark character, and that's really how it developed. It started way back on Pretties for You, but it took us a couple albums to get there.

Yet even in Love It to Death on "Ballad of Dwight Fry," you can hear this vulnerability in Alice's performances. That's what he could do extremely well, and that's why people still love him, still love his shows today. There is a vulnerability. And that vulnerability would vary, into the era when Alice was drinking too much. Glen would be criticized for drinking too much and maybe playing a little bit loose on occasion, but Alice could be falling down drunk forgetting the lyrics and unable to even stand up on stage and people loved him, because of that vulnerability.

Neal Smith on one memorable gig in Detroit:
I didn't even know about it. It was either The Grande or the Eastown—I think it was probably the Eastown. There was a big movie screen that came down from the ceiling. It was a movie theatre at one point. The opening band would sit in front of it. The headlining band had their equipment back behind. The headline band that night was The Who. From behind the stage you could see right through the screen. In front of the screen, because it was pure white there was a light show on it and you could not see behind it.

We finished the show—this was the Love It to Death tour—with "Black Juju." Goose, my drum tech goes, "Did you hear Keith playing along with you?" He said, "He was playing with you, note for note, on 'Black Juju.' I was backstage and you were in front of the screen and he was behind the screen and it was like a mirror image with him playing right with you." With all of the music from Glen and Dennis and Michael, I could not hear the drums behind me as Keith was not mic'ed up. That is the story. Goose said it was amazing. It always reminds me of a scene from a movie. If that had been filmed, it would have been awesome.

April 24, 1971. After a steady two-month rise, "I'm Eighteen" reaches its chart peak of No.21. By this point the band was making $15,000 a show. *Love It to Death* was rapidly going through reissues due to both the label change from Straight to Warner, and due to the cover art, where some thought that Alice's thumb peaking through his clothing, looked too much like a penis.

Alice Cooper:
What a silly thing that was. First of all, what an insult! I mean, they looked at my thumb and figured that's my...my unit! If I woulda known that, I would have had a much longer thumb.

Neal Smith:
Everybody said his thumb looked like a penis. I said, well, if that was my penis, I'd be totally embarrassed (laughs). But I just couldn't believe that; it was one of those fluky things. We had a few things that accidentally happened in our career and that was one of them. All of a sudden they had banned the album, they had to change it and airbrush it out. Give me a fucking break—that's the most ridiculous thing in the world. With Alice Cooper, people were trying to find things that were outrageous. I mean, from that standpoint, if they really thought Alice is sitting there holding his dick in the picture, I wouldn't be in the picture with Alice if he was holding his dick. But at any rate, it was one of those great things in the end.

Also if you look on the back cover, I'm holding a cane. See, in 1968, we had a hunting accident when Alice shot me in the foot. I still have the bullet in my foot. I used to use a cane for quite a while to help me walk. And I still had one of my canes, and I just wanted a prop to use. So if you look on the back cover, I'm sitting on that seat, holding my hands out with the cane going straight down. And then on the front cover, there on the left I had the same cane, but I had it over my shoulders, and I'm draping my arms over it. So that was the first time the cane was used on stage and to this day Alice still uses a cane. So that was the evolution of where that came from. Also on Billion Dollar Babies, *Alice had a cane that turned into an American flag which was kind of cool. And even on* Love It to Death, *Alice was toting a sword.*

April 27, 1971. "Caught in a Dream"/"Hallowed Be My Name" is issued as the second and last single from *Love It to Death*. The song stalled at No.94 on the charts.

Bob Ezrin, on hard rock making inroads to radio:
Because I was living in it and was in that world every day, that was my reality. All of us just felt like we were the true American sound and radio was catching up. I was working with those guys and living with them in Detroit, hanging out with them and Nugent and the MC5 and Jimmy Osterberg, you know, Iggy, and all of these people at that time, and I had produced Mitch Ryder right after the first Alice Cooper album—I did Mitch Ryder, also in Detroit. And so I spent a lot of time there, and from that point of view, being my first real experience in an American city, being into an American city's culture, as opposed to just being a visitor, from that point of view, everything was rocking and hard. Everything was larger than life. The people were loud and brash and the bands were heavy, and to me that felt like the seed of the next revolution. So I just thought this was a true expression of where American youth was. I didn't see it as a dangerous thing to do. I thought it was absolutely natural. And maybe that was good. Maybe in our ignorance, we just stormed ahead and did what we did instead of worrying about what was expected of us.

Alice Cooper on his character's persona:
There were all rock heroes and no rock villains. My heroes were the Beatles and the Stones and all these great bands, and I said well that's great but there's something else I'm missing here. I'll make Alice the ultimate villain. He'll be Dracula, Jack the Ripper, all these guys rolled into one, but he'll be a rock singer, and he'll write these songs that are sort of irritating the parents a lot. And I mean what kind of music fits horror more than rock? It's perfect together. And I was surprised that nobody did it before me.

Michael Bruce:
After Love It to Death, *Bob was determined to prove himself, and he wasn't going to let this be a flop. We really worked hard on Love it to Death. And it was, hey, we're just five guys from Phoenix, Arizona. We used to refer to ourselves as like "the band who couldn't shoot straight" as in that movie,* The Gang that Couldn't Shoot Straight. *You know, the bumbling idiot that makes it big. And we were five of those idiots.*

June 1971. *Love It to Death* is issued in the UK, where it would rise to No.28 in the charts, again, in part, driven by the success of the album's all-important hit single.

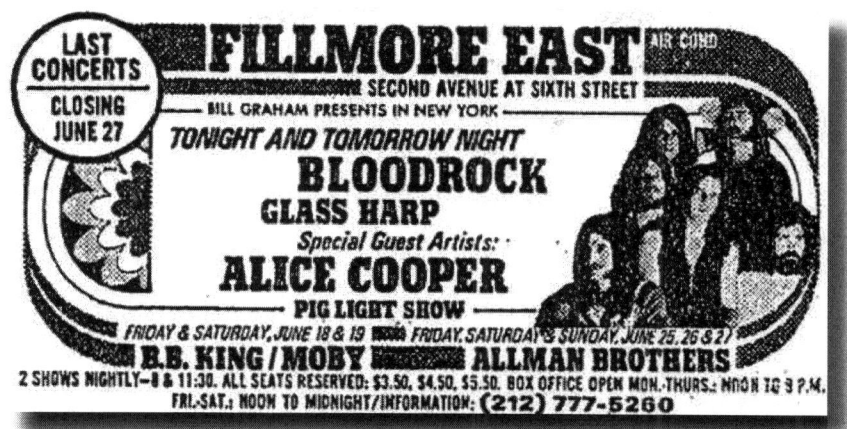

Alice Cooper on "Eighteen:"
"Eighteen" was just a riff we used to jam to, to warm up. I remember when we first started to do "Eighteen," it was in Detroit. We used to rehearse in this dump and everybody had a bottle of Boone's Farm Apple Wine. It was just the worst; I mean, I don't think it's ever seen anything except chemicals. And we'd all have a bottle of that and that was just the chord progression (sings it), and it was a good riff for everybody to warm up and jam a little bit on.

Bob Ezrin kept hearing that and he kept saying, "You know, that's really a good riff." He'd listen to us rehearse and he'd say, "Let's make something out of that." It's one of those things that I would like to say, it was during the war, the end of the war, and there was always that controversy of "I'm a boy, I'm a man." I can go get killed for my country but I can't buy a beer. So "Eighteen" was that juxtaposition of being both. And then, when it sounded like a complaint, then it turns the corner. It says, "I'm 18, I've got angst, I don't know what I am, I don't know if I'm a boy or a man, and I like it!" And that was the selling point of it. It was the fact that instead of "I hate it," it was "I'm 18 and I like it." And everybody related to that and said, "Yeah, I dig being screwed up."

June 26, 1971. Alice Cooper plays the Beggar's Banquet Festival in Toronto, sharing a bill with the Beach Boys, Steppenwolf, Bread, Bloodrock, Lighthouse, Chilliwack and the Old Rationals.

July 1971. Each of the members of the band receives royalty cheques of $8000.

July 3, 1971. Acquaintance of Alice and the band, as well as monumental rock icon, Jim Morrison dies at age 27, in Paris.

July 11, 1971. Alice Cooper play the Long Beach Auditorium, supported by Savage Grace and Black Oak Arkansas. In attendance is a 14-year-old Randy Rhoads who decides then and there that he wants to rock 'n' roll for a living. A decade later, Rhoads would be in a band with Black Oak Arkansas drummer Tommy Aldridge.

July 19, 1971. A particularly robust bill at the Civic Centre in Canada's capital, Ottawa, Ontario, finds Yes and Black Sabbath supporting Alice Cooper. This was followed up in August by additional shows with Sabbath, along with Humble Pie and Edgar Winter Group. This is roughly when Alice started using a boa constrictor in his set, with his first snake Kachina. Apparently the snake had been thrown on stage back in January, and Neal had decided to keep it.

Dennis Dunaway:
I do remember a gig where the bill was Black Sabbath, and Alice Cooper headlined, and there was this opening band that nobody had ever heard of. And I remember walking into the arena and seeing the audience basically people socializing and finding their seats. And this band was on stage that I thought, "Oh man, we've got to follow these guys?!" And it was Yes. And I was thinking, geez, these guys are playing so good and nobody is paying any attention to them.

August 22, 1971. The One Beautiful Picnic festival in Lake Milton, Ohio features a bill that includes Procol Harum, Chuck Berry, the Amboy Dukes, Brownsville Station, Bob Seger and Alice Cooper.

September 7, 1971. Brief recording session at RCA Studios in Chicago where the band work on "Desperado," "Halo of Flies" and "Under My Wheels."

Michael Bruce on the construction of "Halo of Flies:"
I ended up with a lot of song fragments and I used to string them together in sort of a loose format. I'd use them to warm up with and that's where "Halo of Flies" began. And then of course we added other parts to it for the finished song, but I don't remember trying to measure up to Emerson, Lake and Palmer (laughs). We basically made an instrumental with a little vocal part in the middle and it took on a

life of its own. That went back to the band's early beginnings because we used to do jams and Bob used to say it's cool to speed up and slow down as long as you do it together. As far as I'm concerned we were kind of masters at that and "Halo of Flies" was certainly one of them.

September 13, 14th, 1971. Alice Cooper support Led Zeppelin at the Berkeley Theatre, in Berkeley, California.

October 22 – November 7, 1971. The band tour Europe for the first time, beginning on the continent and ending at The Rainbow in London, England, one night with The Who, another night with Arthur Brown.

November 1971. "Under My Wheels," backed with "Desperado," is issued as the first single off of *Killer*. The song is credited to Michael, Dennis and producer Bob Ezrin. Guest guitar on the track is provided by Rick Derringer.

Dennis Dunaway:
We had a lot of positive things going on with outside musicians. Bob wasn't the only one that advocated that. The only time it was ever upsetting was later on when the majority vote of the band was dismissed. Rick Derringer plays the lead guitar break with the heavy effect on my song, "Under My Wheels." We became friends during a six-night stand with the McCoys at Steve Paul's Scene in NYC in '69. Rick was Glen's friend too, and when he stopped by the studio in Chicago to wish us luck, "Under My Wheels" was in progress, so we told him to get in there and plug in.

   Neal always tells the story about Michael and I flipping a hotel couch forward to make a fort for privacy. We spent most of a day under there working up "Under My Wheels." Michael did a lot of woodshedding back in LA and became a much better guitar player. Then he did the same with the piano. And then he applied those instruments to his songwriting. He was extremely persistent with each song. He was loud and didn't care who was around to hear him pounding out parts. He could drive you nuts with it. I mean you wanted to choke him sometimes. But by the time we met Ezrin, Michael was on top of his game. He was also the most aggressive at getting the band to do his songs. If he didn't have an idea, then he was willing to work on mine. But if he had an idea, he was like a steamroller. Sometimes I thought he would sabotage my ideas, which would have been unacceptable if his ideas weren't so strong.

Alice Cooper:
When you're writing for a character, for somebody other than yourself, then it's different. I might write the greatest song that I've ever written and then I will realize that Alice would never sing this. It could be a great song for Guns N' Roses or the Foo Fighters, but it's not a song that Alice would ever sing. Being a songwriter, you just write the song and it comes out the way that it is. If it's usable, then a lot of times we can twist the lyrics around enough to make it sound like Alice, but a lot of times you can't.

Bob and I would sit there and be very objective about Alice. We'd talk about him in the third person without getting personal about it. I would say, "Bob, that whole second section there is not Alice." Bob would listen to it and say, "You know, you're right. Let's change that." If I were writing for Captain Hook then I would be able to do it because I kind of know how he thinks about things, but you couldn't just write anything and have Captain Hook sing it.

Michael Bruce on his role in the band as a guitarist:
Well, I jokingly referred to myself as... you've got the drummer, bass, lead singer, lead guitar player and I was the lead rhythm player. Of course, I was the only other guitar in the band, so... (laughs). But if you think about it, Neal very much so played more from the top part of his kit rather than... he would still have the bass drum, but he wasn't John Bonham? Plus no syncopated type of bass drum parts. He could do it but he didn't have that... a lot of the times it was the writing that didn't bring it out. And then Dennis was all over the place doing runs in the songs. And so my parts were kind of simple—I was the guy that was holding down the fort.

November 5, 1971. The band record a performance for UK music show The Old Grey Whistle Test; the footage airs four days later.

November 8, 1971. Alice Cooper's fourth album *Killer* is issued. Also in early November, the band move into the band house to end all band houses, the 42-room Galesi Estate in Greenwich, CT.

Alice Cooper on Killer:
Now Killer, *by some standards, by real rock reviewer standards, some of them say that that is the best record we ever did. That was the fifth or sixth biggest selling record that year, and that really was just pure*

Alice. We weren't doing anything on that album that we just wouldn't have done naturally, except for the fact that we had Bob Ezrin putting it in a really good package. You know, we would write the song and it would sound really cool, but then Bob Ezrin would take it, and he was our George Martin. He would take the rough song that was a good song, that had three good parts in it, then he would arrange it and get it on tape so it really was good. And that was our Canadian connection there. Without Bob Ezrin we would not... we would have been done. So I always give Bob Ezrin all the credit in the world for any musical ability that we had.

Dennis Dunaway:
My favourite is Killer, *in the respect that that was the first album we did where we knew people would be listening. On* Love It to Death, *we went into the studio coming off of two fairly unsuccessful albums. Even though they made the charts, they weren't putting food on the table. And when we went into the studio for* Killer, *we knew people would be buying the album. So our playing abilities were improving just at a time when we met Bob Ezrin, but then by the time we got to* Killer, *we had learned a great deal about proper studio techniques. Plus we quickly learned how to dissect a song and properly reconstruct it. We were like sponges for that kind of knowledge and Bob Ezrin was a revelation.*

    The song "Killer" came from a vivid dream that I had. I woke up and wrote it down as lyrics. Not long after that, the band was packing up after a long rehearsal day at our farm in Pontiac when I asked Michael to stay after. I played "Killer" for him and we worked it up pretty fast. I wanted it to be longer but Michael applied what he had learned from Ezrin. The next day, we showed it to the others and the band took it to the next level. I love how Glen's and Michael's guitar parts compliment each other on that song.

Many critics went to great lengths to insult our playing abilities. Many of them seemed convinced that our theatrics were just a crutch to smokescreen our deficiencies. If our name had been something like Hurricane Cooper, and we just stood on stage in T-shirts and jeans looking down at our instruments, they might have heard what we were playing. We overshadowed ourselves by giving people a real show. Just wanna hear music? Stay home and put on the record.

As for the approach on "Halo to Flies," early in our career, we prided our ability to assemble medleys of our favourite British bands. We did a Kinks medley, a Who medley, a Beatles medley, and we thought our transitions were pretty clever. So years later, having a bunch of extraneous riffs and melodies kicking around, we decided to apply our knack for segues and we came up with "Halo of Flies." It was the first time many critics finally admitted that we could play. And it proved that the band were self-sufficient in writing our own complex arrangements.

And then "Dead Babies," in this day and age, it's impossible to realize how tough the censors were back then. We were trying to be shocking under the critical magnifying glass of radio stations, advertisers, church groups, parents and even many of the kids that were our age. Plus we actually did have our own sense of decency. It was a balancing act. And as tame as some of our things appear in retrospect— like five androgynous-looking guys with a girl's name—it really was shocking then. It demanded more thinking than the public cared to do, so many just tried to write us off as a joke. Others threatened to kill us. Girls loved us. But nobody could ignore us. As for threats, our entire career was riddled with threats of all kinds. We had so many threats that we became immune to worrying about them.

Johnny "Bee" Badanjek:
After Detroit, they moved to this strange house in Connecticut. I guess it was owned by some old gangster or something. There was like hidden tunnels behind the fireplace; it was like the weirdest house, with tunnels all over the place. It was a huge mansion they rented for the band, and so just before they split up, they were there for a year or so. I think Shep was in New York, and they probably just wanted to be close to the management. They were on the road more than they were in Detroit anyway, constantly touring. So they probably just thought it was time to get out of Detroit.

December 1, 1971. The *Killer* tour ensues, beginning at NY Academy of Music, support by Dr. John and Wet Willie. This marks the first use of the gallows as well as the debut of Alice's "clown" makeup, i.e. solid black with two strong vertical lines rather than the spotty star look.

Neal Smith:
We were very anti-hippie all the time, and the only thing is, as things progressed, we were always decadent, but we were decadent even when we were poor. And so, you know, it was Dennis' idea, when you open up the album cover on Love It to Death, *the most unusual thing was Alice's eyes. And it was the whole inside of the album cover, and when you look inside the pupils, you see a picture of the band. But that idea for the eye makeup came from Dennis. He found a handbill in New York at Carnegie Hall with the eyes on it, and he suggested that Alice try it onstage and we did, and we used it ever since. So that's where that idea... but we were doing that all the time. We just wanted to come up with things that were different. You know, people called us Dada rock in the middle, and in the beginning, and they also called it third generation rock, and they were trying to come up with a name because they just couldn't figure out what the hell we were doing.*

Dennis Dunaway:
I still have the poster. When the band first stayed in New York City, one of our early visits, maybe within the first three, Alice and I shared a room that particular day, and when we got to the room, first thing I would do is look out the window. I'm not sure why, but I looked out the window, and we were about three or four floors up and across the street was the Civic Center in New York City. It's still there. Albert Bouchard lives across the street, by the way (laughs).

  But there was a poster advertising a ballet, and there was like this clown, a white-faced clown, and I thought wow, that's pretty striking that I can see the eyes on this clown from this far away. Because it wasn't a real big poster. So I got Alice to come and look, and he was more interested in television. But later, I kept watching the theatre, and when they finally opened, I went down and asked them for one of those posters, and I brought it back to the room, and I talked to Alice. We went out and found some mascara and came back and Alice did his own version of that kind of makeup. Like I say, I still have that poster to this day (laughs).

  But that's how that started. And the whole thing was the idea of... because when we were in LA, we would drive people out of the room. Which is hard to believe in Hollyweird, that we would be too outrageous for it or that anybody would be too outraged. But they were, just because we were five guys who looked the way we did with our girl's name.

But Neal's right, we were anti-hippie. In LA in particular, there were freaks and there were hippies, and you didn't want to call a hippie a freak and vice versa. Even though there were a lot of similarities back in those days—you know, change the establishment and the way things are done and make it a better world—but hippies by that point had become very, very typical, and were also showing signs of burning out, because of their drug use. And so we found that to be hypocritical. You know, you go to the supermarket and you have to read the ingredients in the food, but it's okay to do heroin—we found that to be totally absurd. And so freaks were of a different order. And even though we drank a lot of beer, we still weren't in the hippie movement.

So yeah, there was a distinct difference between a freak and a hippie. A freak was like the Mothers of Invention. In LA, in particular. You could get away a bit more with calling a hippie a freak. You didn't want to make the mistake of calling a freak a hippie. Even though they had a lot of the same ideals, they had different attitudes about it, and we were more of the freak part of it.

We made fun of ourselves too. We made fun of everybody. We in particular made fun of ourselves. If anybody walked out of the room that was in the band, they knew when they came back that the whole time they were gone we were just whittling them to shreds. And then when they walked back in the room, usually it was Glen Buxton who would say, "Shhh, he's back."

Alice Cooper on the makeup and the evolution of the Alice Cooper character:
Well, to me, it was always, I looked around and said, "Look at all the Peter Pans. Where's Captain Hook?" You know? Look at all the rock heroes; where is the definitive villain? There was no phantom of the opera and I said, I was born to be that. I am not going to be the pretty boy lead singer. I'm not going to be Paul McCartney, this guy or that guy. I looked at myself and said, Alice needs to be the prime villain of rock, the Moriarty of rock. You know, why not develop this character?

And I think that two things that developed the character's look more than anything else was that we had a real fascination with What Ever Happened to Baby Jane?, *the movie*. You look at Bette Davis in that movie and she's like an old, old woman trying to look like a little girl. I mean, she had the white caked makeup all cracking and the black smeared eyes and the red lips, and I went, you know, that is so frightening (laughs).

So that look was involved, and then we saw Barbarella, *and I saw The Black Queen, Anita Pallenberg, and I said, "That's what Alice should look like." You know, a combination of those two. And really, that's how we started shaping the look of Alice, and pretty soon, I realized that nobody had worn eye makeup. No one had become sort of the dark court jester of rock 'n' roll. And I said man, that's just the perfect image for me.*

Nobody had done theatrics. I mean, The Who were the closest thing to theatrics, because of the fact of their smashing the amps up. That was the most chaotic theatrical thing that had happened. And I kept thinking, why can't this show be more visual? Why can't this show be more surrealistic? You know, if Alice looks like this, why wouldn't he have a snake? Why wouldn't he have a sword? Why wouldn't he have a this and a that? And pretty soon we said, since nobody is doing this, and since there's nobody to compare us to, let's just do whatever we want. Let's let the lyrics be the script for the show. So, if I said "Welcome to my nightmare," well, don't just say it, give the audience the nightmare. You know, visually show it to them.

And then of course, we ran up against, at that point, we ran up against the whole world of, "Oh, they're not really good musicians; they hide behind theatrics." And we fought that battle for years and years and years until people like John Lennon and Paul McCartney and Bob Dylan started to say, "You know what? Alice Cooper makes great records." And then we had a couple of No.1s, and very rarely would you find a band that was as theatrical and upsetting to the public as us, like, you know, the Sex Pistols were, with hit records. That was the one thing we had that other bands didn't have, was the fact that we had, you know, 14 Top 40 records.

December 4, 1971. With *Love It to Death* on its 38th week in the charts, at No.145 at this point, *Killer* joins it, entering at No.83.

December 19, 1971. Stanley Kubrick's *A Clockwork Orange* makes its debut, suitably in Gotham, in New York City.

Alice Cooper:
We looked more like Clockwork Orange *characters than we did a band. In fact* Clockwork Orange *used an awful lot of Alice Cooper in the movie. I mean the guy's name was Alex, he had a snake, he carried a cane, he had the glove. I mean there was so much Alice in that movie it was incredible.*

December 27, 1971. With *Killer* now at No.26 on the Billboard charts, "Under My Wheels" enters the singles chart at No.88.

Dennis on the shocking **Killer** *album cover:*
We had this concept: we were going to make every song about a different kind of the killer, and "Desperado" was the gunslinger and "Halo of Flies" had the James Bond/License to Kill guy and whatnot. Even though Michael came up with this incredible song, "Be My Lover," which we were thinking, well, I don't see a killer in there, and you're really stretching to say it's a lady-killer. But that song is so good we couldn't say it can't go on the album (laughs).

So the snake, we thought, okay, the ultimate killers are a shark or a snake. Well, Neal had a snake. Okay, the snake is going to be on the album cover and the handwriting on the album cover is me writing with my left hand because I wanted it to look like a demented ransom note kind of thing. So when we did the photo session with Pete Turner in New York City, who took the band photo on that album as well, we had them do the picture of the hanging at the same time, and then we had them do the picture of the snake for the cover.

Now, Neal was holding the snake and that was not a little snake. So holding his arm out and trying to hold still for as long as it took, Neal started losing his patience with them. Because they would wait until the snake's tongue came out and then they would snap the picture and it would be too late. And Neal kept telling them, "No, you fuckin' missed it!" And he'd say, "Well, you're making the mistake of waiting until you see the tongue and it's too late. Just snap when you don't see the tongue." And anyway, they took a ton of pictures of the snake and when we looked through all of them, all of the contact sheets, there was one picture where the snake had his tongue out and that's the one that's on the cover.

December 31, 1971. Alice Cooper perform at the Winter Pop Festival at Maple Leaf Gardens, in Toronto. Also on the bill are Edgar Winter's White Trash, Dr. John, Sundance, Chilliwack and Crowbar.

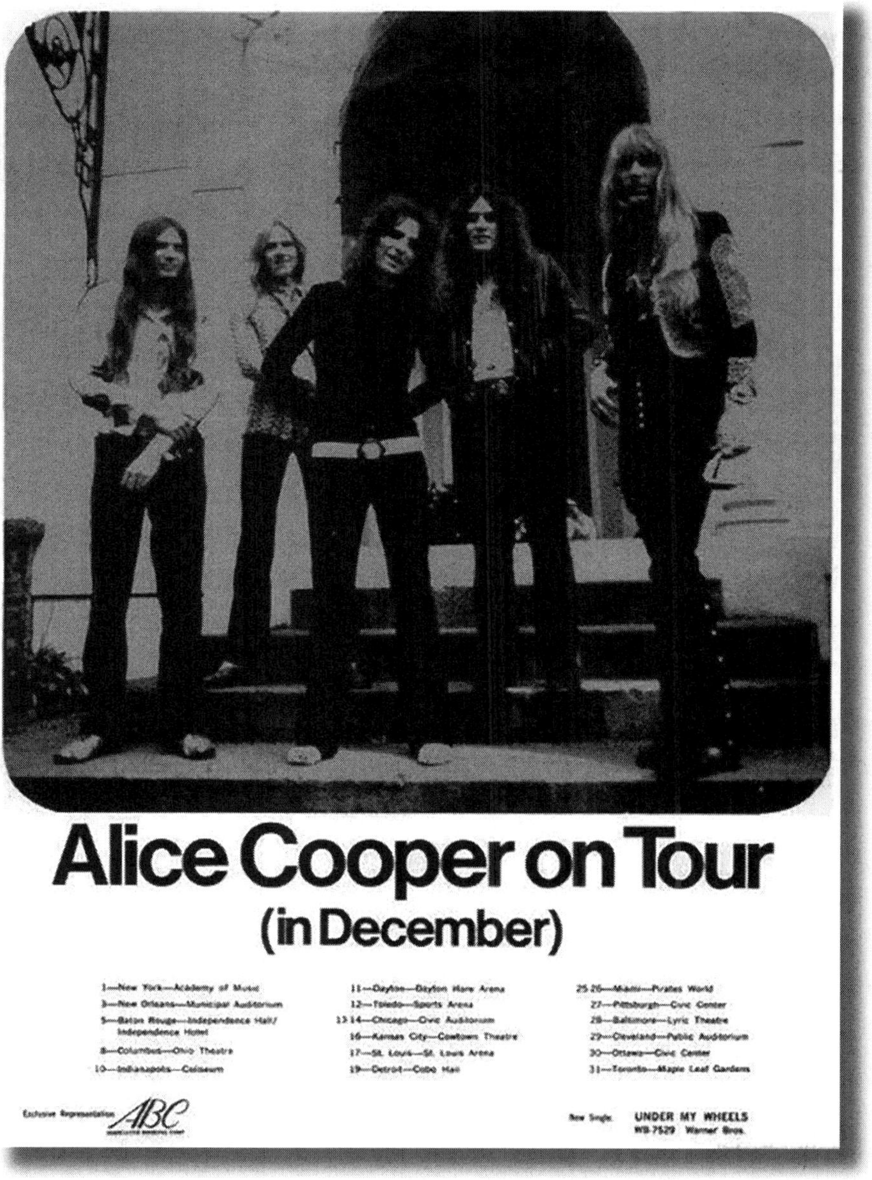
Alice Cooper on Tour
(in December)
1—New York—Academy of Music
3—New Orleans—Municipal Auditorium
5—Baton Rouge—Independence Hall/ Independence Hotel
8—Columbus—Ohio Theatre
10—Indianapolis—Coliseum
11—Dayton—Dayton Hara Arena
12—Toledo—Sports Arena
13 14—Chicago—Civic Auditorium
16—Kansas City—Cowtown Theatre
17—St. Louis—St. Louis Arena
19—Detroit—Cobo Hall
25 26—Miami—Pirates World
27—Pittsburgh—Civic Center
28—Baltimore—Lyric Theatre
29—Cleveland—Public Auditorium
30—Ottawa—Civic Center
31—Toronto—Maple Leaf Gardens
Exclusive Representation ABC
New Single UNDER MY WHEELS
WB-7529 Warner Bros.

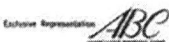

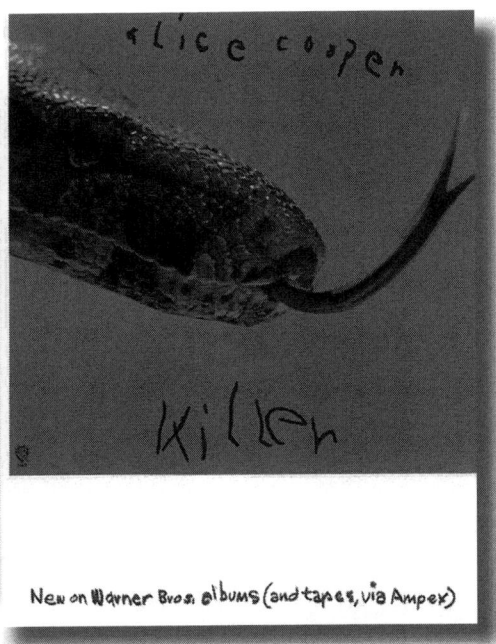

1972

In 1972, Alice Cooper continue their rise due to a constant injection of themselves into the news, through stunt and through achievement. To kick off the year, *Killer* goes gold, and a second deceptively light and campy song from the record makes the rounds as a single, "Be My Lover" harming no one.

As the band shift headquarters to the Galesi Estate in Connecticut (a better kind of band house), they come up with a conceptual follow-up to "I'm Eighteen" in "School's Out," issued and celebrated before the album of the same name would drop. And when it did drop, once more the band would see strong but not stellar sales, the record driven by the fortunes of one hit and really no more (actually less than *Killer*, which had arguably two, two-and-a-half). In summary and in broad terms so to speak, Alice Cooper now had three albums that sold respectably more or less because of one hit single, with, indeed, almost all the rest of the material doomed to be deep, deep album tracks. But of course the band and Shep Gordon, hard workers and enthusiastic participants in life, social animals, make the best of it, pranking Piccadilly Square in London and pouring panties over the Hollywood Bowl.

Into the second half of the year, *School's Out* vaults to No. 2 and the band, like good bands in the '70s did, went back to work, assembling a follow-up album and, just to keep on the tips of tongues, issuing another single in "Elected," this one, again, fortunately working, setting up hopes for continued success once the next record was completed and released. Further success comes when in November, *Love It to Death* joins *Killer* at gold as the band hit Europe for the second time. Alas, however, the heavy workload begins to take a toll as both Glen and Alice find themselves chucking down way too much booze. It affects them in different ways however. Alice copes, remaining the life of the party, while Glen goes hazy and ineffectual.

1972. Dick Wagner commandeers a short-lived and heavy band called Ursa Major, who issue a self-titled debut produced by Bob Ezrin. Gone from the formative stages of the band before the album was famed piano man Billy Joel. Ursa Major toured nationally in support of Jeff Beck and later, Alice Cooper.

Dick Wagner:
Ursa Major *was great, but it never got distributed. We signed to RCA and we were making this record and the guy who signed us and brought us into the label left the label just as our album was finished. And the guy who replaced him was the former jazz critic of the* New York Times *and he hated us! He couldn't stand this kind of music. He was a jazz critic (laughs). So we had kind of a bad transition of promotion there. It killed* Ursa Major. *Bang, that record was no-go and it went cold.*

A lot of people said that it had been a tremendous influence on a lot of bands. And I can see that maybe it was, given that it was 1972. But Bob produced that. He's got great ears. He's brilliant and I learned a lot from him. He was younger than me when we ended up doing that stuff and together we really created a lot of good stuff. I have the utmost respect for his abilities. I remember Bob going around with a fire extinguisher blasting people. He had a habit of doing that kind of stuff, to create as much commotion as possible.

1972. At a presentation at the Hyatt House in LA, Alice Cooper is awarded with the key to the city.

January 21, 1972. *Killer* reaches its peak position of No.21 on Billboard while "Under My Wheels" has moved up to No.59.

January 27, 1972. *Killer* is certified gold, peaking at No.21 on the Billboard charts.

Neal Smith on the evolving stage show:
By Killer, *now we had the big weather balloons that we filled with confetti and fake money. But even before that, the evolution of the sword came from, you know, people would just sit there and weren't really storming the stage. We wanted people to storm the stage. So early on we actually took real money, put it on the sword, dollar bills, and Alice was flinging real money at the crowd. And we did that throughout the history of the band—we always threw real money*

out there. Alice now has fake money on there, but we always had real money. So that's where the sword came from because it was the obvious thing, like a shish kebab skewer; Alice would peel it off and throw it to the crowd.

We used the balloons, and then of course Killer *we added the gallows, which the Warner Bros. props department built for us. And we did that death dirge for "Killer," as Alice was taken to the gallows. We'd come out as characters because now we had recorded music. We had the song "Killer" coming through the speakers, but we're not playing the song. I came out, had the snare drum on, I'm playing the death dirge on a black-draped snare drum, Dennis is the priest—he put a priest costume on—and Michael has a lit torch and Glen is actually the hangman.*

He escorts Alice to the gallows, walks him up the stairs and then puts the rope around his neck and then pulls the lever to hang Alice. So I mean, that's all brand-new stuff that had never been done before. A band actually playing their music, and then going through a theatrical piece for the execution of Alice for the song "Killer." So that was pretty dramatic, and then of course when Alice falls through there and the lightning crashes, and the lights, it actually looked like a lightning storm, and then he chomps on the... after he's hanging there, he's got blood dripping from his mouth and all over his clothes. So I would say that was a big turning point in the violence of Alice Cooper. I mean, the electric chair was one thing but actually having him hanging there and the blood coming from his mouth... rock 'n' roll had never seen anything like that before.

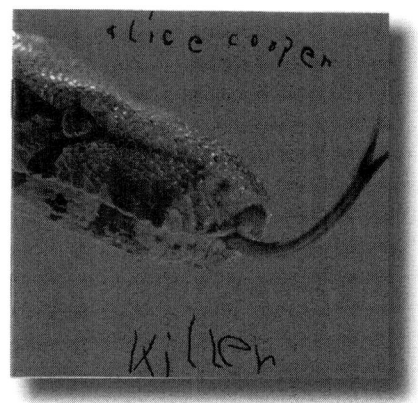

February 7, 1972. *Killer* is released in the UK.

February 19, 1972. The band play the Coliseum in Denver, Colorado, supported by hit comedy act Cheech & Chong.

February 21, 1972. "Be My Lover" is issued as the second and last single from *Killer*.

Late February 1972. The band gather in Joe Smith's Warner Bros. offices in Burbank, CA for a gold disc presentation in honour of *Killers*.

But the physical awards aren't back from the plant yet, so they mug with golds of Jimi Hendrix's *Rainbow Bridge* instead.

March 1972. Richard Avedon takes the famous shot of Alice Cooper naked, with snake, the new one being Yvonne.

Alice Cooper on being provocative and feared:
Here's a guy named Alice, he's got hair down to here, he has absolutely no respect for any authority at all, he's calling his own rules. And that's not bad enough, but they have hit records on top of it and every time that he does something that his parents says, well you're not going to see him, the kids go yes I am. All of a sudden you become the forbidden fruit.

And that's what people are afraid of. They're afraid that their kids are going to start wearing eye makeup and start wearing black top hats and all black goth clothes. And they were right—they did. But all those kids turned out to be doctors and lawyers and politicians; they all ended up being okay. It's just art, but art sometimes really scares people.

March 3, 1972. As part of a north-eastern swing, the band play the Harrington Auditorium at the Worcester Polytechnic Institute in Worcester, Massachusetts. Support comes from Blue Öyster Cult, who begin to regularly share bills with the band.

Neal Smith on the band's shocking stage show:
We just wanted to be memorable onstage; I think that was the first thing. We were certainly aware of Screamin' Jay Hawkins and Arthur Brown, and in those days, in the late '60s, nobody even had a word for Screamin' Jay Hawkins or Arthur Brown, who would come on stage with this big flaming helmet he had on top of his head (laughs) and a big sceptre or whatever he was holding. And lyrically The Doors were doing the same thing. We may have been more influenced by the dark side of The Doors and taking it into a further dimension.

Dennis wrote "Black Juju" and we would all brainstorm. We had the idea of putting the sheets over us; this was even after the door for "Nobody Likes Me;" and we still used the feathers. And we had "Dead Babies," even though it's not about killing babies; it's about parental neglect, child neglect. So we thought okay, we'll just do a theatrical thing for "Dead Babies" and for "Ballad of Dwight Fry," and we'll execute Alice on stage. We'll put the singer in an electric chair. Without a doubt,

1972

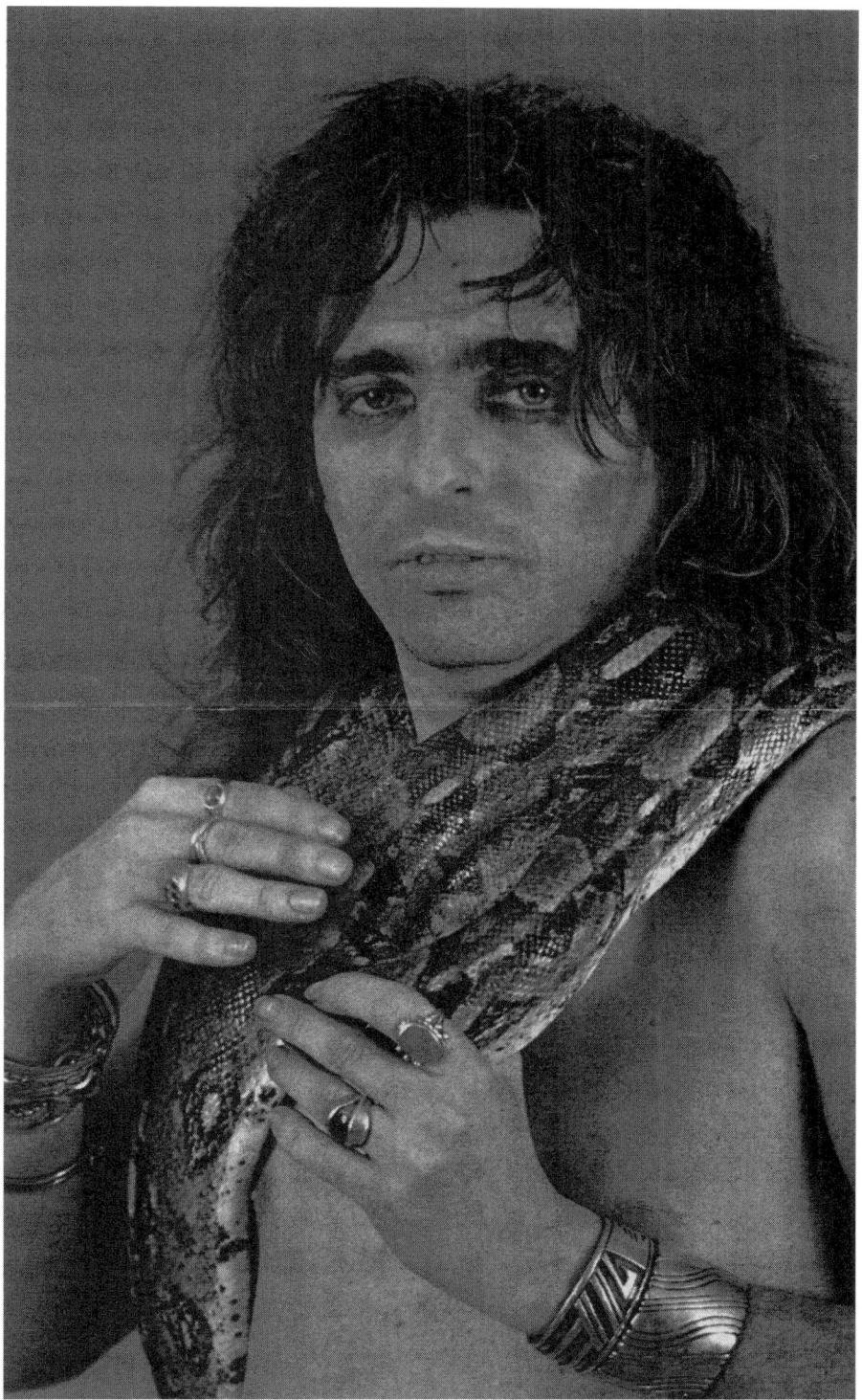

we were big fans of the horror movies and that sort of thing. Our influence went beyond musical to theatrical with movies and Broadway.

March 11, 1972. "Be My Lover" creeps onto the Billboard charts at No. 81.

April 1972. Most of what will become the *School's Out* album is recorded this month, working at The Record Plant in New York, just down the highway from the band's new home base.

Dennis Dunaway:
We had a lot of fun making "School's Out" mainly because we all related on the exact same level. Glen, Alice and I started the band in high school and Michael and Neal went to nearby schools. I'm not sure the historical success of the single detracted from the other cuts though. Royalty checks reflect that many of the other cuts are still getting various kinds of exposure. I thought the album flowed together pretty well. And it has a lot of musical texture.

Alice Cooper on the band's move to Connecticut:
We had done everything we could do in Detroit. We had our first hit record, "Eighteen," out of CKLW in Windsor, through Rosalie Trombley, who still to this day, is as important to us as Frank Zappa was because she took a chance on that song, "Eighteen," which became a No. 1 record there. She was playing Simon & Garfunkel and The Supremes and all those bands, but she heard this record and her son liked it. Her teenage son said that's the coolest record, so she added it. And the next thing you know it got requests and it was a major hit. Now if you were a hit on CKLW, that was the biggest station in the Midwest. That was Chicago, Detroit, St. Louis; that's how big that radio station was. If you got a hit on CKLW, you had a national hit. Everybody looked there to see what was going to be a hit. So we had become a national product because we had a national hit.

Anyway, when that happened we decided New York was more to our liking. LA was still not going to accept us. New York, though, had that underground, the Velvet Underground scene, the Warhol scene. There was actually something going on there, with the Ramones and all this who came a bit later. But when we plugged into New York, then, we were at Max's Kansas City, we were at all these New York things. We had the money now. But we didn't really want to live in New York because it would be very hard to rehearse. So we leased a house up in Greenwich, Connecticut that was a 32-room mansion called the Galesi Estate.

April 2, 1972. Alice Cooper play the calamitous Mar y Sol Pop Festival in Puerto Rico, along with the likes of The Allman Brothers, Bloodrock, Faces, Fleetwood Mac, ELP, Savoy Brown and Cactus.

Carmine Appice:
I remember guys would come up to me and say, "Do you want to snort some stuff?" And I never really did any of that, you know, most of the time. But on this occasion, because we were in Puerto Rico and it was so gorgeous I went, "Yeah, I'll have a snort; what is it?" And I think he said it was mescaline or something (laughs). And I was like high all night; it was ridiculous. And I had to play the next day in the afternoon. And I didn't sleep all night and I was destroyed but we went on and played and had a great, great time. But everybody was smashed. The crowd was about 15,000 people, 20,000. I don't remember exactly, because most of the time I spent was backstage having a good old party with all the other bands. We had this hotel that housed everybody, and we had food fights in the restaurant and we tore up the hotel. Everybody did; it was just pretty amazing (laughs). It was unbelievable; they didn't know what hit them. There was definitely a problem with the hotel security. I guess everybody was billed for the damage but then Rod Stewart got left there, by the Faces, by accident. But then luckily our manager was with us and he bought him a ticket back to wherever he had to go. In terms of bands, I do remember that Mahavishnu Orchestra played, and the Faces were great. The Allmans were there. This festival just happened the one time. I think we got there on Friday afternoon, played on Saturday, left on Sunday. Very cool time.

April 8, 1972. Old manager from the Zappa days, Herb Cohen sues Warner Bros. and the band for royalties from *Killer*, based on his interpretation of wording from the original Alice Cooper contract.

May 16, 1972. Alice Cooper issue the title track from their forthcoming *School's Out* album as a single, backed with "Gutter Cat." The song would become arguably the most beloved anthem of the band's catalogue, reaching No.7 on Billboard, No.3 in Canada and No.1 in the UK. The song essentially single-handedly make the album a success, given that no other singles were floated and indeed, every other song on the album would become deep obscurities in the catalogue.

June 3, 1972. As *Killer* holds ground at No.42, "School's Out" enters the charts at No.88, rising to No.63 the following week. An integral part to the song is the children's chorus. To do this, Alice and Bob had five professional stage kids over to a studio in New York, with their protective and wary mom's looking on. In addition to Rosalie Trombley (immortalized in Bob Seger song "Rosalie," also covered by Thin Lizzy) helping the band out of Windsor, Ontario, Joe Greenberg cites Chuck Dunaway out of WIXY in Cleveland as being instrumental to the band breaking first in the Midwest. As well, hooking up with Michael Quatro as a booking agent out of Detroit aided and abetted the cause.

Alice Cooper on "School's Out:"
"I would say that "School's Out" was... you know, when you're writing a song, and there's a momentum in the song where you know that it's a hit? At times, very apparent, other times not, where you write the song and you say, "Oh, this is a really good song," then all of a sudden it falls off the album and it's a hit and you go, "Oh, great." "School's Out" was designed to be a hit. It was designed to be an anthem. And it was designed to appeal to every single person in the world because everybody has sat through school on that last three minutes before school is out. The longest three minutes of the year is that last three minutes on May 30th or whatever it is. So I said, if we can capture the joy of the kids screaming, knowing they have three months off of school, well, that will be a big hit.

Michael Bruce on Bob Ezrin and his contribution to "School's Out:"
Bob's a perfectionist and he's thorough. There was no detail left undone. Everything from the tempo of the song to how he thought

about the song to what's going on in the song, that was all covered. "School's Out" wasn't just, "Hey, it's the end of school – play it like that." We had a chorus of kids and everything was premeditated and thought-out. Bob was also a child prodigy keyboard player. He's from Toronto and I believe his parents were doctors. He was quite the pianist and we laid everything out on the piano like it was a Mozart movement.

We could have done those albums without Bob, but would they have turned out like they did? Not at all, no way! He was our fifth Beatle. He was our George Martin. When he was done, I was like, "This is what I wanted my song to be like." Take "No More Mr. Nice Guy;" it's basically a rock song, but the way it's done and the way it's produced, it's just done so well that there's not a bad part in it. It was done just right and I take enormous pride in that. It's textbook; it's Rock 101.

We were the culmination of dark and light and that's what we did in our shows. We'd start off with what we called our white set and kill Alice some way and he'd come back, be reborn, and then we'd be in our dark set. And Bob is the one who musically really made that happen. He filled in all the blanks. If there was a part that was going to be, "Okay, make this scary," he'd have the moans or give some sort of idea of how to do the baby thing. He'd do those little vignettes on the piano like, "Mommy, where's daddy?" He made that stuff happen.

Bob takes all of those ideas and puts them in a nice neat package with a title. I used to hate outlines in school because it forced you to focus on writing a paper and come up with a theme, subtitles. I'd want to put the whole thing down on paper and be done with it. Bob was our teacher in that aspect. He taught us how to go through it thoroughly and make a complete piece of music out of it. And I think that's why it's so good.

June 6, 1972. David Bowie issues *Ziggy Stardust and the Spiders from Mars*, probably the definitive, most well-known "glam" album, glam being a mostly UK music and fashion craze that existed from about 1972 to 1975. Stateside, Alice Cooper and the New York Dolls were considered the closest thing to what the likes of Bowie, Mott the Hoopel, Slade and Sweet were doing.

Alice Cooper:
Actually, I invented Bowie. Bowie used to come to our concerts when he was David Jones and he was a little folk singer. And all of a sudden after he saw Vince turn into Alice, he suddenly became David Bowie. So I just want to get the history straight there. I was the first one who

EASY ACTION - The Original Alice Cooper Band

really invented the Jekyll and Hyde character. And then Bowie did the chameleon.

June 19, 1972. The band find out that the 750,000 panties they'd manufactured to be part of the *School's Out* packaging have failed government inspection because they were too flammable. The manufacture figures out how to save the job, with a flame-retardant spray.

Late June 1972. The band work at their new mansion headquarters and at Record Plant on "Elected" just as the *School's Out* album is issued.

Alice Cooper on **School's Out:**
One thing about the School's Out *album that is interesting, was the fact that there was a real Yardbirds presence there, especially with the song itself. If you really listen to the bottom of that song, it's all Yardbirds, which was our biggest influence. And it was the only song I ever did that I was sure was going to be a hit. I mean, a lot of other songs you sit there and you go, "I think, maybe that could be... I'm not sure." "School's Out" was, "Oh yeah, this is a slam dunk right here." If this isn't a hit, then I don't belong in the business. So we were right about that one. That's one in a row there.*

But the other thing with that album, was when we did the reference to West Side Story, *and we did the Jets song and the whole fight thing, we never realized that our audience had no idea what* West Side Story *was. I thought everybody knew* West Side Story. *It was just like part of America to know* West Side Story. *And people would say, "Oh, I love that Jets song." And I go, "Yeah, it's* West Side Story." *"What does that mean?" And I go, come on, you're kidding me. And I realized that 90% of my audience had no theatrical knowledge. I mean, they wouldn't know* West Side Story *from* Bye Bye, Birdie *or any of those.*

I may be the only straight guy in the world who knows show tunes. But I go to a lot of plays and I love musicals, because to me, I do the closest thing to a musical. When I go to see a real musical on stage—and it might be the worst thing in the world; it could be Mama Mia—*I would go, okay, how does this music connect in this theatre, with the way they set this up? And I tell you, I watch the worst stuff and go, oh, I know how to connect that up. I think of something on stage. With me it's going to be something like a dead body on stage that's going to be flung around. And I would pick up something from a show that you*

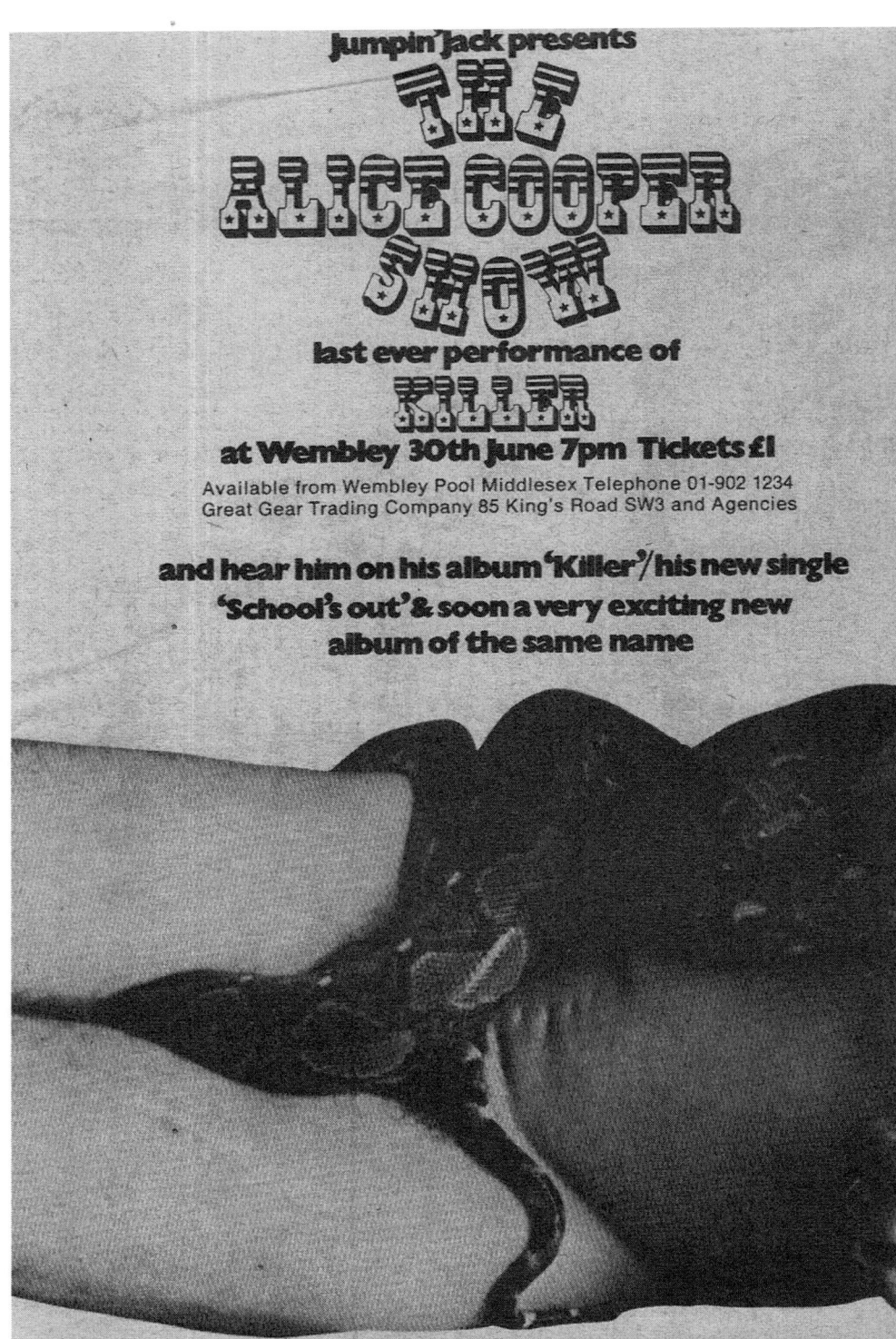

1972

would never connect up with Alice Cooper (laughs).

I'm telling you what. We've already had offers on taking Welcome to My Nightmare to Broadway and re-doing it as a new version of it, and that may happen. So that might not be that far away from being a reality. I would love to take it to the West End of London and just do it over there in London for a month and then on Broadway for a month. And then, you know, take it to a town and do it for two weeks at a time, a week at a time, in each town.

But back to the album, "School's Out" was really the biggest hit. I mean, there are a lot of what I would call stage hits on there. There are a lot of songs that the audience wants me to do. There's about five or six songs I get requested for all the time on that. And there are 28 albums. If I just did one song off of each album, that's a full show. So I've really got to pick and choose what songs I'm going to do.

Michael Bruce on School's Out:
That was great. That was one of the more fun albums to make and Glen was really on the mark. We rehearsed and did some recording out in LA and we did some recording in New York. It was a fun album to do and was the most band-like experience. Songs like "Blue Turk," "Gutter Cat vs. the Jets," Bob brought in that West Side Story *element and we loved it, and I liked "Luney Tune." It was just the real spirit of the band, some of our blues with our New York sort of feels.*

That and Killer, *the band was still pretty much intact and I think that after* School's Out *we started working really hard and we were doing like two albums a year and we started leaving Glen behind. I don't think he could keep up and I just don't think he was prepared to work that hard. He either couldn't or didn't want to.*

Dennis Dunaway, on the assembly of "Elected:"
"Elected" was recorded, pretty much, everything except the vocal, at the estate. I remember the actual take that we got on the recording. Because I remember when we got to the end, and I started doing this high bass line, and later in overdubs we added horns, with everybody in the band following the bass line. The song was on its way out, and when I started doing this bass line, I knew that that was the take, that we had finally gotten the take, and I had chills going up my spine, thinking, "Wow, we finally nailed it."

Neal Smith on "Elected:"
The nucleus of that song was "Reflected" from Pretties for You. *In fact,*

"Reflected" was originally called "Elected!" And the agreement that we had as a band is that anything we wrote on Easy Action or Pretties for You, we all share the songwriter's credit equally on it. Whether someone wrote a song, I think Dennis wrote "B.B. on Mars," but we all took credit, because it was the early stages of the band and we all worked on all the songs a lot, equally as much. A song like "Apple Bush," that was a song I had written, but it was the whole band that made it come to what it was on the album. And then anything that would be spun off from that era, whether it was recorded or not—as I say, "Elected" was like a rewrite of "Reflected." And because that was a rewrite of "Reflected," it still fell into that category, so that's why everybody's name was on it.

But yeah, we brought it back out, dusted it off, rearranged it, and changed the feel a little bit, but it still had a lot of the characteristics of the original song, and then changed the name to "Elected." After "School's Out," which was a timely song with the ending of the school year, the election was coming and we wanted something timely, because we'd found kind of a formula with that, first with "I'm Eighteen" to "School's Out," now "Elected." So that is why we chose to use that subject; it was working for us, and nobody else was really doing it to that intensity that we were.

Late June 1972. The band try a new prop, a 20-foot cannon which was supposed to shoot a dummy of Alice across the auditorium. It malfunctioned at one of the band's rust belt shows and was quickly sold to The Rolling Stones, so Mick could sit atop it.

June 28, 1972. The band arrive in the UK and record a performance of "School's Out" for *Top of the Pops*.

June 29, 1972. A famous stunt in Alice Cooper lore finds a truck festooned with a photo of Alice on a billboard "stalling" in Piccadilly Square. Shep says that this was staged in a panic because ticket sales were poor and something had to be done to generate some press. A driver was found who was willing to get arrested, and in fact the faux breakdown of the vehicle was staged three times.

Alice Cooper:
We pulled every trick in the book in England. We stalled a photo of Alice half-naked with a snake around him in Piccadilly Square on a Friday afternoon. Stalled a truck and stopped London. It was the cover of the

London Times the next day. It was a pure Hollywood publicity stunt. But the British loved that. The British love to be put on like that. When they saw the show, we gave them the show they wanted. It had everything they were expecting in it. Everybody thought we were from England because we were such a big hit over there, and actually we were from Detroit.

July 23, 1972. Alice Cooper play one of the most memorable gigs of their career. The venue is the Hollywood Bowl. Supporting were Captain Beyond, Jo Jo Gunne and Wolfman Jack, who rode in on a camel and introduced the band. A helicopter broke the law by flying too low (and was fined for the dangerous manoeuvre) as he dropped thousands of pairs of paper panties over the crowd, in celebration of *School's Out*, each copy of which came wrapped in a thin cloth pair of panties. Bernie Taupin recalls being there with Elton John and the two of them leaping up to grab the panties as they fell from the sky just like the rest of the crowd.

Dennis Dunaway:
I couldn't say we had made it until we played the Hollywood Bowl. When we went back to LA as a successful band and played the Hollywood Bowl, that was the night I said, well, I have to admit that we've made it (laughs). Elton John was there that night, and he was backstage raving about our costumes. And that had a lot to do with his... all of a sudden, he was flamboyant from that night on (laughs).

Neal Smith:
He came over to Alice and I and said, "Thank you for showing me what rock 'n' roll is all about," and from that second on he was glitter.

July 28, 1972. *School's Out* reaches its highest point on the charts, No.2, locked out by *Honky Chateau* from Elton John, who had been in attendance at Alice's Hollywood Bowl show the previous week.

August 1972 – January 1973. Alice Cooper and Bob Ezrin work at their Connecticut band house, The Galesi Estate in Greenwich, as well as The Record Plant in New York and Morgan Studios in London on tracks to be used on their forthcoming sixth album.

August 5, 1972. Alice Cooper play the Akron Rubber Bowl in Akron, Ohio, supported by J. Geils Band and Dr. John, memorable due to a reprise of the helicopter panty-drop stunt.

1972

September 2, 1972. Alice Cooper play a triumphant show at Varsity Stadium in Toronto, Ontario. The show, so loud, with 24,000 in attendance, making it the highest grossing show at that venue up to that point. Two nights later, the band play the Montréal forum in Montréal, 18,000 in attendance.

September 19, 1972. "Elected," backed with "Luney Tune," is issued as an advance single from *Billion Dollar Babies*. Issued just in time for the November US presidential election, the song hit No.26 on the charts the week of the vote. As promo, the band created a story-themed music video similar to those that would become big business in the '80s. The song is a loose rewrite of "Reflected" from *Pretties for You*.

Dennis Dunaway on "Elected" and "Luney Tune:"
"Elected" was a natural follow-up for "School's Out" because of its similar potential for repeating airplay. Every time school ends, they play it. So what about every time there's an election? It was pretty simple so I might say we all thought of it together. And they both continue to get periodical bumps in airplay. I didn't like that video because like Glen said, "Even the chimp's in it more than the band."

Because our controversial image was repellent to parents, and therefore advertisers, we had a rough time getting anything filmed, or on television. So the money wasn't invested there. But I know we could have introduced some bold ideas if we, as a band, would have been left to our own invention, and so we did videos. But unfortunately, every time a camera was around, outsiders would be there to impose their interpretation of what they thought Alice Cooper were all about. And with all due respect to their talents, they missed it completely. Why would we record "Black Juju" and project a sexually threatening image with a sinister stage show, and then ride an elephant like the Monkees? It was embarrassing and damagingly counter-productive to our cause. How can you shock people after that?

As for "Luney Tune," John Lydon of the Sex Pistols is always citing that as the scariest song he's ever heard. I wrote that song and Alice wrote the bridge. I still have the very original lyrics, which also may have come from a dream. I have lots of notebooks filled with what I call my dream poems. Alice used lines from those poems in many songs. I wrote the song on bass and Alice delivered the lyrics as I had imagined them, with convincing sincerity. We had one of our rare disagreements over the line, "Couple shots and I don't feel no pain." I'm not sure why I didn't like that—it's a strong line.

November 2, 1972. A show at the Hofstra University Auditorium in Hempstead, NY is filmed for the first *ABC In Concert*. When the show aired on November 24th, some affiliates yanked coverage, shocked at the opening act of the program. For those who ran the footage, complaints were numerous.

November 4, 1972. The band arrive in London, England and proceed to Morgan Studios where they work on some of the material that would appear on *Billion Dollar Babies*. The famed photo shoot used in the gatefold of that record also takes place, conducted by David Bailey at his studio. Shep says that the money used in the gatefold of the album had to be flown over from the States and delivered under heavy guard with guns.

Dennis Dunaway on the Billion Dollar Babies *cover art and packaging:*
I don't see anything shocking about it myself. It was just a snakeskin wallet, and I guess people got shocked because it had the crying baby. Alice is holding the crying baby, which was baby Lola, whose mother, Carolyn Pfeiffer still works for Alive Enterprises after all these years. She

worked in publicity with the Beatles, with Derek Taylor. That's where we got her from, and that was her daughter. It was so blatantly, "Hey, we're rich (laughs), and we're rock 'n' roll." We had a picture with a big gigantic pile of money, and a crying baby with Alice Cooper makeup on. But overall, it seemed pretty mild to me.

    The white clothes and the rabbits, that actually came from an idea I had when the band lived together all the way back before Love It to Death, going back to that concept of the white and the black on that album. Cindy, my wife, who was Neal's sister, at the time had rabbits on this farm that the band was at in Pontiac, Michigan. And I got this idea for the white part of the album which I thought would be the back cover, all sitting in a white bed wearing white, and we would have these bunny rabbits in bed with us.

    So it would be the opposite of the dark. See, I wanted to contrast happy and innocent and dark and evil. So we brought in a photographer and we did this shoot. I have seen some of these pictures crop up all these years later. But at the time the guy wanted to be paid a few hundred dollars, and we're like, "You've got to be kidding, man.

Look in our refrigerator. We don't have any food! Take pity on us and do a spec deal." And the guy wouldn't do it.

And I was so pissed-off, after we went through all this trouble. I told him, "Well, we're going to redo this picture someday, and then we're going to use it and you're going to be sorry." And so eventually we got around to it. We even got rabbits in London. That was David Bailey, who photographed the Beatles and all kinds of people. And that shot was taken in London. But the night before, I was up all night, because Cindy was in my room sewing, making those outfits, because she made all the clothes for the band. But she was up all night and I'm trying to do a photo thing at nine o'clock in the morning with no sleep. None of us had any sleep, really; we were partying in London. But the hard part about that photograph was trying to get that much American money in England.

November 6, 1972. *Love It to Death* is certified gold in the US, having peaked at No.35 in the charts.

Neal Smith on success:
I was the first guy in the band to buy a car and it was a Silver Cloud Rolls Royce. That was a goal of mine. That was in late '72 after School's Out. *When I left school in 1967, I had a picture of a white Rolls Royce next to my bed and eventually it happened.*

November 10 - 26, 1972. The band conduct their second European tour, supported by Flo and Eddie. Opening night in Glasgow (the only UK show) includes a riot by 300 fans, an overturned limo and the first three rows at the venue vandalized. Shep recalls Alice refusing to fly over to the UK because they didn't have any Budweiser beer there. Shep confirmed that he was right and got a connection to look into it, an American who was opening up the first Hard Rock Café there. Eventually some was acquired from an American base in Germany and the tour was back on.

November 13, 1972. After the band's show at the Olympia Theatre in Paris, Omar Sharif throws an after-party to which the guests were asked to arrive dressed as Raquel Welch. Later, in 1975, Welch (who Alice called Rocky) would fall for Alice hard, who was now in love with Sheryl and had to spurn her advances, despite Shep urging Alice to try keep her entertained and show up to her events, given that Shep was now managing Welch and wanted to keep her happy. Alice recalls one incident where he and Dick Wagner were golfing at the Doral Park Country Club in Florida with some bankers, and out of the blue, Raquel runs up to the cart and says, "I'm your caddy today!" Also, according to Alice, at this Olympia Theatre show, somebody jumped up on stage and rushed Glen, throwing a burning guitar at him.

December 1972. Alice is admonished by manager Shep Gordon about his alcohol intake and he flies off to Jamaica for a rest and rethink. Meanwhile, Glen in hospitalized in London and once back home in Phoenix he is re-hospitalized with a pancreas gravely damaged due to alcohol abuse. Buxton never quite recovers and his participation in band matters is reduced.

Author Gavin Baddeley on Alice Cooper's psyche:
Alice Cooper is more heavily influenced — at least he's said he's more heavily influenced — by things like TV, films, soundtracks and so forth. He's very much an American decadent. Unlike the European decadents of previous generations who smoked opium and read poetry, he drunk Budweiser and watched TV all day. But the results are a kind of dissolving personality, a descent into depravity and confusion.

But of course his motivation has changed over the years. I think even he'd be the first to admit that. During the '70s, with the band's first major success, he was drinking more and more, losing contact, perhaps, with a lot of what we call real life. The show itself certainly was shocking; it was very much that they wanted to get people's attention.

I mean, one of the things he describes is that in the early years they'd do these various shows and they'd be the one band that would empty the room in minutes. And it sort of worked out. That was something to be proud of in a perverse way, and it was also the thing that attracted the attention of Frank Zappa. Later on, I think it was largely a commercial decision on their parts; it was putting on a show. It was the Grand Guignol. I mean he used the term Grand Guignol about his stage show on a number of occasions.

One could say that part of Alice's mental degradation is represented by or seeded in the prosaic version of how the name came about. Alice Cooper just sounded so all American, and Alice Cooper, the character, was sort of about the side of being all-American that people didn't like to talk about. Alice Cooper is a persona being separate from Vincent Furnier, the preacher's son, who he was off stage.

My suspicion is this became increasingly important for him as his problems with alcohol became more and more pronounced, and he was having problems differentiating between different sections of his life. And if you look at some of the albums from this period they talk about the trouble of, you know, coming back down to earth. And a lot of popular musicians will tell you there is an issue whereby they don't like to talk to anybody after a performance. Because it's such a powerful, powerful thing, and that you can't maintain that level of intensity 24 hours a day, seven days a week. And this is pronounced if you're playing a character like Alice Cooper. What he does on stage is not something you can do in your private life and hope to remain sane.

Michael Bruce on Glen Buxton:
Funny guy; you know, he played the spoons or whatever other kind of hardware was laying around. Funny story, we were downstairs rehearsing, and his high E string, the real thin one, kept popping out of the bridge, the saddle on the bridge. You know, he would play it and it would flip out. So I said, "Glen, you gotta get that taken care. You don't want to have that happen when we're playing." So a couple days later, we're playing along and I go to him, "Did you get that fixed?" He goes, "Yeah, yeah." I went over and looked at his guitar, and he drove a nail in his guitar right next to the string. If that gives you any indication... (laughs).

And then he cut a hole in his Gretch and put a Fender pickup in there. There's nothing he wouldn't do; you know, he could do anything. It was all right as long as you got what you were looking for. He was an interesting player. As we started doing less cover stuff as we were changing from the Nazz days and Spiders... we used to do four sets and then we would do one original and then two original and then three original. He was really fine on the covers but it was a little harder for him when we started writing.

December 12, 1972. The band return home to the east coast after their European tour, whereby Alice gives Bob Ezrin the *Billion Dollar Babies* from overseas. Ezrin takes them to The Record Plant in New York City and continues to build the record.

Dennis Dunaway on recording the album in various locales:
I'm not sure I would describe it as being more difficult or easier, but we had a mobile truck parked in the driveway of an estate in Greenwich, Connecticut, and it was one of the first studio albums recorded with a mobile truck, I mean, early on. I don't think it was the very first one though. So the whole house had... you know, there was a microphone

in the hallway because it had a certain amount of echo. There was a microphone in the solarium because it had a certain amount of echo, and we basically talked to a video camera, which was kind of early on technology. And we recorded most of the bed tracks right there.

I mean, we did the vocals at the Record Plant East in New York City, and we also recorded a lot of the vocals at Morgan Studios outside of London. But when the band was doing a European tour over there, we realized we needed one more song for the album. So after the tour, when everybody had the flu, we rented a hotel... well actually we rented rooms in a hotel, but as it turned out we were the very first people who stayed there, and we had the entire hotel to ourselves, and we wrote "Generation Landslide." And then we went back to London and recorded that. I was very happy with the way that album came out. I loved "Generation Landslide;" I thought that could've been a hit for us.

But being in various places is what a band does, so that wasn't a problem, especially since we recorded most of the tracks in our own house. As for other players, Rockin' Reggie was a friend and a good influence on Glen. We knew Mick Mashbir ever since our Arizona days. Bob Dolin added what we were looking for in keyboards. Steve Hunter is a very unimposing guy. He fit in better than Dick Wagner, who is a nice guy but he just didn't get our humour. His severe sort of seriousness was foreign in our world, and it created an awkwardness all around. Ezrin insisted on his involvement, and he certainly could play, so we went along with it. We all liked Donovan and we were honoured that he sang. We just tried to keep doing what we had always done—keep moving forward and try to stay focused on each task at hand.

As for outside material, "Hello Hooray," Alice and I chose "Sun Arise" for Love It to Death so weren't against outside material. For Billion Dollar Babies, we were trying to come up with a good opening song so Bob's suggestion to do "Hello Hooray" was a welcome solution. Of course, we did it much different than the demo that we had heard. But it turned out to be stage show opener too. The fog would roll out and then this song would start and it would be the introduction to the set. And then we used pyro where Alice would point his cane at the audience and this flame would shoot out above their heads. And that would kick the show off.

But you know, we were safety-conscious. This wasn't really pyro like a charge; this was more like flash paper, and actually it was flash paper, like magicians use. We could have used lasers, been the first band to use laser beams, which Blue Öyster Cult ended up doing. But we were concerned about the safety factor that was in question in those days, so we passed on that, as well as other things. Our show kind of had this dangerous look to it, this aspect, but we didn't really throw anything into the audience that would hurt anyone. A lot of people threw things back that would hurt us. I mean, Glen went to the hospital one time because someone threw a hammer and hit him in the knee. Neal got a dart in his back one time, Michael Bruce had an M80 thrown and it blew up right next to his head, in Toledo.

Back to the album, "Generation Landslide," we had just finished a European tour and we were all sick and exhausted so we went to the Canary Islands to rest. "Rest" was management's code for finish writing the album. Like I say, we were the first guests to stay in a brand-new high rise hotel on the beach. We had our equipment set up on the top floor where, unfortunately, men were still working on the hotel. So, with the sounds of hammers and saws all around, the Alice Cooper group wrote "Generation Landslide" together from scratch. It proved that Alice Cooper was still at our best when we were left alone.

Neal Smith on "Generation Landslide:"
Unlike "Billion Dollar Babies," that's a perfect example of a song that did start with a beat. We had finished the Billion Dollar Babies album, and we had recorded most of the tracks in New York. We recorded some of them at The Record Plant in New York. We had recorded some of them at the estate in Greenwich Connecticut, and then in Morgan Studio in London, where we stayed at the Brinks Hotel. We needed one more track for the record and we were on tour in Europe, and we took some time off. We went down to the Canary Islands, and there was a brand-new hotel. We were going down there to write the song. We went from London to Canary Islands, just specifically to write one song.

And we said, well, where the hell are we going to be able to actually rehearse in a hotel? It's impossible. So we found a hotel that was just almost completed in construction, and all the penthouses on the top floor weren't really finished yet. They were okay, had electricity, and they were finished to the point where we could go in and use one as a rehearsal area. But it wasn't really ready for somebody to stay in the room. So we stayed in a hotel, and took the equipment up there to use as a personal area. And we spent the day and didn't come up with anything really great.

And then somebody suggested, or I suggested, well let's just try a little bit different beat. So we really didn't have any ideas. There was nothing going on. So I just started going (sings the drumbeat), and Michael started strumming chords, and then in like 15 minutes the basic idea for "Generation Landslide" was written. Now, that one specifically, the drums inspired the song. "Billion Dollar Babies," like I say, that didn't happen. That was pretty much straighter, and then I came up with the idea for the intro to the song, and that really solidified the song. So "Generation Landslide" was written around the drums.

And I love Alice's harmonica playing. He's a great harmonica player; he should play it more, but he doesn't. He played on "Eighteen" and he'd done it on a couple of tracks, but I don't think he did any on Killer or School's Out. So on the guitar solo, we were hugely influenced and knew a lot of Yardbirds songs. So the break in the song was inspired by The Yardbirds and the solos that they would have, where they'd go "Bum bum," then they'd stop and the harmonica would play—it was like an old blues thing. And we'd never tried anything like that as Alice Cooper, even though we knew those songs for years. Lyrically, I think my two favourite songs are "My Stars" and "Generation Landslide." And it was such a great song to play drums on too; just let the kit run right through there.

EASY ACTION - The Original Alice Cooper Band

1973

Parallel to the theme of Alice as "the world's most interesting man," the Alice Cooper band packed more living into 1973 than any band in any of their given super nova years. Okay, maybe not (Kiss had quite the 1976), but let's just go with 1973 as an incredibly energized super nova year for Alice Cooper.

First off, the band is methodically imploding. Alice and Cindy move out of the band house down to Manhattan. Cooper also gets involved with Salvador Dali for a loopy hologram project, inconsequential save for the fact that it's just more thrown on the pile of the cult of Alice, band optional.

The big news is that in February, Alice Cooper issue what will be their biggest album. And why is it big? I'd say it's a combination of it being their time, the fantastic and decadent packaging featuring provocative images of snakeskin, babies in makeup, piles of money and the band in virginal white, and the fact that the album contained, to some degree, four hit singles versus the usual one to two.

An extravagant tour ensues, the band's biggest and best, aided by magician The Amazing Randi, but further cracks appear with the addition of a keyboardist and more shockingly, Glen Buxton being ghosted by guitarist Mick Mashbir. Nonetheless, surprisingly little is discussed in the press about any of this. The band are plastered all over the newspapers and magazines and the album goes gold.

And then, as testimony to how much sensual and information overload five bodies can stand, before the year is out, *Muscle of Love* will emerge. Turns out there is indeed a limit, and the album is not great, it is to be the last for the original band, and the record is never toured. "Teenage Lament '74" is issued as a single, but it's never a runaway success, soon to be joined by the impressive and impressively heavy title track as the only songs to live on in classic rock rotation.

January 1973. Alice and his girlfriend move out of the band house and into a penthouse suite in Manhattan. The seeds of a rift between

Alice Cooper, the man and media maven, and Alice Cooper, the band of school chums from Phoenix, are sown.

January 16, 1973. Alice Cooper issue as a single "Hello Hooray" backed with "Generation Landslide." The dramatic and glammy concert anthem would reach No.35 on the Billboard charts, after entering at No.72. Alice Cooper's version of this song is nearly unrecognizable as the Rolf Kempf original or the purely folky Judy Collins rendition. The lyrics are the same but Alice Cooper completely overhaul the melody, the tempo, the rhythm and the arrangement.

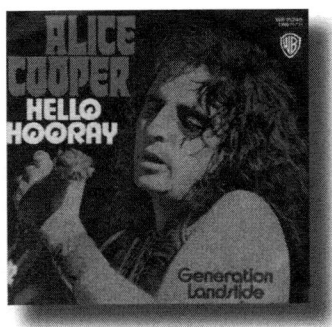

Neal Smith:
Rolf Kempf. Of all the albums we recorded, there were only a couple of other songs written by somebody else. And that song was presented to us. I still have the reel-to-reel tape with the original song on it; I guess Judy Collins did a version of it just before we did. We didn't normally do someone else's material because we were such avid writers, ourselves, but for the beginning of the album and for the beginning of the Billion Dollar Babies *show, it seemed to be perfect.*

It was a great track; Bob liked it, so we played it and learned it, and it sounded great. It was a perfect intro to our show. It really said what the band was all about, and what we had done and what we had accomplished. And the lyrics were all written by him. Alice stood aside as a lyricist—and Alice is a great lyricist—and went with the lyrics that were written, and it worked perfect. So, it opened the show. And on the album, as the song fades out, there's cannons that are firing, very, very subtle in the background.

February 1973. The band rehearse for upcoming tour dates. Bob Dolin is brought in to play keyboards and guitarist Mick Mashbir is brought in to compensate for the fading skills of Glen Buxton.

Mick Mashbir:
In May of 1972, I drove across America on my way to London and ended up staying at the Cooper mansion for a couple of weeks. I knew Michael Bruce and Neal Smith from playing together at parties, etc. in high school. Later when I lived in the desert, Mike or Neal would come by

and we'd jam on Kinks or Yardbirds songs. Are you getting a picture of the influence of the British Invasion on musicians in Phoenix? (laughs). After a couple of weeks I went off to London. The Coopers followed a few weeks later to promote School's Out. We hung out some more, and then they left. I had been living in a tiny studio for about three months when I got the telegram to "Come back to work on the new album." I was stoked. London was starting to happen for me musically but I personally didn't understand the warm beer concept (laughs) so, it was time to go. I felt no hesitation at all. In fact, I felt it was destiny being fulfilled.

About two years earlier I went to see the band in Tucson, Arizona for the Killer tour. I bought some really good street acid — don't try this at home, kids! — and had a great time. Rock security wasn't what it is now. I looked like one of the band so I headed backstage after the show. The guard opened the door for me, no questions asked! Anyway, while talking in the backstage scene I had this very strong feeling that at some point I would have a real reason to be there. I could have been a guitar roadie, but fortunately for the roadies, it didn't turn out that way.

On my flight back to America, I thought about Glen, since he was a lead guitar player and so was I, and wondered how he felt about me coming in to play. The first thing I did when I arrived back at the Cooper mansion was go directly to Glen's room. I knocked on his door. He opened it and said, "Mick! What are you doing here?" I said, "I came back to play on the new album." He said, "Cool!" and that was it.

After a couple weeks of rehearsal at the Cooper mansion, the Record Plant mobile truck showed up and we began recording Billion Dollar Babies. We had a pretty difficult time getting any decent takes. Part of it was probably the new chemistry. This was the first record that Glen hadn't shown up for. I'm sure that weighed heavy on their minds. By the end of the second week things were going so poorly that Bob Erzin wanted to pull the plug, but it was decided to press on once the band got to London.

We arrived in London and started recording at Morgan Studios the next day. Name any famous English artist and they all recorded at Morgan. The change of studios made a big difference and things started to come together. We started listening to rough mixes in London and you could hear the magic in the tracks. Morgan was the site of the infamous superstar jam with myself, Alice Cooper, Neal Smith, Keith Moon, Marc Bolan, Harry Nilsson and Rick Grech. Even though I started that jam, as usual I am in none of the pics or articles. It began during a break while I was talking with Marc. I started playing a riff similar to his hit "Bang a Gong" and he asked if he could play Michael Bruce's guitar. I said yes and off we went. Rick Grech ate a couple of my peyote buttons, picked up Dennis Dunaway's bass and Neal sat down at his drums.

We had been playing for about an hour when a highly inebriated Keith, Harry and Alice showed up. Bob Ezrin was very excited! This was the era of super group jam records and he figured he had one of his own beginning to form. Well, he set up a mic for the three singers, started rolling the tape—here comes genius! Well, the first thing out of Keith Moon's mouth as a singer was "I blew a dog." I was bummed he wanted to sing instead of playing drums. I think Neal would have given up the drum chair for Keith, no problem. Anyway, it all went downhill from there. Ezrin got pissed-off, stopped the tape and threw everyone out of the studio! So much for that super-duper session.

After a couple more weeks we went back to New York and finished the album at The Record Plant. As far as what makes the album so great? It must have been my involvement (laughs). I think a fan could give you a better answer than I can. I do know though, that the record was a victory lap for the band and our playing skills were well honed and our overall confidence was up, which contributes greatly to the vibe of any record.

But yeah, it was actually Mike Bruce that made that happen. GB was basically on strike. He didn't want to be in the same room as Michael or Bob Ezrin and they were rehearsing for the next record. Mike was also looking to the future because he didn't know what GB was gonna do. He knew I would fit in with the other guys from Phoenix. I ended up playing on every track except "Elected," "Sick Things" and "Generation Landslide". My favourite song was "No More Mr. Nice Guy". I was happy with all my parts. GB was around as little as possible. We were recording in the bands mansion and he didn't bother to come downstairs.

Neal Smith:
When we did the Billion Dollar Babies tour, Bob Dolin was the person who played keyboards. You know, Michael Bruce had always gone back and forth, as far back to "I'm Eighteen," between guitar and keyboards. He's the one who played it on the record, and he played it live on stage. And he would go back and forth from his guitar to keyboards. So, by the time we got to Billion Dollar Babies, we could afford to have a keyboard player on stage. And so Bob Dolin was a friend of Mike's from Phoenix,

and I don't know who else might have known him, but he's a great keyboard player, so he ended up on the Alice Cooper *Billion Dollar Babies* tour in 1973.

And Glen really did not contribute anything, unfortunately, on the *Billion Dollar Babies* album, except smashing his guitar on "Sick Things." He was having some health problems and alcohol abuse problems, and the demons of rock 'n' roll were really starting to take its toll on Glen. I mean, he could still play "I'm Eighteen" and he could still play "School's Out" pretty damn well, but the new stuff he wasn't keeping up to speed with it.

So we had two guys come in to play songs on the record. I think Dick Wagner was there, Steve Hunter was there, and they came in because that was kind of the Nimbus 9 camp. When Alice went out to do *Nightmare*, he used all those same studio guys on it. So I mean, we still had the feeling of the band, but just sort of the frosting on the cake was those guys. Which was fine. Because I like the stuff Dick Wagner did on "School's Out" and "My Stars," that's his solo on that one. But Mike Bruce is also playing on a lot of it as well.

The point I'm making is that Glen was not able to play a lot of those songs when we went on the road. So we went and added another guitar player, Mick Mashbir, who was a friend of mine from high school in Phoenix, Arizona. Mick and I knew each other a long time. I knew him from high school, but we all got to be friends with him after high school, and he was in a couple of bands out in Arizona who were great local bands. So we were lucky to get him to come on the road with us, and he had a great look, and he's a really easy guy to work with, and a great guitar player. So he came on the road with us and he filled in the gaps where Glen wasn't able to play. So that's how they ended up in the band, as backup musicians with the original Alice Cooper.

Illusionist James Randi on joining forces with Alice Cooper:
I was in a magic shop in New York City on 34th Street, and one afternoon I'm talking with some colleagues there. The phone rang, the proprietor took the phone call and he turned to us and he said, "Anybody here want to work with a rock artist?" And he didn't mention any names or anything. Frankly if he said Alice Cooper I wouldn't have known the difference. But I said, "Yeah, tell him I want $100 to talk to him." And the other guys laughed and everything, and then turned back to the phone and he put his hand over the phone, and he says, "Okay, he'll pay." And I said, "Hey, damn, that's okay. Just wants to talk to me; he wants to talk to me, I'll do that." I said, "Where is he?" And he said, "He's

so and so by the Enterprise" and whatnot. So it was just frankly down the street. I was near 8th Avenue, I should say, at the time.

And so I hustled myself down there and I found the place appropriately decorated with dead plants. The potted plants all over the place, they were all dead. Purposely done, I found out later on. That was the sort of atmosphere to the place. I walked in and introduced myself to Shep Gordon and we hit it off right away, and he said, "What do you think you could do for us?" And I gave him a whole thing, and I said how I could get in touch and get a hold of an original Will Rock guillotine. That wouldn't mean anything to you—technical term in the trade.

So as I say, Shep and I hit it off very well, and I described what I could do. And he said, "Okay, what do you want for it?" And I said, "What are you offering?" And he made me an offer which was very, very satisfactory. And I said, "Fine, you're on; we're in business." And he told me when the tour started, he invited me to go... where was it? It was some place north of the city, in Connecticut, where they were holding fort. They had rented an old mansion there and pretty well wrecked the joint from what I saw. Somebody had put a hole through one of the walls so he could see the TV in the next room. But that was sort of the way of groups in those days.

Dennis Dunaway on meeting James Randi for the first time:
The band was in a hotel room in NYC and we were all sitting on a bed watching television which was typical of the band, especially Alice—he's still glued to the screen whenever he has any downtime. The TV was the god, it was always on, we all liked it and we all got a lot of ideas for the band from television. All of a sudden there was a guy who started talking in the back of the room and one by one we looked around to see who the heck it was and it was him. We had all decided that we wanted to do something different and he just happened to be a powerful personality that stuck, I guess. He came in and started doing magic tricks and stuff. Randi is a great self-promoter.

Alice Cooper on the band's love of sensationalism:
Well, we were the National Enquirer, where other bands were the LA Times and the Chicago Tribune. Alice Cooper was the Weekly World News. We were the "Boy Born with Dog's Head." We were more exciting, much more sensational. And I understood the power of the press. I was a journalism major, an art and journalism major in school, and I totally understood what sold papers and that was sensationalism. So Alice Cooper gave them sensationalism.

You know, I wasn't stupid. I was saying, if I have an image like this, I'm not going to sit back and be subtle about it. We've got to be outrageous. But, we have to be able to pay it off with great songs. It's like that in sports. If you get 20 rebounds a game, yeah, then you can have leopard-skin hair. If you can knock out anybody in the ring, then you can call yourself The Greatest and be as outrageous as Muhammad Ali. Same thing with music. If you can deliver hit records and hit albums, you can pretty much do anything as outrageous as you want to.

February 14, 1973. ABC re-airs *ABC in Concert* and the complaints pour in yet again.

Dennis Dunaway:
The Alice Cooper group had a lot of detractors. We had a lot of people who hated us and weren't afraid to let us know it any chance that they got. So it was hard to all of a sudden think that we had all of a sudden made it. And then also, because we were putting so much of our profits... all of our profit basically went back into our massive staging. No band before had their own stage, or even lighting on the road. If you think about it, Hendrix, The Who, none of those bands; they would show up and use whatever lighting was available and whatever staging was there. So, a lot of our money went back in.

February 17, 1973. The New Musical Express gives away an exclusive flex-disc version of "Slick Black Cadillac," as the Alice Cooper team continues to work the UK market, regularly buying ads in the UK music weeklies and doing a high volume of press.

February 18, 1973. Alice continues to make good use of his ties to New York City, getting an invite to a performance by George Burns, who he give an "Alice Cooper Living Legend Award." Cooper also had one made for Jack Benny, who he also met that night, but that award had yet to arrive. Also around this time, Alice and Shep meet Salvador Dali and his wife Gala over dinner at the St. Regis hotel to discuss Alice's likeness being used in a hologram project Dali was overseeing. Gala instructs the duo not to discuss money with Salvador, in fact, only to respond to things he brings up. Gala pours Dali hot water, after which he pulls a jar of honey out of his pocket, pours some in and snips it off with a pair of scissors. Gala eventually takes Shep aside—Salvador would only call Shep Mr. Blenly—and they leave the room to talk money. In subsequent meetings, always at Trader Vic's at the Plaza Hotel, Dali pays for dinner only with his autograph, by signing a napkin.

February 26, 1973. Alice makes himself available to Salvador Dali for the technical work necessary to create the Alice Cooper hologram. Cooper is wearing over $1M of jewellery borrowed from Harry Winston. Subsequently there's a presentation at a museum, with national press in attendance. Rather than pay for the making of the hologram, the Cooper grant cede rights to it to Dali and take three holograms. The work, called "The First Cylindric Chromo-Hologram of Alice Cooper's Brain," can be seen at the Dali museum in Spain; as well, one is in the collection of the Dali museum in St. Petersburg, Florida.

Dennis Dunaway on the growing fame of Alice at this point, over and above that of the band:
I fully understood Alice having his own celebrity status and I had no problem with it. That's what we had strived for. The problem came with the decision to cut us out. Out in the real world, I was excruciatingly quiet, but the band knew me as a relentless crusader for a crazy cause. How else would you talk a preacher's son, a football linebacker and two punks from Ohio into wearing sequins?

February 27, 1973. Alice Cooper issue their sixth album (in four years), *Billion Dollar Babies*. The album would reach No.1 on the *Billboard* charts and hit No.1 in the UK as well. Canada would respond with a No.2 ranking and Germany, No.9.

Excerpts from the Warner Bros. **Billion Dollar Babies** *press release:*
In Alice's own words, "Billion Dollar Babies *is a reflection of just what*

the album title implies, that the group's current success has afforded us the freedom and environment, to the extent of overindulgence in many fashions, to put together a total representation of ourselves as being the by-product of the affluent society from which we've come."

Production began on Billion Dollar Babies in mid-October of 1972 with Bob Ezrin joining the group and their 16-track mobile unit at the Cooper estate in Greenwich, Connecticut. At this early stage Alice Cooper had an abundance of material but no real theme for the album. Basic tracks were laid down and recording in Greenwich went on until the first week in November when things were interrupted by the European invasion/tour which established the Coopers as the number one rock attraction throughout England, France, Germany, Holland, Denmark, Sweden and Switzerland. It was on this tour that the whole "billion dollar baby" concept came into being and that was due largely to the high level of respect Europe had for Alice Cooper as well as the lifestyle that the group have begun to maintain. Everything was first class for Alice Cooper, and for the first time in their career they saw all around them the visible proof of the seven hard years of belief in what they were doing all of sudden paying off, not only monetarily but respectfully as well.

Side one of Billion Dollar Babies opens with the only cut on the album that was not written by the group, and it's the first single from the album, entitled "Hello Hooray." The single was introduced to Alice Cooper by their producer Bob Ezrin, and they immediately picked up on it because of its Broadway feel. The song was written by a Canadian singer and songwriter named Rolf Kempf. Alice's personal reason for liking the record was because it was done in a ballad fashion and is a powerful as well as unique song on this album. The second cut on side one is called "Raped and Freezin'." This song is basically a three-minute and 15-second Tennessee Williams story about a guy hitchhiking that gets picked up by a woman. The poor kid gets raped and is let out of the car naked to the world in Chihuahua, Mexico.

"Elected" is the next song, and this top 20 hit is nothing more than Alice living out his fantasy of running for President. "Billion Dollar Babies" is a three-minute, 39-second sexual exploitation song and according to Alice, is a further adventure of the character that Alice has portrayed in all of their previous albums. This song is that character confessing some of his sexual fantasies. "Unfinished Sweet" is a six-minute, 17-second story of a person going to the dentist and the changes that that person goes through while being done in by the

EASY ACTION - The Original Alice Cooper Band

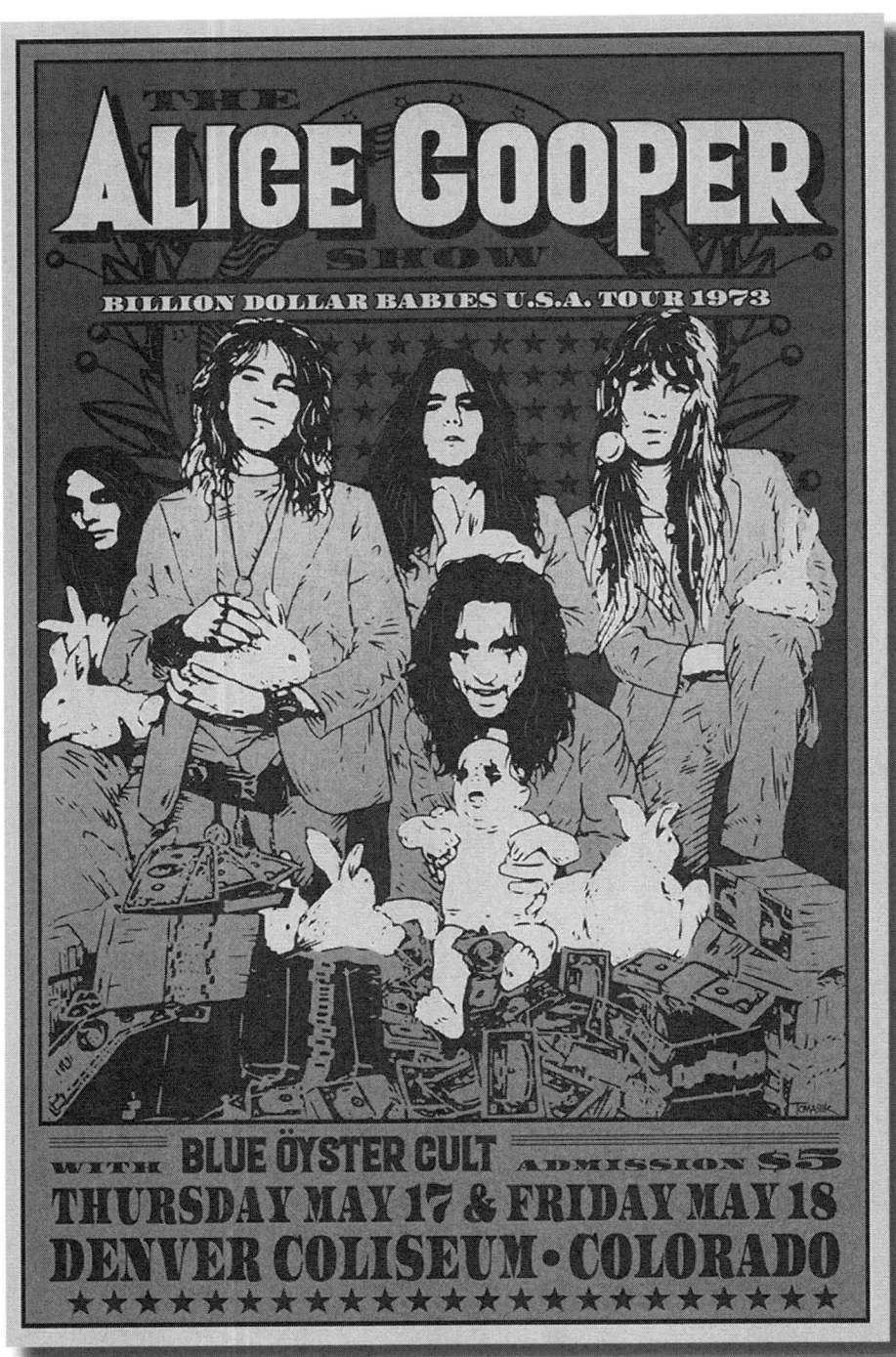

dentist including a drilling sequence, a tooth-pulling sequence and a dream sequence due to the over-abundance of gas the person has received.

Side two opens with a three-minute, five-second rocker called "No More Mr. Nice Guy," a story of a nice young rock star that has been verbally killed by the press. His personality changes because of what all the bad press has done to him. "Generation Landslide" is a four-minute, 31-second Alice Cooper song of America and American things. The song is a decadent statement of America today as seen through the eyes of the character on all Alice's albums.

"Sick Things" is a four-minute, 18-second Bela Lugosi tune mainly referring to mass audiences taking on one individual personality and that personality becoming far more perverse than any performer could attempt to be. "Mary Ann" is a two-minute, 19-second tune which shows a very melodic side of the Coopers. "I Love the Dead" is a five-minute eight-second song about necrophilia, plain and simple, and is the final cut on the album. An interesting note about this song as well as all the others on the album is that Alice wrote the lyrics within one hour of recording the song. He said that by doing this he was able to keep the album as fresh and current as it could possibly be, and it was to him quite an interesting way of doing things.

Alice Cooper on **Billion Dollar Babies:**
It was probably the most timely record we ever did; School's Out *and* Billion Dollar Babies *were just so timely. They hit at exactly the right time. We were at the very top of our popularity. All of a sudden* School's Out *broke everything wide-open. That was a No.1, and then* Billion Dollar Babies *followed it up. When those two things happened right there, suddenly there was a new respect for Alice Cooper. All the rock critics that said, "Well, maybe, just by accident this group could have a hit. And maybe, just because their show is so good, and because Alice is so bizarre, okay, we'll give him that."*

But when we followed up with Billion Dollar Babies, *all the critics were saying, "You know what? This is the best album I've heard all year." All of a sudden, even the musicians, who were always, "So what, Alice Cooper?!," they were now going, "Hey, these guys are good." And to me that was important. Because I knew that the show was going to overshadow the music. And when they started actually loving the music, that's what I really cared about. It's a no-brainer that they're going to love me getting my head cut off. If you hate Alice Cooper, you're going to love that. But when they actually played the record and said this is* my favourite record, and when you get guys like John Lennon saying "Elected" was his favourite record, that's great. That's the kind of recognition you've always wanted.

Dennis Dunaway on Billion Dollar Babies, plus Michael Bruce's increasing dominance with respect to the songwriting of the band:
We all wanted the same thing—to make great records. It didn't matter who came up with the best idea for a bridge or a lyric. We tried every idea and voted on what was best. That's what got us to the top. The problems came when that democracy fell to dictatorship.

For instance, four of us did not want "Mary Ann" on Billion Dollar Babies. We had some killer rock songs and the best one of them should have been where "Mary Ann" was. Betraying our long proven rule was a major problem, and damaging. And as that type of thing escalated, so did our resistance to it. But Alice wasn't resisting. And the more he was separated from the rest of us, the more we saw our band, and all of the benefits of what we had all strived for, being taken away from us. And the louder we rebelled, the more they called us out-of-control rock star egomaniacs that they had no choice but to replace. We just wanted our band back.

But "Mary Ann" was actually played by a keyboard player from Nimbus 9 recording studios, Jack Richardson and Bob Ezrin's studio, in Toronto Canada. He was one of the guys who worked with the studio and did a lot of keyboard tracks whenever they needed something like that for The Guess Who and so on and so forth, a really nice guy. Personally I was fighting tooth and nail to have another song put on the album instead, because I thought we had some great songs that we were bumping to put that on. Like "Woman Machine," that ended up on Muscle of Love, although I also don't know if they were really as good as I thought they were at the time.

But I really thought we had more band songs, that would likely become something people would remember the band for. Even though in retrospect, I like "Mary Ann." Actually, I wrote a bass part for that. I had worked diligently to come up with something different, which actually reminded me of an early song that Michael Bruce did on the Easy Action album. I think it's "Below Your Means," which has a part where Michael reminds you of a little Mozart guy, playing piano, a spoiled brat kid, and then the bass does this little comical run. Okay, well, for "Mary Ann" I had a similar thing, kind of a very Broadway bass part gone crazy. But as it turned out, we decided that for texture, we wouldn't record the bass part. I'm kind of sorry that we decided that *actually. I would have liked to have recorded that. But time was of the essence as well.*

And then we also had "Sick Things," which Bob Ezrin and Alice wrote together. Ezrin was on piano, and Alice came up with the concept and the lyrics and everything. And then when we recorded it, when we went to Morgan Studios outside of London, we decided that we wanted to get more bottom on the bass. So we actually set the track up and I played the bass part really fast, and then we slowed it back down, so the bass could have more bottom.

At that point I also re-did the bass tracks to the movie, Good to See You Again, Alice Cooper, *which didn't have all the shtick in it at that point, but it was basically the live concert that we did in Texas, where they had a technical problem with the bass tracks, and I had to redo all of the bass for that soundtrack. This was an actual movie release, but it was only released briefly. You know, rock movies are generally not successful.*

And the last song on the album, "I Love the Dead," has one of my favourite bass parts I ever wrote. That one had a lot to do with Dick Wagner, actually. He played a lot of the guitars on it, and some of the great guitar lines in it were Dick Wagner. So we had that new influence. The band was very tight amongst ourselves. Usually everything that we did was the band in a room, and anybody else was kind of an outsider. But then when Ezrin came along, he was accepted as a part of the band, and when Dick Wagner came along, he was accepted as a member of the band. And so was Rockin' Reggie. So we were like that. It was a tight clique, but we didn't keep people away if they were into it and they had creative ideas that we liked.

Neal Smith on "Mary Ann" and "Sick Things:"

On Easy Action, *there was a song Michael wrote called "Beautiful Flyaway" that was very Broadway, very theatrical, and so we thought that with everything we had on* Billion Dollar Babies—*"Sick Things," "I Love the Dead," "Raped and Freezin'"—we needed something a little lighter. But it had to have that Alice Cooper twist on it. So if you listen to the lyrics you certainly know what the twist is on that. But again, that goes in to the theatrics of what Alice Cooper was and what we could do musically as well as theatrically.*

And "Sick Things," there was a huge ballroom where we would actually rehearse our live shows. And the fireplace was so big you could put a small car in there, and there was like 40-foot ceilings. We'd bring all the equipment up and do our full rehearsals right there, before we would go on tour. But we'd also use that room to record. We'd made a drum riser about ten feet high, put the drums up there, and then put microphones all around this big monstrous room and that was the drum sound we got for "Sick Things." I'm just banging away doing these big rolls across tom-toms that are echoing in that room and it was just monstrous. There was just no way could you get a bigger sound than that—maybe in the Grand Canyon or something!

Michael Bruce on Billion Dollar Babies:
Our Sgt. Pepper *(laughs)*. The quintessential Alice Cooper album. "No More Mr. Nice Guy" was a tune I had written and had been around since Killer but it was just not a song that would fit on any of those albums. But when Billion Dollar Babies came around, it was its time, and that song—and "Billion Dollar Babies" really—set the mood for the album and then we built it from there. I think it was more of a public album like we were celebrating our success. It's worldly and in-your-face at the same time.

It's got great pieces like "Mary Ann" and Alice wanted to put his macabre twist on it and yet the album had songs like "No More Mr. Nice Guy" and "I Love The Dead." It ran the gamut. But each of the albums were so distinct that even Muscle of Love, and not doing it with Bob Ezrin, was distinctive in its own way because it wasn't Bob Ezrin. It was Jack Douglas and Jack Richardson who were people we worked with all the time with Bob. It was the same sort of thing, but without the big theatrical piece. Each album seemed to have its own character to it. I think it's what The Beatles had going. Each album had a real character and a flavour to it that stood out. When you listen back to Rubber Soul... we weren't doing it to that extent, but we were on that track.

But yeah, we also had on there "I Love the Dead." From what I remember, that was a song that was worked up by Bob, Alice and Wagner together. But they didn't have an ending to it and I came up with the major chord change (sings it). The up, cheer-y part I wrote and I noticed I didn't get any credit on it, but that's okay. Those guys were working so much on the feeling of the first part of the song that they never got to where the song was going as a whole.

I had written a lot of stuff with the band and "I Love the Dead" is a good example where I didn't get any credit on that because people thought that I wrote so much of the stuff that it's not going to matter "to Michael." I wrote some stuff for a couple of Neal songs and Dennis' song "Black Juju." I worked with them but didn't get any credit because that was my job in the band. I was one of the writers and I was on salary to do that. If I didn't like the song they'd come up with, then it was my job to work on it whether or not I got any credit.

Dick Wagner on working with Alice for the first time, resulting in "I Love the Dead:"
They were looking for more accessible music than what they had been doing all their career which, some of it, was a little bit in left field. Then Ezrin stepped in and they did "I'm Eighteen" which was very accessible. They wanted more of that and they hadn't been able to come up with anything until I came in and did the stuff that I did and it turns out they were ballads. I wrote some of the rock stuff too obviously 'cause I'm a rock 'n' roll player.

I knew Alice from before because we had met in Detroit. We met when I was in The Frost and he came backstage to see me one day and later that year I was flown out to Greenwich, Connecticut to the mansion where they were living and wrote "I Love The Dead" with him out there. From then the relationship just developed. So, was I afraid? It's always scary to sit down with a new person and write because you don't know what to expect. It was the perfect collaboration between Cooper and I. It was immediate because we would just start laughing at shit. We would laugh and laugh until we'd settle down and then we'd write a great song. We'd always come up with these weird titles, have a good laugh and then make great music.

Alice had the idea. I just sort of started playing the music, and wrote the music. He came up with the title, and when you're singing "I love the dead," what kind of music are you going to write? (laughs). There's only so many ways you can go. I sold my interest in that song to them because I needed money at the time. My name isn't even on the credits on the album. That's a point of contention, but life goes on. It's the first thing that I wrote with Alice.

Mick Mashbir on Michael Bruce's contribution to Billion Dollar Babies:
I know that Mike presented a lot of the songs in finished form, lyrics and all, like "Be My Lover," and if Alice felt they fit what he and the band were trying to present, then he would leave the songs as is. If the lyrics didn't fit, Alice would rewrite them. I can't give you any specific examples of the rewrites but I know that it frustrated Michael and that led to his desire to express himself with a solo album. The easiest way to understand this is, Mike embraced the Beatles' music, and the rest of the guys were a Stones band before he joined. I remember that during the tracking rehearsals Alice didn't sing. He sat and listened and

worked on his lyrics. What competition there was led to a more creative working situation, as it often does in bands.

February 27, 1973. The band perform a dress rehearsal gig at the Capitol Theatre in Port Chester, New York, no audience, to work the bugs out of the difficult *Billion Dollar Babies* show.

Illusionist James Randi on Alice's show and its effect on the fans:
You've got a character that's called Alice Cooper, and it's not Vincent Furnier. It's Alice Cooper, and you've got to develop the character and the character always takes on the character in tune with the music that's being played and the themes and such, so that's all part of developing the character. You're in show business, not just going out there and doing music.

I'd never even been to see a hard rock show before in my life, frankly. I knew nothing about it. The kids were eating it up and they caught on. About one-third of the way into the show they were catching on. It's all a put-on. It's an act. The dolls, the chickens, the whole thing and everything, it's an act. And they loved it. Once they caught on to the fact that this is all a big extravaganza show, literally a show, then they felt more at ease with it. There were some kids that were die-hard idiots, of course. They were all doped-up and they were exposing themselves and tearing their clothes and doing all kinds of crazy things, but they were gotten rid of by security pretty fast.

But most of the fans, they laughed at it, you see. At first they didn't quite know whether to laugh or to be scared or whatever, but then Neal would be winking at them and... well, Neal was quite a good character in the show, too, and Dennis Dunaway, still a very good friend of mine. He would always carry on. He would get close to the crowd and say personal stuff. He'd call down to the front row and say something like, "Are you terrified?" Things like this, so he lightened it up. And they left very happy. That was a very happy audience. They wouldn't have left early. You couldn't have gotten them out of there with a can opener.

And Alice kept it going, on stage and off. He was always very conversational and everything, and he was busy, busy, busy. Press all over the place and all kinds of problems with the show to get it onstage that night, sometimes. We'd travel during the middle of the dead winter and we had all kinds of problems. We all pitched in. I even shovelled snow along with the rest of them when we had to. It was a cooperative deal. We all worked. We never asked about why we were doing it. We did it because the show had to go on.

Mick Mashbir on getting Bob Dolin into the band:
I'd only seen Bob play in one band and Mike Bruce wanted a keyboard player for the live show, so we auditioned him. Bob was a gifted player with a fabulous ear. On tour we got along quite well since we were the hired guns. Whenever there was a press conference at the hotel, the local promo man would show Bob around town so we would not be interviewed by the press. On the tour everyone from both bands got on tremendously. The openers Flo and Eddie hired Bob and me about five years later.

March 1973. *Billion Dollar Babies* is certified gold, however platinum wouldn't be achieved for another 13 years.

***Guest guitarist Mick Mashbir, on touring* Billion Dollar Babies:**
The tour was a great experience. For me, it was like taking the express elevator to the penthouse and paying for your own room. That's a whole other story! (laughs). I had only been playing in bars and clubs and in the middle of the Phoenix desert before that. Having said that, I was more than ready to take that ride. At first the band wanted me to wear a gorilla costume! I was having none of that, but looking back on it, I probably would have gotten more publicity out of it. But no one would have known what I looked like.

The first night was a humbling experience. The crotch of my pants split as I climbed up to the stage. But as far as Glen was concerned, he was secure in his place in the band. I was just a supplemental player to him. We got along just fine. I remember once we got to the gig and everyone piled out of the limo and went in the back door. Glen and I went to the trunk of the limo to get our guitars out. We both had the same workingman approach. We carried our own guitars.

Anyway, the limo driver starts to drive off! We're screaming and chasing him. Finally he backs up, opens the trunk and we get our guitars. He drives off again. Glen and I get to the back door, it's locked and no one is there. It's one of those glass doors. We look at each other and start banging the glass with our guitar cases, hoping someone would hear us. Oops! The glass shatters, we open the door and just as we step in, someone comes around the corner, "What happened to the door?!" "It must have been some fans," we said as we shuffled off to the dressing room, laughing the whole way.

Neal Smith on the Buxton/Mashbir drama:
On the last two albums, Billion Dollar Babies *and* Muscle of Love,

Glen's only contribution was smashing a guitar on "Sick Things." That's all he did on those two albums which is a lot like what Pink Floyd went through with Syd Barrett. They got another guitar player and went on, but we couldn't figure out how to do that with Glen. Dennis and I started working with another guitar player, Michael started working with another guitar player and Alice started working with other guitar players—everybody did it, but we couldn't do it as a band.

Mick Mashbir played on Muscle of Love. He had been on the Billion Dollar Babies tour, he had been on the Muscle of Love tour. He went down to South America with us, so he was already in the organization, but he was being paid to come onstage with us and play the guitar parts Glen didn't know. Glen still played "School's Out" and "I'm Eighteen" and stuff, but there was a lot of pressure with everybody to try and figure out what the fuck we were going to do. Other bands had done it and moved on easy, but Glen was such a huge part of this band. After the fact, there's ways we could have done it. Was that 100% the reason for the break-up after Muscle of Love? I wouldn't say that, but I think it had an awful lot to do with it.

Michael Bruce on Glen and his deterioration:
Another occurrence that I always thought really put the nail in his coffin was that first trip to New York. You know how the movie Blade Runner, I think it is, takes place in this hotel that has the old-style elevators with the wrought-iron cage; it's a hotel in New York. And we stayed there and they had these huge rooms that had like three doors on them, eight beds inside.

And we went in to crash. I remember we got in really late and all of our luggage and guitars were sitting there, and in the morning, Glen's guitar was gone. So we were pissed-off and we decided to check out. And we went down to sit in the lobby and right across the street was the Howard Johnson's. So we get something to eat, and when we came back, somebody had stolen his suitcase out of the lobby. Just his. I mean, what are the chances? You have all that luggage sitting there, that they would get Glen's. Somebody was, you know, a serious fan or they didn't like him; I'm not sure which (laughs).

But think about it. He lost his sound, he lost his image, all his clothes, and it was really hell for him, you know, during that time. I remember him experimenting with different guitars and he just couldn't seem to lock in. We would play shows and he would end late or start early and have feedback. And he was really struggling with it. But I think that was another factor that wasn't a big help to his psyche at the time. Plus his other extracurricular activities. It was not a good time. We persevered through hoping he was going to get better and it didn't really happen.

March 1 - June 7, 1973. Alice Cooper mount an intensive Canadian and US tour in support of *Billion Dollar Babies*, main support coming from old pals Flo and Eddie. Stage props would include dolls, mannequins, Alice's famed guillotine, as well as a surgical table, dentist rill, axes, whips, a bubble machine and a new snake named Eva Marie Snake.

Illusionist James Randi on life on the road with Alice Cooper:
The show was an 'I love the dead' sort of thing. He was perpetuating

his character. And I was quite taken with it because it was a very, very professional group. I didn't see any dope being used at any time. The roadies were always into pot and whatnot, and that's okay, but I didn't... Alice was boozing pretty heavily at that time, but beer only. Never anything stronger than that. But I never saw any dope being used; I never saw anything really nasty taking place. There's stuff I wouldn't approve of and wouldn't have liked to see, but I was in approval of everything I saw and I got along very, very well with everybody there. They liked me and I liked them and we were a good working team. And we had to do some very strange things, but it's a long story.

But I was concerned about his consumption of beer. They would pop open a can for him, give it to him and he would chug-a-lug, put it down, and they'd take it away and give him a fresh can right away because he was always afraid of somebody putting something into the can. Which could have happened. It could have happened, theoretically, so he was very cautious about that. And he was a little concerned about the fact that he was consuming a lot of booze, and the next morning he would pretty well almost always be hungover, and he was feeling a bit bad about that. I felt he was very uncomfortable with that.

Anyway, I hit it off well with the guys and everything. Glen Buxton gave me a lot of problems because he was always high and the guys knew it and they came to me first and said, "Glen will always be little dopey and a little crazy. Just try to understand that." Shep had determined to keep him for the Billion Dollar Babies tour, because he was advertised and he was in all the photographs and such. But they hired Mick Mashbir to play the guitar from a back room doing Glen's part, and Glen never knew that he wasn't being heard on the system. It's a strange story. They actually had him surrounded with monitors and little speakers on the stage pointed up at him and he was hearing himself. But he wasn't hearing what Mike was doing from the back room, and that was going out to the audience. Very sad.

Dennis Dunaway on the Billion Dollar Babies show:
I'm not sure it was so shocking other than this totally outrageous band had made it to the top. We were doing the guillotine at that point, but it was the same formula that we used before with the light and dark. We would kick it off really kind of positive with "Hello Hooray," which, if you were in the audience, this big giant bank of fog would roll off the stage and then we would all be standing there wearing white playing this ballad, an arena-type ballad, and then do some rockers.

And then all of a sudden everything would shift gears and we *would change into dark clothing, and I would switch from a white bass to a black bass and everything would do that same shift of gears into the dark side of things. Alice would be an evil type of person, and then he would get caught and punished for his crimes.*

And in the end he would come out in white tails and a white top hat and confetti would drop and all of a sudden everything would be positive again. So we would have this happy ending kind of comeback. People came to see this thing everybody was talking about, and they were seeing something they had never seen before. Even people who had seen us before would see something they had never seen before.

That was still a heavy duty time with the animal rights people, where it was impossible to convince them that we didn't kill animals onstage, that we never intended to do that. It was just an accident that happened—that plagued us forever. And so there was a lot of that still with officials. Plus because of the Jim Morrison profanity thing, it was common in those days for promoters to withhold a fairly large amount of your pay, and if any foul language went out over the microphone, if Alice had said a four-letter word, which he never did—Alice has never cursed. Then the promoters would keep that money.

So Alice got around that where he would go to the front of the stage and say, "What's the dirtiest word you know?" And he would

hand the microphone into the audience and they would say the dirty words (laughs). And on those nights, quite a few nights, it would end up with the promoters and everybody arguing whether or not that was a loophole or not (laughs). But Alice did that more just to bug the promoters for trying to withhold that money than anything.

But we never got any heavy banning by the religious right or anything, because Alice's father was a minister himself. And it was almost impossible to be shocking in those days, with the amount of censorship and everything, although we basically found a lot of loopholes. It seems tame by today's standards, but back then it was quite shocking that we would have a song called "Dead Babies." But we would get around it by making the lyrics about parental abuse. The message was moral. But all people tend to hear is the chorus, "dead babies," and then Alice has a baby doll on stage. We had to be shocking without being banned, and that was the hard part. It was very hard. And so it was safe enough that we were able to get away with it.

Neal Smith on the notorious nature of the band by this point:
Well you see, Alice kind of sweeps that under the rug a little bit, but we were getting death threats. We were getting banned from a lot of cities. The founding fathers, the mayor or the first selectmen from some cities would come see our show. And I mean, it got more negative publicity than it was really threatened. Once the Toronto incident with the chicken came out, they said Alice Cooper bit the head off a chicken and drank the blood from the neck. That's the kind of stuff, once it's out there, once it's out in the press, people believe a lot of this bullshit.

And it was great for us. It was phenomenal. You can't buy that kind of publicity. But the fact is, the show was basically theatrical and we weren't harming anything. There was one article I read saying there were baby ducks and chicks on the stage, and with our big platform shoes we were just smashing them to pieces. In actuality, we had stuffed blown-up animals of little bunnies and teddy bears and we smashed those onstage, but they weren't real animals. So it's always interesting how the press interpreted sometimes what we were doing on stage.

But no, there were death threats. We definitely had death threats. Plus the fact that people couldn't figure out whether we were gay. I mean, I was shocked when I found out that a lot of people in Canada thought that I was a girl. They thought that the drummer for the Alice Cooper band was female. And I can attest, that's not true (laughs). I'm not gay and I'm not female. But there was a lot of fear about the band.

They didn't understand it. They couldn't put a label on us and they couldn't figure what the hell we were doing. When we were with Frank Zappa that was one thing, but all of a sudden we have a hit with Love It to Death *and "I'm Eighteen" and* Killer *and "Under My Wheels," all of a sudden this band that everybody thought was going to go away is selling millions and millions of records and the songs are going up the chart, into the Top 50, the Top 30, the Top 20, and then "School's Out" was in the Top Ten. We became a real threat.*

There were some cities in the Bible Belt that banned us. But also the mayor would come to see one of our shows, and they would say, "Oh, it's not that bad," and we would go ahead and play the city. I think Utica, New York was one of those cities. So it was always an issue. But we were not going to change what we were doing. By the time we did School's Out, *I mean, I was carrying three handguns with me because the threats were so severe. But in those days, you could just throw them in your bag and walk on the plane with that and nobody would check anything. And I would sleep with them under my pillow.*

And I had Kachina, my boa constrictor with me. That was another thing that we added to the show was my pet snake Kachina. So she was always with us, and then we wrote the song "Is It My Body," and right around Killer, *we decided to bring the snake on. And she traveled with us anyway. If you are on the road with us and we were paying for your food you had to work somehow (laughs). So Kachina came out and she made the cover of the* Killer *album.*

March 15, 1973. Because of a cancelled show in Knoxville, TN, the band return home to Connecticut for a short break to work on songs for the next album. Alice, however, returns to New York City.

Dennis Dunaway on the band's songwriting process:
It would depend on the songs. I always maintained that Alice Cooper was the name of the band, and all of the songs were written by Alice Cooper, which meant all five members. And everybody had a lot to do with the songwriting. There are hardly any... there are a few songs that pretty much Michael came in with the song and we added our parts, but most of the songs were gone over, taken apart and dissected and reassembled hundreds of times over until we got the song just the way we liked it.

Alice's contribution, a lot of times, if we went into the studio and didn't have any clue what we were going to do, we would start by jamming and Alice would sit in his chair with his beer can sitting on the floor and a pad and pencil, and he would be thinking about what the song should be about or whatever, and we would be playing, and then all of a sudden Alice would jump up and say, "Okay, how about if the song goes (sings some chord structures)," and then he'd direct us like Burt Bacharach. Burt Bacharach is one of Alice's heroes. And so even if Alice seemed quiet in some respects, in other respects, whenever he had an idea, it always seemed to work. It always seemed to be a valid direction for the song to go. And usually his talent lies in coming up with the concepts for the songs.

You know, back in those days, I was trying to come up with a book of poetry, which was based on dreams. All these nights of playing and not getting back to the hotel room until three, having to get up at eight and stuff, what would happen is, we would rarely have a sound night of sleep. So when I would start to fall asleep, I would start to have a dream or something, and I got in the habit of forcing myself to get up and try to write a poem related to that dream.

And I had a whole book of those, and Alice always kept that book by his chair, and he would sometimes just be paging through it and he would see some lyrics that would inspire him, and he would take the concept of the poem, and a lot of times just pull a lot of lines out of it and turn it into a song. Some of them were pretty abstract ideas, but he would make them more relatable to people. "Killer" was a song like that; that one, the lyrics are pretty much a dream poem, as I called them."

Alice Cooper on the songwriting process:
Well, Dennis is so clever. Dennis has always been the artist in the band. By the way, he's a great artist, graphic artist. He always came up with the weirdest stuff. All the stuff on any of the early albums that was really out there was Dennis. All the stuff that was really commercial was Mike Bruce and myself. When it came to songs like "No More Mr. Nice Guy," that was a single; that was Mike Bruce and me. Mike Bruce wrote a lot of those riffs. We were very open about… you know, we blueprinted "Substitute" by The Who there. When it came to things like "Blue Turk," that's Dennis and me.

All the trippy stuff was always Dennis. He was a big Pink Floyd fan. He was the first one that came to me and said, "Listen to this." It was Piper at the Gates of Dawn and I listened to it and went, "Wow, that's really cool. That's the best psychedelic band I've ever heard." Dennis was the guy that could have joined Pink Floyd and fit right in. Dennis was every bit a Roger Waters, or even maybe bordering on Syd Barrett, *just very creative, very smart, and a great showman onstage. He used to bring in Stockhausen and all this electronica and we would sit and listen to it. I wasn't always interested, but I would sit and listen to it with him.*

March 21, 1973. "No More Mr. Nice Guy," credited to Michael and Alice, is issued as a single off of *Billion Dollar Babies*, backed with "Raped and Freezin'." The song reached No.25 on the US charts and No.10 on the UK charts. A full court press is put on the hit record, with announcements of TV ads for both the UK and the US.

Michael Bruce:
Well, it's funny, "No More Mr. Nice Guy," that's my song. I wrote it, and

that song was written back when Killer was happening, and of course, it didn't fit that album. It didn't fit School's Out—maybe it could've fit School's Out. But then Billion Dollar Babies came along. Well, "No More Mr. Nice Guy," the music on it, that part stayed the same because I wrote the whole thing and it was perfect, I must say. The whole song was like, "I used to be such a sweet, sweet thing—that was just a burn. Break my back just to kiss her ass and got nothing in return. All my friends told me, man, you're crazy for being such a big fool. But I guess I was, because being in love made such a fool. Now I'm no more..." See, really, that's life. But then Alice re-writes it and changes it into a song about the press. Great, if you're the lead singer..."

Dennis Dunaway on "No More Mr. Nice Guy" and "Raped and Freezin':"
"No More Mr. Nice Guy" is pure Michael Bruce. Other than ideas for bass parts, like me playing some unusual notes in it that made the chords sometimes sound like they changed when they didn't, or changed to a chord that had different textures than it normally would have, had I just played the root note. You know, Michael came in with that song, played it, and that was one of those things that was kind of a done deal. When you finished it and heard it, you knew it was right. Michael always had—and still does—that crystal-clear guitar sound that just cuts through.

And Mike Bruce had a very offbeat sense of humour. He was funny. So, when we were driving around in station wagons, hotel rooms, year after year, all together all the time, long hours on the road, I think what held it together was a highly entertaining sense of humour within the group. I was the guy who, if I said something, the conversation stopped because I was so quiet. But my sense of humour is so off-the-wall, it's kind of like, people just think about it rather than laugh. However, I was the one who was the observer. And I contend that I remember a lot of things that nobody else in the band remembers. And I remember it much more clearly, because I was observing instead of doing (laughs).

Now the flipside of "No More Mr. Nice Guy," "Raped and Freezin'," that song kind of came together at the end. It's also definitely a Michael Bruce chord structure, which I always really liked, because Michael's chords, a lot of times, had a swing feel to them. And his chord changes, he would land on chords and stay on them long enough to allow the bass the room to do things, as opposed to chord changes that are coming so fast, the bass doesn't have much choice but to comp the chord changes. And "Raped And Freezin'" was one of those kind of good *feel songs where Alice, of course, enhanced Michael's lyrics. And then I think it was Bob Ezrin's idea, at the very end, to have the 'ole' from the bullfight come in.*

Neal Smith on "Raped and Freezin':"
The character in the song, Alice I guess, gets picked up by somebody while he's hitchhiking. And of course it has a south-western kind of Mexican flair in the music, which, I always loved to bring a different feel in as far as the percussion went. And of course we were from Phoenix, Arizona, so from "Desperado" on Killer *to "Raped and Freezin'" on* Billion Dollar Babies, *once in a while some of the things from the areas where we lived in different parts of the country would filter into our music.*

April 3, 1973. A press conference and party take place in NYC for the

opening of the Dali Hologram Exhibition.

April 21, 1973. *Billion Dollar Babies* hits No.1 on the charts.

Dennis Dunaway:
When Billion Dollar Babies *hit the top, we were already deep into* Muscle of Love. *But by then, the band were buckling from pressures far more severe than that.*

April 28, 29, 1973. The band film performances in Dallas and Houston for the *Good to See You Again, Alice Cooper* concept film. Meanwhile, "No More Mr. Nice Guy" is at No.55 on the singles chart while "Billion Dollar Babies" is at No.3.

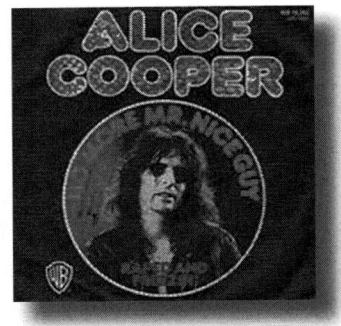

Alice Cooper on "Billion Dollar Babies:"
"Billion Dollar Babies" was actually a song that was written off the drums. It was a drum riff. Neal comes in and goes (sings it), you we wrote the song directly off that riff. And we used to do that a lot. Dennis Dunaway would write a bass riff, let's say on a song like "Blue Turk," and we would write the song around a bass line, and this time it just happened to be off the drum riff.

Everybody was very good about contributing original things. And then we let Bob Ezrin take a 15-minute bit that we did and tear it down to three minutes. He would take the best stuff out of it and say, 'Okay, now we're going to put this song together.' And we would listen to it and of course, we would go, "Out of all of that music we just played, we get this three minutes?!" And he would go, "Yeah, but that's the hit."

And "Billion Dollar Babies" was basically just making fun of ourselves. Here we were, the most hated band in Los Angeles, couldn't get a job. Went to Detroit, met this guy Ezrin and all of a sudden we're the biggest thing in the world. We were voted No.1 band in the world and we were just making fun of ourselves—here we are, billion dollar babies. And it was also a bit of a play on words from the old Busby Berkeley movies.

Michael Bruce on "Billion Dollar Babies:"
I told Neal that I'd go to music stores and hear those drums. But it has a lot of little riffs to start as opposed to one monster riff like in "Smoke on the Water." It's a solid song and when I hear it today it really holds up. It's so powerful and it couldn't be denied. We were hot at the time and it could be about 'billion dollar baby' meaning you got it so you flaunt it, or about a girl. It had a lot of different faces that could be put on the song. And those lyrics, it's hard to remember them, "Slimy little monster greasy as a weasel in the alley been infected by the rabies"—it's a mouthful, but Alice is a word creator. He does great lyrics. More than anything what I really miss is having somebody who can get up there and sing and create great lyrics for a piece of music. That's one thing I really miss about working with him.

Neal Smith on why he isn't credited on the song "Billion Dollar Babies:"

Because I didn't write anything except the drum intro to the song. That was the hook, but the original song, as we were working it out, the song pretty much had a straighter beat to it. A friend of ours, who you'll see on some of the credits, Rockin' Reggie Vinson... he was a good friend of Glen's. His name is on a couple songs on School's Out, and he did some background vocals with us, and he's a good songwriter and a good guy on his own.

The original idea for the song... I can't remember its name, but it was called "Rag Doll" or "Rag Doll Girl" or something. But it was a straighter song, and then we gave Alice the idea to go in that direction and then he came up with some great lyrics on it. And then I did that beat. I had always heard this different movement on it. So as we were working it out, the song didn't start out with that beat. I think if "Billion Dollar Babies" would have gotten written by everybody in the band, and our friend Rockin' Reggie wasn't there, it would've been a different story. But it was his song, and it was part of my job to add to it. It's a great question, as a matter of fact. Sometimes people think the song is written around the intro, but it's not. Still, the song came to life when I finally put that part on the intro.

But yeah, I had always loved the Rolling Stones intro from Charlie Watts to the song "Get Off of My Cloud." I thought that was very cool, and as a drummer I always used to like to write songs for drummers, because people listen to songs and think, "That's cool." But if I was a drummer listening to an Alice Cooper song, what would be cool about it? And I always tried to have something special in there that would get someone's interest.

So this one gave me the opportunity. And I'm a rudimental drummer; I learned all the rudiments when I was first trained, early in my music education. And I always loved flams; "Mississippi Queen" and some other great songs had a big flam all the way through. And "You Drive Me Nervous" from Killer *was flams all the way through the song. For people that don't know what they are, it's like a double stroke; you use both sticks with one syncopated just right after the other on a single stroke, and it sounds like 2 hits at almost the same time. It's one of the basic rudiments of percussion.*

So I wanted to have a drum intro, and we were fooling around with the idea of songs that would feature different guys in the band in the beginning, in the intros to a particular song. And I pretty much had liberty to do whatever I wanted to a song. Bob Ezrin heard the song being a little bit straighter played all the way through the song, but I liked the idea of this flam intro and then sort of keep it going through

EASY ACTION - The Original Alice Cooper Band

1973

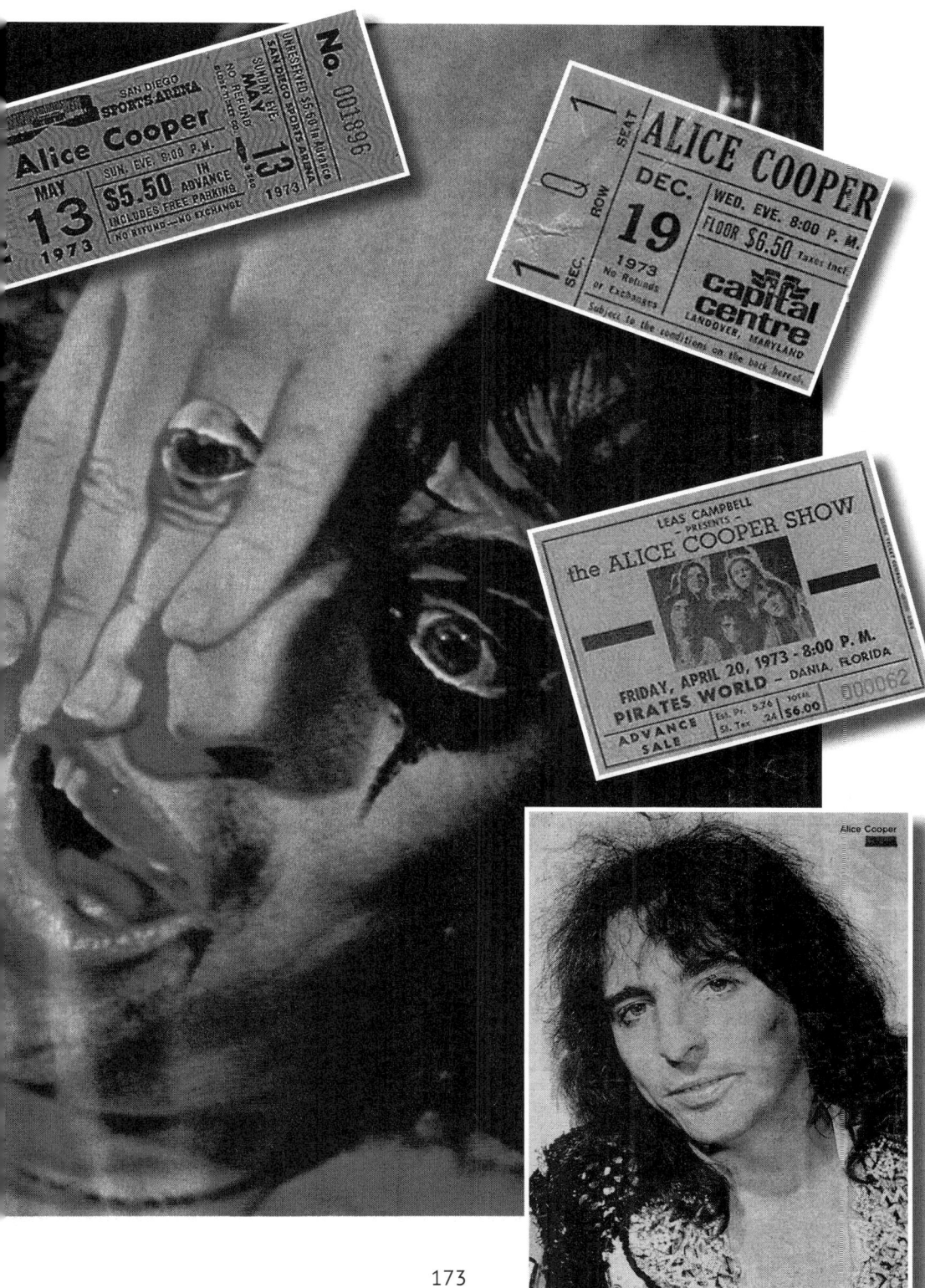

the song. And Bob said, "Well, ya know, if you're going to play it, you have to play it perfect." And I did play it perfect and it ended up being the intro to the song as well, and gave it a certain flashy character and feature that I think helped it stand alone. "Billion Dollar Babies" is such an interesting song and interesting album.

Dennis Dunaway on the song's Cooper/Bruce/Vinson credit:
Rockin' Reggie, whose name is Reggie Vinson, was a friend of the band, who we met in LA. But he lived in Detroit, not far from the Pontiac Farms where the band lived, when we wrote the Love It to Death and the Killer albums, and he became a very close friend of Glen Buxton, and he used to hang out at the house all the time. And then when the band moved to Greenwich, we called him Rockin' Reggie; Alice tagged him with that name. And actually Rockin' Reggie is the one that tagged Glen with GB, who... everyone called him GB, pretty much from then on.

But we were writing the Billion Dollar Babies album, and we knew that we wanted that to be the title of the album—Alice had come up with that name. So we knew we wanted that to be the title of the album but we didn't have the song. And Rockin' Reggie, and Glen wrote this kind of ballad-y country and western-flavoured song. First of all, it would be good to know that Rockin' Reggie wrote incredible songs, where you would swear that it was Roy Orbison. I mean, his voice has that range and that style.

But anyway, so we're at the estate, trying to work out this song one morning. Back in those days, we would rehearse about ten hours a day, and we would start reasonably, around noon. But anyway, everybody is sitting down and we're running over this song over and over, and it was a good song, with a nice...and then I said, "I don't know if this has got the fire that we need for the title track of the album." So I kind of jumped up and said, "Okay, we've got to light some dynamite under this song." And then I had Bob Ezrin and everyone in the band looking at me, "Okay, what's the idea?"

And here I am standing up and making this little speech about it, and I didn't really have a clue (laughs), so I just turned the bass amp up and played this riff, just started making up this riff. And then the next thing we knew, we had Glen doubling the riff, and that song kind of changed radically, because of that bass line. But Neal hadn't gotten his drum part together. He was working on that drum part, but it wasn't tight; it wasn't together. We were in the studio actually recording the song, going for takes, and the drum part still wasn't together.

And Bob Ezrin decided, well, we can't keep just running through this, trying to get this drum part together, so he told Neal that he wanted him to straighten the beat out, so we could get the take. And Neal refused; he stuck to his guns. "No, no, I know I'll get this; just stick with me." And he did, within a couple more takes, and he nailed that, and I think it's one of his most creative drum parts.

As for recording, Donovan was in the studio, Morgan Studios outside of London, and there were a lot of people there. Rick Grech from Blind Faith, Keith Moon was there, Harry Nilsson, Mark Bolan, Flo and Eddie, you know, Mark and Howard, and anyway, it was sort of a celebrity bash going on there. But we had brought Donovan in, specifically, to sing. He sang some of the verses and doubled on some of the choruses of Billion Dollar Babies. Great guy too. I mean, he was into it and very professional, as you expect I guess.

Keith Moon had on like these, you know those Groucho glasses with the nose, okay? He had those on but the nose was a penis. And he had had a few drinks that evening. As a matter of fact, so many that he could hardly sit on the drum stool, let alone play (laughs). And Harry Nilsson was also drunk and kept falling on the control board, and we kept kicking him out because he messed all the dials up; he could hardly walk. But when Harry Nilsson sat down at the piano and started playing and singing, here's this beautiful voice and all and these incredible songs coming out of him.

That song was verging on heavy metal but we were never comfortable with that term. Alice in particular always put down heavy metal, which is ironic, because of some of the styles of music he's gone to since then. Which I don't criticize. I'm just saying, he always seemed to be the one that always puts it down.

You know, heavy metal by the time we were coming up was getting a cliché connotation, as were things like drum solos. So we didn't do a drum solo. Neal did on "Halo of Flies," but normally when you would have had someone's drum solo, we did it with the bass and with a whole different kind of a feel than what some other drummers were doing at a time. And also, when we did do a drum solo, when it really did come down to drums, I had this idea for everybody in the band to play the drum solo. So everybody would grab sticks and we would stand around his kit and we would all be pounding out this pagan beat while Neal did the soloing in between. Actually, Alice's band used that idea on later tours.

Illusionist James Randi on his duties during the tour:

When Alice went out there and he had to make these big fountains of flame come from his fingertips I had to equip him with the two devices strapped to his fingers that did those things. So I was the last one that would speak to him before he walked onstage, and then he would march up the stairs looking like the Frankenstein monster and out onstage and "School's out forever" and all that sort of thing, and boom with the flashes.

So I had a number of duties to do, but the two parts I played were the mad dentist and the executioner, and in both of them I was completely disguised and I did not get listed in the program. I didn't want to be listed in the program. I didn't want to be somebody's second banana because I'm used to running my own show and I didn't want to take a second seat, so to speak. But during the interviews and the press and the media meetings and whatnot I was there and I was doing silly tricks for them. Fluffing the thing up, you know.

May 5, 1973. Alice Cooper takes the tour to his home state of Arizona, playing Tucson, and according to James Randi, Phoenix, possibly on the 6th or 7th (although in the quote below, he may be describing the Tucson show).

Illusionist James Randi:
I'll give you a little episode to chew on. When we came to Phoenix, Arizona, Alice came to me with a very worried look on his face. I said, "What's up?" He said, "This is my hometown." I said, "Yeah, I understand that." He said, "My mom's going to be here." I said yeah. "My mom doesn't know what I do. She knows I'm a musician but she's never heard any of the records; she's never seen the show." And I said uh-oh. And he said, "Yeah uh-oh. Would you sit with her during the opening of the show and as much as you can, any time you're off stage would you go and sit with her? We'll put her in the third row or so and you'll have a reserved seat there, and just soothe her." And I said sure.

I had to babysit his mom. And a lovely lady. After all his father, as you probably know, was a Mormon minister and the mother was very much a member of the family and that sort of thing, and I knew she was going to be in for quite a shock. So I went and sat with her and introduced myself to her. I sat down unnoticed from the audience.

And then the show started, and Alice came out onstage with the torn costume and the smeared makeup and everything, and she sat there and said, "Oh, Vincent, oh why is his shirt torn like that?" And I said that's part of the costume. "Oh, well he could get it fixed, you know."

And she was extremely, extremely naïve at that point. And then when he started to attack the dolls and stomp on them and whatnot, she said, "Oh, why is Vincent doing that?" I said, "It's all part of the act. He's just having fun with the kids, but remember it's all an act. It's just an act." And she said oh, my. She was quite shocked by it and quite subdued by it, and rather disturbed.

And then I went and did my dentist stuff, and I came back to sit with her again after changing to regular clothes again, and that was before the executioner thing, and I sat with her and looked at her, and she was laughing and chortling and carrying on. She loved it. She sort of settled into it and said oh, okay, it's an act. I guess he's an actor and that's my kid up there. And she was quite happy with it.

And when I went to the audience to rescue her right after the guillotine when Alice came marching out with the tails and top hat and everything, resurrected, I went and grabbed her and took her backstage so she didn't have to deal with the crowd, and she was quite pleased. And at his 60th birthday party, which... was it last year? I've forgotten now. I was invited out to Phoenix to celebrate that, and I went out there and I met the mother again. She remembered me, and she said, "Oh, my, you don't know how happy I was to see you." She said, "I didn't know what was going on. I thought this was some sort of a monster I'd raised, and you talked me out of it." So it was a very good arrangement. I had a hell of a time.

Dennis Dunaway on a notorious snake incident, rumoured to have taken place in Knoxville, TN:
Yes, the famous one was when the snake pulled up missing, because it was in Alice's bathroom. They couldn't find the snake and we had to move on to the next gig. And the next thing you knew, we read in the paper that it had come up in a different room in the hotel, in Charley Pride's room. He freaked out because the snake came up out of his toilet, and evidently it had gone down the toilet in Alice's room.

But as far as any other problems, I'm not going to be able to remember the name of this stadium, but I think it was in Pasadena, wherever the Queen Mary used to be parked, in California. Anyway, our snake had just eaten or something, so right after it ate, or right when it was ready to be fed, we wouldn't use it on stage. But we had this big thing there, so Warner Bros. said they would supply a snake.

So they put this... there was this big basket on the floor of the limousine, and the band was in the back of the limousine, and we're riding to the gig, and everybody is kind of bored and stuff, and it was like, "Well, you wanna look at the snake?" "Nah, later." "Ah, you wanna look at the snake?" "Yeah, let's look at the snake." And we look in this basket and it's solid snake. This was the biggest snake I'd ever seen in my life. It's like, "Whoa, wait a minute, what's going on here?!"

And during the show, when the roadies got this snake out of the basket, there were like five guys trying to manhandle this snake out to the stage. So they walked it out to Alice, Alice sang to the snake, and then they went backstage and spent the rest of the night trying to get this snake back in the basket. That one wasn't a boa constrictor; it was an anaconda. That thing must've been... I bet it was 20 feet long (laughs).

June 1973. British MP for Pontypool Leo Abse attempts to get Alice Cooper banned from the UK, offering the band valuable free press. The notorious Mary Whitehouse, name-checked by both Deep Purple and Pink Floyd for her censorship antics, gets involved as well. Meanwhile, Michael Bruce crafts plans for a solo album and Alice swans about town hanging out with celebrities, often at Max's Kansas City. He also travels with his girlfriend Cindy to Acapulco.

Alice Cooper:
We just said we're going to go to England. All right, "Eighteen" was a hit over here and it got to be a hit over there. And already the urban legend had started in England about, oh, I heard that he kills cats and eats them and things like that. Incredible. We didn't have the internet then so it was all urban legend. By the time that we were scheduled to go over, they had tried to ban us. Mary Whitehouse and Leo Abse said, "No, Alice Cooper's not coming to play in England." Thank you! They couldn't have been better. We sold out every ticket at Wembley, the record went right to No.1 and the public said how dare you tell us what we can see and what we can't see, right?

Illusionist James Randi on the cultivation of the band's bad reputation:
I think it was Baltimore where Shep Gordon called a special meeting. He said, "Oh, we're in deep shit now." I said, "What's the matter, Shep?" He said the mayor of Baltimore, who was a young fellow in his early 30s I guess, had given Alice a key to the city. And that's the last thing that Shep wanted. He said, "No, the parents have got to hate him! They've got to want their kids not to go and they've got to forbid their kids to go. That makes sure the kids will go. They'll find a way of getting there if the parents absolutely forbid them to do it!"

And that was Shep's psychology. He wanted them to be against Alice—that is the adults—to be against Alice and to despise him and hate him and the whole thing, and so he fostered that image. But when he found out the mayor wanted to give him the key to the city, he didn't know what the hell to do.

Shep was in heavy control. Shep was just wonderful. I had to admire him. He was in control at all times. He cooperated with the media and such, he knew the media were our friends and whatnot. What they would say would influence attendance and he tried to direct what they would say. Of course, he was doing the PR thing. Shep was a wonderful, wonderful manager. I mean just top-notch. Alice couldn't have asked for a better guy.

But Alice Cooper made his own news. As soon as he arrived in town... well look at the plane. The plane had on its tail a huge dollar sign, on both sides. And I used to sit up front with the pilot, who was a fellow named Kirk, and on the door was Alive Enterprises. Captain Kirk, the Enterprise. Get it? But that just happened to be a coincidence.

But I'd sit up front with Captain Kirk, the captain of the ship, the pilot, and we would have a lot of laughs, and I'd listen in on radio interceptions. He'd gesture my attention out the window to another plane that was flying... I say alongside, but that's half a mile away. You could see the plane there and the pilot would come in and say, "Hello, unknown aircraft to the starboard. This is TWA flight 466 to St. Louis. May we ask what is your airline, the dollar sign on the tail? We don't know that airline. We don't have it in our books here." So he'd get on and say, "Oh, this is Alice Cooper." They'd say, "Alice Cooper?! Oh wow!" Get all excited (laughs). That's just part of the joy I had in working with this group. They were wonderful people, wonderful people.

June 8, 1973. The band move back to Los Angeles (in piecemeal fashion), with Alice moving into a house next to conservative firebrand Barry Goldwater. Co-manager Joey Greenberg and road warrior Charlie Carnel, now legends in the business and part of the organization since the beginning, leave the fold. Rumours start flying that Alice has legally changed his name to Alice Cooper, further staking claim on the brand for himself.

July 1973. Lou Reed issues his *Berlin* album. Producing is Bob Ezrin and the guitarists on the project are future Alice Cooper axemen Steve Hunter and Dick Wagner.

August 1973. New York Dolls issue their self-titled debut. Like Alice

Cooper, the band represent a hard rock sound married to a glam look, although by this point Alice Cooper had been methodically dismantling their glam visuals since 1969. Indeed with the "hot mess" that is the New York Dolls, androgyny and decadence collide and explode, and what's more, the band is American. Again, similarities with Alice Cooper.

Neal Smith:
I actually I knew David Johansen on a social level hanging out in the city. I liked their image. It was like Twisted Sister and The Plasmatics. You had your Dolls and the Ramones and all that vibe coming out of New York, which was great. But I really didn't think they could play; they were a flash in the pan. They were an offshoot that our inspiration, our influence started to create. People that may have been reluctant to do something, to go in a kind of a transvestite or gender-bending direction, have long hair and be kind of effeminate but still tough, still hard rock 'n' roll, I mean, I thought that was all healthy stuff. Because rock 'n' roll has no limits.

Late August 1973. Neal marries his girlfriend Babette.

Alice Cooper on Neal:
Neal Smith was the epitome... if there was ever any drummer that challenged Keith Moon as far as ego, it was Neal Smith. Neal Smith was not only six-foot-six, but he would wear the six-inch heels. And with blond hair down to his waist. You know, he would call up Keith Moon and say, "How many drums do you have?" Keith would say "32;" Neal would say, "I have 33." Then he would stand up on his drum set. Now you have to picture him. He's already seven feet tall, in all chrome, and that hair. And then he would lift up his arm as high as he could and twirl his stick. He was the ultimate show drummer. He wasn't as good a drummer as Keith Moon, of course, but he was the epitome of what I call the glam drummer of all time.

Neal Smith on his showmanship:
I'm 6'3", pretty big on the drums, and I had like a six-foot arm span. I have huge arms and people say, "Your playing looks like an octopus." But I think, one of the biggest things that I had influence on were the huge drum sets. Let's face it, Keith Moon's first drum set was seven drums and my biggest set was 21 drums. I was watching an Elvis special from 1973, and the drummer had a set of Premiers or

Slingerlands. The guy had three mounted toms on the bass drum, so even Elvis' drummer was inspired by it. So, you know, nobody had three toms mounted on the bass drums. Because Slingerland kind of flipped out when I told them I wanted three drums on one bass drum.

I think that's the stuff that Alice misses today. The other dimension. I also used to do the real spinning of the drum sticks. Not a lot of drummers do that. What they do, I call it a wuss-ass little thing between the fingers. It's like a little windmill or something. But I judged myself from what I played more than how I looked on stage. But I think I had a lot of energy on stage. I still do. I think I bring some charisma to the stage.

Early September 1973. While in Toronto to rehearse at Nimbus 9 material that will emerge on *Muscle of Love*, the band are presented with platinum awards for Canadian sales of over 100,000 copies of each of their last four albums.

Neal Smith on the title, Muscle of Love:
We brainstormed and we talked an awful lot about what we did musically and theatrically—we did it every single day—and as far as the ideas and where they came from, it wasn't Alice by himself, it wasn't me, it wasn't Glen, it wasn't Dennis or Michael—we were all throwing out ideas all the time. So we were in the great Northwest and playing either Oregon or Washington state, and we're in the airport driving back. This is when we're getting ready to record Muscle of Love. *And Glen was passed out; he was lying on the limo floor and I think I had my legs over him. He was too out of it to even get in the seat, which often occurred. And I don't know, no matter what, Glen was always engaged in the conversation, and we're talking about somebody, and Glen said, "Oh, they can suck my muscle of love." And that's where the title* Muscle of Love *came from.*

If we threw it out and we liked it and it worked, nobody thought any more of it. So that's what we created. And as far as the press went, man, we gave them so much to work with. A band like ours, they could just spin it and take it off on their own. So yeah, we had a lot of publicity. But basically it was all true stuff. We weren't making it up—except when Alice said he was Eddie Haskell. He was just so bored talking about the same bullshit every time, about the snake and about beer.

Mid-September 1973 – October 12, 1973. Back in LA, the band work at The Record Plant and Sunset Sound on tracks that will comprise their seventh album, *Muscle of Love.*

October 4, 1973. Alice work with Ronnie Spector and Liza Minelli in New York City on backing vocals for "Teenage Lament '74."

October 12, 1973. Police raid the band house in Greenwich and arrest Michael Bruce, Bob Dolin and Mick Mashbir for possession of cannabis with intent to sell; four pounds of the stuff is confiscated.

Dennis Dunaway on the band's relationship with drugs over the years:
Well, we were able to function (laughs). In the real early days, the Pretties for You *days, we were probably like most people in Hollywood, California in the '60s; we were pretty spacey, even on stage. But soon after that, the band really got more professional, going in the studio and stuff. We went in straight and we worked on music straight, in the studio or on stage. However in the later days of excess, that changed for some of the members and not others. To this day, Neal and I pretty much believe that the inspiration comes from the music. Even though people fool themselves and think that the inspiration comes from drugs, you don't need drugs — drugs in the long run hinder you.*

October 19 - 22, 1973. Alice travels to Japan, to do some TV and to promote the forthcoming *Muscle of Love* album. Reported to be the largest press conference ever for an entertainer, Alice's pow-wow with the press was attended by an estimated 200 reporters.

November 19, 1973. The original Alice Cooper group issue what would be their last album together, *Muscle of Love.* Quite impressively, it is the band's seventh album in just a little over four years. Jack Douglas and Jack Richardson share the production credit after the band split with Bob Ezrin, the breaking point being Michael's refusal to accede to Ezrin's request for changes to his song, "Woman Machine."

***Dennis Dunaway on* Muscle of Love:**
I like the album except it really needed Glen. That's why it didn't flow like a complete album. But he had dropped out entirely by then. And for the first time ever, I found myself going against the majority vote, which was to replace him. But the band began as friends and I wouldn't have

given up on any of them. I wouldn't want them to give up on me, and I refused to give up on Glen. We all loved Glen, but the Don Quixote in me refused to allow the big business machine to rule over friendship. I knew he would be lost, and as it turned out, he was. My insistence on keeping him only added to the fractures in the band.

As for the songs, "Hard Hearted Alice," I really like the lyrics on that song. The chorus may have held a more biting significance to us in the band. It had a two-fold insinuation. I've always felt the recording was too soft and whispery. The live version had a lot more dynamics when the guitar solos really kicked in. And although this looks like an album of shorter songs, because of their complex arrangements, "Muscle of Love" and "Man With The Golden Gun" seemed longer than their actual running times. "Crazy Little Child," I thought the style of that song was too typical for us but I liked the challenge of going for that classic bass playing, which I got Jack Richardson's guidance on.

Jack Richardson of course is credited as the producer of Muscle of Love, but Jack never gets credit for co-producing Love It to Death and Killer. The band didn't vote for Bob's departure. This is what happened. We were rehearsing at Nimbus 9 studios in Toronto. We were happy to see Bob walk in because we had just worked out a song. But as soon as we started playing "Woman Machine," he stopped us to make changes. We hadn't even gotten past the intro!

Michael confronted him over it, emotions escalated, and Bob got insulted and walked out. There was no vote and no reason to think it was anything more than a temporary flare-up. But somehow, it turned out to be beyond our resolve. In the end, Muscle of Love shipped fine but a lot of record stores returned them to Warner Brothers claiming the box had a defective stain on it, and of course the stain was intentional. And some stores didn't like the depth of the box because it took up too much space per unit in their record bins. Those returns were a major blow to the album's momentum.

But yeah, Muscle of Love was different because Jack Richardson produced it without Bob Ezrin. Jack Richardson produced The Guess Who, who are renowned in Canada, but like I say, Jack Richardson also produced Love It to Death and Killer. Bob Ezrin was the little boy wonder apprentice. In fact, Richardson was the man who made sure the album came out a viable product.

I don't know, we kind of had a feeling that we were getting back to the way we had worked before we got so on the road-oriented. You know, we were putting out two albums a year, plus coming up with a new concept and new staging and new costuming and everything for each tour, to promote each album. So that had to happen twice a year too. Plus I don't know if there were any bands doing more gigs than we were. We were doing like 65 shows out of 90 days-type thing, and our days off sort of thing we were either traveling to the next city or writing an album, to go back into the studio.

Muscle of Love *co-producer Jack Douglas:*
It was the death album. It was the last group album and everyone knew it, so it was a bit of a downer. The fun part was that we were doing it at Sunset Sound, which is a great studio; I loved it. And the other thing about it was that I had a chance to be hanging out with John Lennon during his adventures in Los Angeles.

Mick Mashbir, *on his uncredited work on* Muscle of Love:
I wrote the verse in "Never Been Sold Before" and co-wrote "Hard Hearted Alice" with Mike. I knew nothing about the music biz so I didn't really know what to ask for. The album credits were on the book cover insert and I was credited as "additional guitar." Shep didn't want the public to know that GB wasn't involved. My favourite moment was when we have been trying to get a basic track for "Muscle" and Neal kept fuckin' up the take. Then after about a dozen or so tracks, I fucked up and Neal threw an empty vodka bottle at me. There was a lot of tension because this was the follow up to Billion Dollar Babies. *As for the production change there, Jack's style and vibe was much more rock 'n' roll than Ezrin's. Don't get me wrong, Ezrin was a trained musician with a lot of talent, but he just wasn't fun to work with. If you can't have fun while workin' or playin', what's the point?*

But in the beginning I was just happy to be a part of it all. After the Billion Dollar Babies *album and tour, GB won an award for his slide work on the "Slick Black Limousine" flexi-disc. That was my work that got me thinking that I might be getting the short end of the stick. During the recording of the* Muscle of Love *album there was talk of making me a permanent member but Alice left the band before that could happen.*

As for why Glen is credited on the album, there were a bunch of writing sessions with only the band. I was not asked to be there. GB was there but I don't know what he contributed if anything. They were trying to get him back into participating and probably thought giving him songwriters credits was a way to keep him interested. But, since he didn't know how to play any of the songs when we were rehearsing for the Muscle of Love *tour—I had to teach him the songs—I don't think he actually "wrote" anything.*

Michael Bruce *on* Muscle of Love, *and music versus theatrics:*
It was a good album, but it's just unfortunately about the box, although it did go to No.20. The box probably should have been lost after the first shipment of records because it was hard to merchandise. You learn

these things after, but that's show biz. As for that photo shoot, we were kind of like sailors on a holiday letting it all hang out. That's kind of where the idea for the cover came from.

And the music, it was the material we had at hand. When the Stones do an album, it's basically a collection of what they've been doing for the last year or six months or whatever. And maybe it's because there was such concentration of stage energy, but I certainly didn't think Queen did a stage show for any of their stuff. But their stuff was certainly very theatrically-oriented. Because I always looked at the sales of the records. You don't hear too much theatrics over the radio do you?

So it's the musicality of the album that to me said it all. We got to No.1, and when you look at all the people behind us when Billion Dollar Babies went No.1, it was pretty impressive. So that's the bottom line. We were selling theatrics when people came to see it, we were selling records when people came to buy records. And they were buying our records so I think it was like love and marriage—can't have one without the other (laughs). It was a partnership of music and theatrics.

But the neat thing was that you were always wondering what the band was going to do when they came to town. And when you think about this, could this have happened ten years later when MTV was out? We would have had to make videos of what we were doing and then you would have lost the whole element of surprise. I think we made it in the time that was our time and it kind of was over when it was over.

Neal Smith on Muscle of Love:

Bob Ezrin, unfortunately, did not get to work with us on that album. I love a lot of songs on that album. It shipped a million copies, and I think 800,000 sold but they had to ship some of them back. Which was in part because of the packaging—they weren't expecting this funny box. There were a lot of people that sent them back because they thought there was a stain on the box. Well, that was intentional, but some people were too freakin' stupid to understand that. So, there were some logistical problems with it that had never occurred before.

But I thought the album was great. I would've loved to work with Bob on it, but we worked with Jack Richardson and Jack Douglas, two really good friends and two great producers. I never thought there was anything wrong with the album; I still love it to this day. "Muscle of Love" is one of my favourites. I'm crankin' out double bass drums on that song all the way through and it's got nice changes.

The only thing I didn't really like on that album was "Crazy Little Child." I thought that, for us, was a little bit out of the norm. Even though for my solo stuff I've recorded songs like that, I think for the Alice Cooper group, I just never really saw where that fit. With "Mary Ann," I understood how that worked, but something that was that different?! It was a cool song in its own way, but I think if it had been replaced with another song it could've changed the colour and the character of that whole album.

Now I don't think anyone in the band wanted us to be a disco band, but a song like "Big Apple Dreamin'," there was a place called The Hippo in New York, a discothèque, in the early to mid '70s. It was actually called The Hippopotamus. We would go there and hang out when we were in New York, because we lived in Connecticut, and where we lived at the time was only about a half-hour drive in to the city. So we would hang out there a lot, be in there a lot on the odd days.

And we thought it'd be a goof to have a song where, it's not with a disco beat, but it's like the Stones when they did "Miss You," just sort of a nod to the music scene that was going on at the time. It was an experiment for us, and I think it's kind of a cool song. And again, an experimental song for us—we weren't that kind of band. But we were always willing to listen to stuff. Lyrically, it was interesting, that's for sure. And then "Woman Machine" is great because of all the percussion. That was a fun song to do, experimenting with different percussion.

Photographer Bob Gruen:
I took a lot of pictures for him. Not so much the album covers but publicity pictures for a number of years. But that sailor shoot, yeah, that's mine. That was their idea, to set up as sailors. They did a short tour in December kind of with a sailor theme, the way sailors drunkenly come ashore and take over the town. We come into your town, want to party it down, that kind of feeling. I mean I just showed up there, they were in sailor suits, so I took pictures.

That's the thing about Alice; he has all kinds of props. It's like a theatrical production. He acts out every single song. In the early days it was a bit more low budget but they were very effective tricks. There's one part of a song where he would take a feather pillow and he had a high-pressure air can, like it looked like a fire extinguisher or something, and he would cut a big hole in the pillow and then hit it with the air from the gas can and literally blow feathers all around the room. Within a second he filled the entire Fillmore with tiny feathers.

And then he would swing a spotlight around his head—again, a simple trick that cost a dollar for a spotlight that you gaffer tape an extension cord at the back—and he would swing it around his head so the light was alternately hitting the feathers and hitting the back wall and swinging around so it would just flash on these feathers. So you had all these thousands of little dots flashing in front of your eyes. Very effective, and the whole thing cost less than five dollars. All you need is a new pillow and some more air every night.

He had all kinds of things. At the end he would hang himself. I think in the early days he had an electric chair. He ended up finally graduating to a guillotine, because Alice plays a lot of roles of nasty, evil people, and he gets punished for it. There's a moral to the story— he doesn't just get away with being an evil person. He advocates evil things and then he's literally executed onstage.

November 25, 1973. Alice meets Lemmy for the first time, at a Hawkwind after-party in New York City. Alice and Lemmy would become notorious denizens of the Rainbow Room on Sunset Strip, but Alice in the late '70s and early '80s, Lemmy in the late '80s until his death in 2015.

December 1, 1973. Black Sabbath issues their fifth album *Sabbath Bloody Sabbath*. Two points of interest: 1) the record's album cover would successful out-frighten anything Alice Cooper would ever do and 2) Geezer Butler, quipping about the vinyl shortage at the time, said that the record was delayed because all the vinyl was getting used up making Alice Cooper records.

Dennis Dunaway:
I don't remember the vinyl shortage but the price of oil definitely went up. And we were on the road and there was the truckers strike, because of the high cost of fuel. We had two semis on that tour, and whenever they would pull into the gas station, there would be all of these truckers picketing. And then they'd have to tell them, "Oh man, this is for a band, rock 'n' roll" and everything, and then they supposedly—this is what I heard—they would be allowed to fuel up. But we had a few gigs where we had makeshift staging. Because we actually had two sets of stages. One would go to one city and set up and do the gig, while the other one was driving to the next city for the next show. And that was a really tough tour because of that.

December 7, 1973. *Muscle of Love* is certified gold, while entering the *Billboard* charts this week at No.76, while *Billion Dollar Babies* was still charting, down at No.158. Concerning sales, in addition to people reacting negatively to the faux water damage stain on the *Muscle of Love* album cover, there was a problem with getting enough records into the stores. Instead of rack-jobbers pushing a dozen copies into a store, there would only be, say, five, because that's what fit in a rack. Then there would be a lag until the album would be restocked. As well, fewer copies fit in the standard cube boxes used to ship records, adding to the cost and the confusion. Ultimately, there was an element of the packaging causing a supply problem rather than a demand problem.

Neal Smith on dealing with the label:
Warner Brothers was always a struggle. If you talk to Dennis or Alice or Shep--especially Shep—every album, they wanted to release us. "Well yeah, 'I'm Eighteen,' Love It to Death, *that was a fluke.*" Love It to Death sells 500,000 copies and goes gold. "That's a fluke. That's the end of you guys." And we'd say one more, so we do Killer, *and it goes gold and platinum, with "Under My Wheels." "Oh, that's a fluke. It didn't really have a hit as big as 'I'm Eighteen,' so I don't know why it sold so many, so we don't give a shit." "Okay, one more." "School's Out" goes double platinum, one of the biggest singles they ever had. And they still think it's a fluke, so we have to renegotiate again to do* Billion Dollar Babies. *I mean, it was always like that.*

December 8 – 31, 1973. Alice Cooper perform what is known as the *Billion Dollar Babies Holiday Tour*, a North American campaign that becomes, essentially, the tour for the *Muscle of Love* album. The set list to split evenly between the two recent albums, with a few earlier hits at it on. Support comes from ZZ Top.

Illusionist James Randi on his guillotine prop:
Alice was quite interested about the history of the guillotine we were using there. That beautiful guillotine; it's the only one of its kind. It was invented by a man named Will Rock, R-O-C-K, a magician of olden times. And I'm talking about the '20s now. And he was famous for this one particular illusion. For many other things too, but he had invented the idea because when—I'm calling him Alice. I do that with the public, but we called him Coop of course—when Coop would have his head fastened in there, he would sing the final lines of the song, "I Love the Dead," and he would be looking out at the audience and they would see that was his head in there, and I'd be holding him by the hair, holding his head up so they could see him. And then I'd simply drop the hair and I'd stand back and look at the audience, and grab the rope and pull the rope and the guillotine blade would come down. And the head that went into the basket was Alice Cooper's head, the real head. Of course Alice was attached to the other end of is as you might imagine, but it's a startling illusion.

And the audience in the front row would gasp—"Oh Jesus!" They thought it had gone wrong. But it hadn't gone wrong. And I'd reach into the basket and pull out the dummy head that we had moulded with the hair and the blood coming from the neck and whatnot, and I would slap it in the face and drop it back into the basket, but it was very, very realistic. It was so realistic that it really shocked the audience. I mean they'd really go wow! A huge shout would come from them when the head went in the basket.

But I knew what I was doing, I got there, I set up the guillotine, I tested it. Made sure that we had four safety gimmicks on it so that it couldn't possibly approach his neck at all, and Coop trusted me. He got into it the very first night and he said, "It's all in your hands." And I said, "Yeah, or it's all in your neck." But no, he was very confident with what was happening, and we didn't add anything else to the show. We had to improvise a few times because some things went wrong. Other things didn't arrive, props didn't arrive and things like that, but we always made it.

And the stage they use these days is much less than the big stage show we had. We had a plexi-glass stage, solid plexi-glass, two inches thick all over the place with mics coming up from underneath it. Spotlights and whatnot rotating like crazy. All kinds of wonderful effects. They can't get that into the theatre by just unpacking the show and putting it into a theatre, you know? Because when we went to these places we were always in big coliseums and places and we would move into just a bare area there and we would construct—they would, I had nothing to do with that—they would construct a huge plexi-glass stage that occupied a couple trailer trucks. It was huge. It was a big, big, big production.

And they were doing very well. They were doing so well that in one of the cities in Europe—I've forgotten which city now—they weighed the money. They actually weighed the money because they didn't have time to count it before they left. Shep was in a hotel room there and he had a scale. We were all laughing. We thought it was so damn funny to weigh your money, you know? They'd have 100 of whatever, kroner notes, and they'd say, "That's 15 pounds, 100 kroner notes; I wonder how much that is? And they only weighed it to get an approximate figure.

Dennis Dunaway on the Billion Dollar Babies stage:
We took our entire stage. The whole stage was ours. The stage was made out of plexi-glass with steps that lit up, that bands have copied since then. The Stones I think even copied that idea. But we had an entire stage that had multi-levels. We had two semi trucks to fit it all in.

We also had our own lighting, which we had taken on the road since the really early days, because we used to take the old iron theatre lights, from theatres that didn't use them anymore. These things weigh a ton. And then Charlie would shimmy up of the posts and clamp the things on, put all of the lighting up like that. These days you have hydraulics and the lights weigh nothing; you can just pick it up with your little finger. And then they have vari-lights where the computer changes each light to whatever colour you want, which isn't what we did.

We had tons and tons of stuff that had to go up on the scaffolding, which our roadies also shipped and set up night after night. We took our own PA, which actually we rented from ShowCo, but that wasn't... we weren't the first band to take our own PA with us, but we were one of the very early ones. And this staging also has scaffolding that went way up high.

We had giant mirror balls—this was before disco. These things must've been four feet in diameter, and then we had chrome and gold mannequins hanging up in the rafters, which I still have in my basement at home. And we had these boxes with stars on them. And it was like a gold box with giant gold glitter on it, and then a white plexiglass star, and then the lights would flash inside these boxes. We had those as well.

But the other props, the more important props, were the mannequins, which I thought were extremely effective. They got chopped up nightly with a hatchet by Alice, which had certain connotations that I'm not sure that the show has now. You know, a rag doll isn't the same as a mannequin. It doesn't have the same powerful imagery and so forth. But I still have the mannequins. I still have the little baby doll mannequins and most of them have hatchet chops in them.

And then we had the guy impersonating Nixon. Oh he was great. I don't know how much he got paid but hanging out with him was a blast; he milked it. One time we were walking with him down the street and there was a traffic jam in New York City and he walked out into the street and started directing traffic and you could see people looking at him going, "Whoa," and they would all do what he wanted them to. When he would go to a restaurant, he would just walk in and point to a table and all these people would see him, freeze for a minute and then the whole place would be abuzz with everybody hustling (laughs). He had a blast with it. If he was sitting still and you would really study him then you could see the differences, but because of his boldness and he would always keep moving, he would really look like Nixon.

Mick Mashbir on the final spate of tour dates with the band:
First let me say that touring in the winter in the Midwest and Northwest is not pleasant. Some days the weather was so severe that

I didn't expect anyone to show up at the arena, but the fans did. We were using a modified version of the Billion Dollar Babies *stage and because of the storms the stage didn't make it to the gig, but the equipment did so we performed as a flat stage rock band. I think those were some of the best shows for me and the band. It was the first time I could go to the edge of the stage and engage the fans. It was hard for Alice because he relied on the props to do his thing and they weren't there. When we went to Rio, we were a flat stage band and we kicked ass. I wish there were some bootlegs of that show. Actually the state of the band was cool because the* Billion Dollar Babies *book hadn't come out yet. I was sharing a house with Mike and Bob Dolin and we continued working on songs in our home studio. That is where I began teaching myself to produce and engineer.*

December 11, 1973. "Teenage Lament '74" is issued as the only single from *Muscle of Love*, achieving a middling No.48 on *Billboard*. The other songs from the record would essentially fade into obscurity, save for the heavy rocking title track, which would become a modest but perennial success at classic rock radio.

1973

December 13, 1973. A show in Toledo, Ohio is halted after only ten minutes when a riot breaks out. The trouble begins when fireworks were lofted onto the stage at ZZ Top's set, and then once Alice Cooper started, a flurry of projectiles prompted the band to walk off and not return.

December 23, 1973. Shep Gordon, who recently had picked up Helen Reddy as a client, throws a party for her at the Troubadour in LA. In attendance are Micky Dolenz, Harry Nilsson and John Lennon. The core of the "the Hollywood vampires" takes shape, referring to Alice and his circle of friends who became drinking buddies about town.

December 26, 1973. Very frightening hit horror movie *The Exorcist* opens for business. Alice attends the premier with the movie's female star, Linda Blair. The two are essentially the top horror stars of 1973, working with different media.

EASY ACTION - The Original Alice Cooper Band

1974

Bizarrely, the Alice Cooper band finishes up at work by playing a clutch of dates in Brazil, April 8th in Rio to be their last. Alice meanwhile finds out how famous he really is, by doing mainstream TV along with a sort of promo/press solo tour of Europe, on behalf of the band still at this point, early in the year.

Kiss issue a debut album and Aerosmith issue their fine second record, *Get Your Wings*. New York Dolls and Montrose both issue their second albums too. Alice Cooper, with their boxy and somewhat tepid melange of radio-friendly rock propositions, recorded only sensibly, all of a sudden don't sound as bold as they still look.

A goofy movie called *Good to See You Again, Alice Cooper* doesn't help the cause although a greatest hits album keeps the façade up and at 'em. Still, behind the scenes, the band is breaking up — slowly. Everybody seems to want to spread their wings and make solo records. No one knows at this point how horribly ineffectual Dennis, Glen, Neal and Michael will be at this, how almost nothing comes of it for decades, and how any record that did manage to fall into record stores would suck.

Nay, it is only Alice who would make this work, something Shep instantly realized as quite likely, with his manager hat on, knowing full well that Alice the complete man, with the name Alice Cooper, is thereabouts 80 to 90% of the band or the brand or the talent at hand, in the eyes of the public.

So, not like he absolutely was thrilled with the situation, but good-natured Alice rolls with the punches and goes back to work, now faced with building a solo career, even if a small part of him might have thought it was temporary. Put together with Dick Wagner, connected by Ezrin, Alice gets to writing what will become, arguably, the record tied with *Billion Dollar Babies* as the best (or at least historically most well regarded) to bear his now legal name.

February 1974. Lou Reed issues his *Rock n Roll Animal* live album. Lou's band includes four future Alice Cooper collaborators, guitarists Dick Wagner and Steve Hunter plus bassist Prakash John and Finnish/Canadian drummer Pentti "Whitey" Glan.

Dick Wagner, on his style versus that of Steve Hunter:
In some ways, we come from the same school. And having played together so much, it's hard on some of those records to tell who's playing what. I think he's more of a technically proficient guitar player and I might play a little more... I don't know if you would call it soulful. I'm more of a rock 'n' roller than he is but he can certainly play rock 'n' roll, obviously. He's got a little more country roots, a little more blues roots. I have blues roots too but I really came up as a rock 'n' roll guitar player.

Steve Hunter on his style versus that of Dick Wagner:
Well it's a little difficult for me to compare against Dick because whatever it was that was different about our playing is what helped us played well together. I think his tone, generally, tends to be a little brighter than mine. Mine's a bit darker and warmer and his is more a searing, singing sort of tone. And the two of us, because of that difference, played well together. You didn't have to think about it too much, because we just worked naturally together and it just seemed to work from the get-go.

As a player, I like to be melodic. I mean, for me, the guitar is a very, very expressive instrument. Because of the nuances it's like a singer. There are so many nuances and so many ways of singing a phrase, and the same with guitar. I love playing melodies on guitar. That was my main love. And that love came out of blues, because blues solos, normally, are pretty melodic. You could almost always sing them. That has been my mainstay, that's what I'm about, that's what my playing is about, and it's a feeling and emotion thing. And I think that's some of the reason why I got hired, especially in the '70s.

And again, tone, I had a friend of mine say, "You know what your tone sounds like? Your tone sounds like a great big black woman singing." And to me, that was the highest compliment that anybody has ever given me on my tone. And I thought oh, okay, that's a woman tone. So it's a woman's voice, and that's what it's always been to me. When somebody said that, I thought, how cool is that? So maybe that's how I would describe my tone.

Early February 1974. Alice takes Cindy on a vacation to Mexico where they both get food poisoning. Alice golfs, having been introduced to the sport on a recent trip to Hawaii.

Mid-February – Early March 1974. Alice is busy being a celebrity. He films a segment for game show *Hollywood Squares*, he films an episode of *Snoop Sisters*, he and Helen Reddy present Stevie Wonder with a Grammy, he meets Elvis, he attends a Kiss record release party, and he generates salacious rumours due to his nights out with Liza Minnelli. Shep and Alice both regret doing the *Hollywood Squares* gig, Shep saying that it showed too much of the real Vince.

Alice might have continued down this path if Bob's and Alice's first plan for Alice's next phase had seen the light of day. The plan was to do a movie about a rock star, named Steven, who is also a pilot, and who crashes his private plane in the snowy mountains. After a couple of months, he has to cannibalize the girl who was with him, with whom he was having an affair. He emerges from his rescue a cannibal serial killer who wakes up and finds that what he thought was a nightmare actually happened. Alice and Bob flew up to meet with director Daniel Mann in Vancouver, where he was filming scenes for *Journey into Fear* on a boat in the harbour. Nothing comes of the Alice vehicle, but Bob and Vincent Price bond over Ezrin's Montecristo No. 2 cigars, with Bob also telling Price that he'd like to put him in a hot rock 'n' roll song one day.

Dennis Dunaway:
I think the day that it lost a lot of its impact was when Alice went on the Hollywood Squares *and* The Muppet Show. *All of a sudden the curiosity factor of, "Who is this?" and "Is this guy for real?" was answered. The answer was no, it's a character; it's not a real guy. But that didn't matter to us because it was entertainment. We were evolving and would have continued to evolve, especially if the band had stayed together long enough to sign that next record deal, which would have brought us the money we needed to do some of our phenomenal concepts that we, up until then, just never could quite afford to do.*

February 18, 1974. Kiss issue their self-titled debut album. All of a sudden, Alice Cooper have some competition. The significance of Kiss' entrance onto the Alice Cooper timeline is that the original Alice Cooper group is over and done with before Kiss even gets going. Still, over the next essentially two-and-a-half years, the battle for the shock rock throne will be waged between Kiss and the Alice of *Welcome to My Nightmare* fame, with the head-to-head not really gathering in intensity until after Kiss' *Alive!* hits in May of 1975. Shep recalls that much of the Alice Cooper band's tour apparatus and supplier base simply shifted over to Kiss, as people associated with the now defunct group looked for employment. He recalls that this was a deliberate procedure, through consultation between himself and Kiss manager Bill Aucoin.

Neal Smith:
Ace Frehley was a good friend of mine, and he still is, and he told me one time plus I heard him say in interviews, "Alice Cooper band, they had one Alice Cooper with the makeup and we wanted four Alice Coopers on stage." And so maybe we didn't take our individual images far enough to really stand out as far as the press went. Still, the bigger the band was getting, everybody individually was getting more attention as well, because I gotta tell ya, Dennis and Glen are two of the most interesting characters on the planet.

Kiss drummer Peter Criss:
Number one, Jerry Nolan from the New York Dolls was my closest friend. I don't know if people know that but we grew up together in Brooklyn. We went to school together. He gave me my first drum lesson. I was jealous, actually, when he got the Dolls because they were so cool. They were such a force in New York to reckon with. Everyone loved the Dolls in New York. It's funny, New York was the only place in the world they were famous. I think their album Too Much Too Soon *was a good title for them because that's what they were.*

But Jerry was the type of guy for who image was extremely important. As important as the music, I think more so with those guys. Looking great, they looked adorable. They looked like chicks with the eyeliner and the chick boots. We tried it, but we looked like we were in drag. Looked like four guys in drag. Gene's a big guy. He looked like an old whore from some whorehouse.

So we realized that makeup, the glam, didn't look great on us. It wasn't going to fly for us. But we knew we wanted to do something that no one else ever did in the world, and we had a chemistry to it, and we wanted to be the Beatles. We wanted to be four guys that each one of us was like John, Paul, Ringo and George, and everyone loved each one of us separately, but all together they loved us like immensely. And we thought, wow, what a great idea. It was kind of like when we saw Alice

Cooper. He was the only one who had makeup on. No one else did. So we thought what would it be like if four guys had the makeup on and the four guys all shared the limelight?

Casablanca Records' Larry Harris
To show you how they upped the ante, we were with Warner Bros. in the beginning with Kiss's first album, and so was Alice. Alice was on Warner Bros. Well Warner Bros. before the first Kiss album came out actually approached us and asked us to ask Kiss to take the makeup off. And we were kind of incredulous because it was, wait a minute, you've got Alice Cooper, he wears makeup, what's the problem with Kiss? Well Warners felt this was over the top and it was too much makeup. And of course we said no, we're not going to do that.

But actually Neil Bogart, so he could cover himself, did say to Bill Aucoin, by the way, Warners asked if you'd take the makeup off, and Bill said absolutely not. So Neil could go back and tell Mo Austin, oh no, the band said they wouldn't do it, even though Neil knew they'd say no anyway. But they wore just that much more. Alice had some makeup on. You could still tell his features, and what did he use, a boa constrictor or something? Big deal. You can walk in the streets of certain cities in America, whether it be San Francisco or LA, in those days, especially San Francisco, and see people with a boa constrictor walking around in the street. And Alice's thing lasted only a short period; I mean him being that outrageous.

March 1, 1974. Aerosmith issue their second album, *Get Your Wings*. Dick Wagner and Steve Hunter play on "Train Kept a Rollin." The album is produced by Jack Richardson and Ray Colcord, with Bob Ezrin credited as executive producer.

Alice Cooper:
It's funny, if there's one band, musically, that's the closest band to Alice Cooper, it would be Aerosmith. When I talk to Joe and Steven Tyler and all these guys, and we talk about our high school days and our 20s, what our roots were, it's exactly the same. We learned every Yardbirds song there was and so did they. If we went into a room and somebody said, you know, "I Ain't Got You" by the Yardbirds or "Shapes of Things" or "Happening Ten Years Time Ago," we learned those songs and they said, "So did we" (laughs). So I could tell by Aerosmith, how their records were, their influence. You know, they listened to Them with Van Morrison, they listened to The Kinks, they listened to The Who. And everybody was influenced by The Beatles.

Dick Wagner:
I think I played on four tracks on that album, actually, including "Same Old Song and Dance." Steve Hunter played on it and so did I. They used us because we were more advanced, we could come up with the stuff more quickly, whatever, and Joe was still learning. I mean, he's a great player now. But it takes a while to get to the stage that Steve and I were playing at, because we both had been doing it a long, long time. We're both on "Train Kept a Rollin'." We're doing the solos and I think we also play on the rhythm tracks too, but Joe also had rhythm tracks on that song.

March 10 – March 21, 1974. Alice takes his celebrity tour overseas, after a band tour was cancelled. He hangs out with Dutch soccer pros (one of which presents him with a gold record for Dutch sales of *Billion Dollar Babies*. In Finland, he winds up meeting Colonel Sanders of KFC fame, and then in Paris, he is spotted nightclubbing with Aristotle Onassis. In London, he drinks with Bernie Taupin, practicing for when both would do that and more back in Los Angeles as part of the Hollywood Vampires.

March 30 – April 8, 1974. The band perform five dates in Brazil. The April 8th show in Rio De Janeiro would represent the last show ever of the original Alice Cooper group.

1974

llusionist James Randi:
That was a close one in Brazil. The kids almost started to die like flies. They were all being pushed by a massive crowd. I never saw such a big crowd of people. They were being pushed up against the supports at the front, the three-quarter inch plywood. And we had to reach down, literally reach down and grab some of the kids and pull them up onto the stage because they were getting crushed. It was a bad scene, very bad scene.

Dennis Dunaway:
We just plain got driven into the ground. We were working so hard, we just couldn't do everything. And also the other thing that is a distraction from art is when you become that popular, how do you sleep when there's people knocking on your door all night? How do you write a song, how do you discuss, even, a song at a breakfast table like we did before we got so popular, when there's a whole bunch of people standing there asking you for your autograph?

It's a bittersweet thing, but it's a wonderful thing; it was our goal. But it makes it very difficult to be able to keep focused on the project at hand, which is the art of it. We did as well as we could but there's a tendency for things to get very complicated as far as logistically being able to sit down. I mean part of the chemistry of that band, and I think any good artistic collaboration, is friction. Because we were all passionate about getting the best thing. And it was all for the right thing, but we had loud discussions and we could drive people out of the rehearsal room. It wasn't anything where we were really upset at each other. We were just voicing our concern for my idea. I think my idea's the best, you think your idea's the best, and then we'd discuss it and try both ideas, and then everybody would vote.

And then the good thing about it was if my idea wasn't the one that we used, that was the end of it. Same with everybody. That was the end of it. But try to do that at a table when there's a bunch of strangers standing around you. There was a lot of that, and the difficulty of being able to sleep. You were in different time zones all the time. You were traveling and moving this giant stage. We didn't have the crews then that people have that set up a show like that at Madison Square Garden these days.

Michael Bruce on the factors contributing to the end of the band:
I really liked Muscle of Love, *but by that time Glen was kind of out of the picture. I think we were going in a direction that Alice didn't feel as comfortable with. I remember Shep came in and said, "Oh, this is the end, man." "What's the problem, Shep?" "Oh, the album just went to No.10; you know, we just had a No.1." And it was ruining his day. You know,* Billion Dollar Babies *was No.1. And that plus the fact that he lost a publishing lawsuit with Herbie Cohen regarding the early material.*

So he was like moving on, moved out to LA. And even though he was still managing us, Alice is out there. And then we get the phone call, he doesn't want to work with us anymore. And I think it was just the writing on the wall. You know, by that time we'd built Alice Cooper up into a namesake, a household word, and he wanted to move on and Shep was ready to do that for him. Even Deborah Harry, in her book, she says the same thing. Shep was constantly trying to get her away from the band. And that's, I guess, what managers sometimes do. They develop that person into a star rather than all the guys in the band.

We had agreed that we weren't going to stop until we were all millionaires. And I think Alice and Shep forgot that we wanted to be millionaires too (laughs). I think back now—I'm going to be 70 on March 16th—our future wasn't carved in rock. It was more like etched in sand. And I think that we weren't going to go past Billion Dollar Babies *even though* Muscle of Love *was the band reaching out, trying to prove itself.*

Alice had become sort of like a Frank Zappa. You know, it was all about him. Any interviews and stuff, he would talk about everybody on the planet before he ever mentioned anybody in the band. And it was disheartening, because we came up through the ranks of the first couple of albums, I sang, and jokingly we used to refer to Alice as the lead maraca player in our band. He wasn't playing an instrument. And he didn't always sing either, you know?

But I have to say, he became a great lyricist and a very, very good singer. But the thing is, we just felt like we wanted to express ourselves a little bit broader, musically, than, you know, Alice stabbing at the heart of the love generation and stuff like that. Which was provocative and it made for great print, but you know, it was just another kid rebelling against either his parents and/or the country, with like when we did "Elected."

But I would write a song like "Desperado," which, I did a lot of lyrics on that, but even the more melodic stuff and softer stuff that we did still had his view of the world. And we wanted to say something, the guys in the band. I know Dennis did. He was very frustrated. Neal did. We basically wanted to take a year off to see what we could do. We were very naïve of the fact that Alice doing a solo album... I think we all thought he was—and this is crazy that I even entertained this thought—but we thought he was going to do his solo album as Vince Furnier (laughs). That wasn't going to happen.

May 1974. *Good to See You Again, Alice Cooper* premieres, after which further editing happens. Essentially this turns out to be a soft launch. Also this month, Alice and Groucho Marx strike up a friendship and an episode of *Hollywood Squares* Alice shot in March airs, with more staggered throughout the coming months.

***Neal Smith on* Good to See You Again, Alice Cooper:**
We had done so much to create an image for the band intentionally and unintentionally that when the movie came out... the lights, the sunlight and we're outside, I was like, "What the fuck?" We've done all this for years to create an image and an attitude and this was like a home movie. It's not very Alice Cooper-ish as far as I'm concerned. When did we ever say we were into comedy, and very, very bad comedy too, by the way? It is what it is and I'm glad it's finally released.

Dennis Dunaway on the evolution of the live show:
We could afford to carry off more of our ideas as the gigs picked up. But obviously it was, okay, well, we executed Alice in an electric chair, what are we going to do next? So that led to the gallows and that led to the guillotine and it would have kept escalating had the original band stayed together, or been allowed to stay together, rather, and moved into the era after we would've signed our first lucrative contract. We could've taken it to the sky but that didn't happen, so unfortunately a lot of ideas prematurely bit the dust. But every tour that we did, every album that we did, and every album cover and the way we dressed, was designed to fit a particular album. It kept evolving just like it did in the days of the VIP, when the band kept changing. And we were the only band that did that, although the Beatles did that. They influenced us as well, because it seemed like every time the Beatles put out a new album they looked like a different band.

June 1974. Reports surface that Alice is planning a solo album, while both Neal and Michael are well along on solo projects. Various sides to the story as to why the band would break-up are offered below, but Shep is adamant that a clutch of problems contributed. He says that the band needed convincing night after night at the end to do the show with full theatrics rather than just go out in jeans. All the years of being disrespected as musicians had built to the point where they wanted to make it all about the music, Mike and Neal in particular. Dennis, famously framed as the artist or the Dali in the group, could have gone either way but ultimately sided with the band. Glen by this point was so hobbled by booze and, posits Alice, downers, Seconals, that he barely ventured an opinion on anything.

Shep also figured that Alice was doing all the work, that the band wouldn't do interviews, the guitars were being played by outside players, the guys would only continue if they were allowed to make solo albums, and that they didn't think Alice was a good singer or lyricist. Furthermore, Shep figures it was the band that broke their gentleman deal that they would continue until they were all millionaires.

Financially, at this point, Shep figures that each equal partner had about a quarter million dollars to his name, so they were far from their goal but not exactly broke, which is sometimes how he characterized the situation (and certainly a truism of sorts most of the time pre-*Billion Dollar Babies*).

There are various reasons that the band was not as well off as the hyperbole would have it. First, they were selling gold and barely platinum but not astronomical numbers of records. Second, the show was very expensive to put on—which the band was all too aware, another point of contention in the break-up being the reticence of the guys to invest in something as elaborate as *Welcome to My Nightmare*. Finally, huge paydays for concert performances were not the norm yet. With ticket prices of only a few dollars, Shep figures at the high end, for a marquee show of the day, a band might get $50,000, and indeed even a tenth of that for a marquee act performing only a few years earlier, at the turn of the '70s.

Dick Wagner:
I really don't know the story in that. He became Alice Cooper. Because originally the whole band was called Alice Cooper and he became the persona. The way it was approached to me was that he wanted to go solo and just be Alice Cooper and that he wanted a better band to be able to play better places. That he wanted something better, something more sophisticated. I don't know if that's all true or not.

August 1974. Warner Bros. issue *Alice Cooper's Greatest Hits*. The album features a Jack Richardson/Bob Ezrin remix of the tracks (most notable on the three *Killer* selections), and a subsequent refloating of the remixed "I'm Eighteen" as a single.

The theme of the artwork suggests that what we're seeing is an auto repair shop that turns into a dancehall at night. Underscoring this is a picture of a business card that reads: "BIG AL'S Garage & Speakeasy. REPAIRS DAILY, DANCING NIGHTLY." As for the staff of the place, Al does front ends and vocals, Mike does tune-ups and plays guitar, G.B. does lube jobs and also plays guitar, Denny does brakes and plays the bass and finally Neal specializes in rear ends by day and drums by night.

Pacific Eye & Ear's Ernie Cefalu on the **Greatest Hits** *cover art:*
Drew Struzan did the outside and Bill Garland did the inside. Two different illustrators, which makes that piece even more desirable, because Drew's only worked on the same piece with another illustrator three times. The first one was the first Star Wars *poster, when he worked with Charlie White, who could draw figures. So Charlie did the background and Drew did the figures. So that piece and two other pieces, Black Oak Arkansas' Early Times that we did. Bill was very much a very versatile illustrator, like Drew, and Drew was a mentor to him, and we all worked at Pacific Eye & Ear together, and they did it like an animation cell. Drew did the background, and then Bill did the cartoon characters on an overlay.*

But what happened was, we did that album cover, we submitted it to the record label, and the record label said, "Well, you know, you're going to have to change... anybody that is still alive, you have to take out." So we had to change 23 faces. And it wasn't just as easy as going in and changing the face. You had to find somebody who was the right

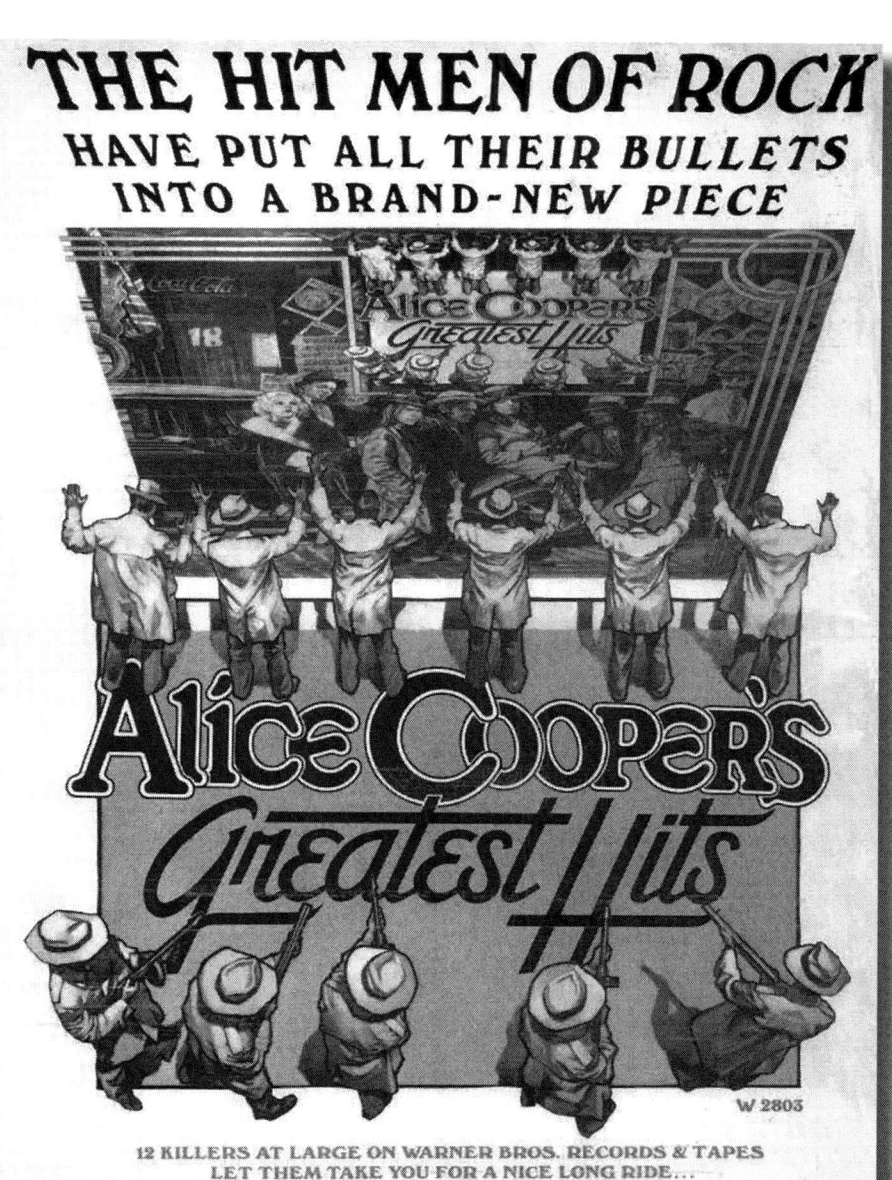

physical height and weight. For example, on the front, I think we have Judy Garland dancing with Alan Ladd. Well, originally it was Mickey Rooney. Judy Garland and Mickey Rooney were teenagers together in movies—all the Andy Hardy movies and stuff—and they were sort of a known couple so it was a no-brainer to have Judy Garland dancing with Mickey Rooney.

Well, when they said Mickey Rooney is still alive, you can't have him in there, you have to change it, we had to find somebody who is his same height and weight and physical makeup. So it wasn't just as easy as changing heads. And those two drawings are graphite pencil. So it's not that easy to work with graphite, once you start erasing. So it was really tedious. You can't just go in an take the face out and just redraw it over. You had to lift the graphite that was on the board off, and then redraw on top of it. So it's an interesting cover. It was really neat watching Drew do the work.

Late August 1974. Dennis weds long-time girlfriend Cindy. They are still together 45 years later. Meanwhile, Alice is in Toronto working with Bob Ezrin and session musicians on his first solo album. Work winds up mid-September.

September 18, 1974. *Good to See You Again, Alice Cooper* receives a full-blown official launch with extensive merchandising and ad campaigns.

November 12, 1974. After a steady climb, *Greatest Hits* reaches a lofty No.3 on the Billboard charts. But, alas, the band that crafted these anthems is no more.

Michael Bruce on the breakup of the band, beginning with Glen Buxton:
You can't say the situation with Glen wasn't a factor. On the other hand you can't say that was the only reason. He just wasn't doing his job anymore and we tried to get him some help, but he just didn't want it. I think everybody decided to go on their own. I know I did and when we wanted to get back together, I don't think Alice wanted to do it without Glen. So, he just went on and did his own thing, which in the long run turned out pretty good for me being one of the main writers. Every time Alice plays, he's promoting the catalogue, so I've done well. He's kept it alive.

But Glen wasn't really doing his part and when we went in to do any recording he wasn't writing. He was just doing whatever Glen would do and then we'd go into the studio and have these songs written and there would be no Glen part. So Wagner or Steve Hunter or Mick Mashbir or Bob Dolin or whoever—we had a bunch of different people come in, not just Wagner—would come in and they would provide something that Glen would do. Glen carried on and he was on the Billion Dollar Babies tour 'til the end, but his participation was somewhat limited. But for Muscle of Love, Glen was ill and in the hospital and when he came out we didn't know if he'd know his stuff or not and we basically had to be prepared either way, so that was why Mick Mashbir came in.

Dennis Dunaway:
I didn't want to, but being completely driven into the ground physically and emotionally, we had no choice but to take a break. We all agreed to take one year off and then we would get back together and do our next Alice Cooper album. That wasn't unreasonable, and it was a solid investment for the band's future. Never in a billion years would I have thought that Alice would take the ball and run with it.

"School's Out" was the biggest selling single in the history of Warner Bros. Records. Our Billion Dollar Babies album was No.1 in the US and the UK. We were on the cover of Forbes magazine for topping the Rolling Stones' and Led Zeppelin's tour records. We had worked incredibly hard for a decade. And I've never squandered any money away. So we were questioning where the money was, which is very different than wanting to cash out. Their eventual story, that "they wanted to cash out" rationalization, came way after the "they refused to do theatrics" campaign, which was the first excuse. But yeah, first it was the idea that after our break, we thought we would all return refreshed, sign a significant new record deal, and finally have the funds to do what we had always strived toward.

But the initial breakup, I think the original band members were the last to know about it. And really, because I think we were kind of being kept on hold in case people rejected Alice as a solo artist. Or in case the record company rejected Alice as whatever. So we thought the Battle Axe album was going to be the next Alice Cooper album. We sunk so much money into that gigantic stage, and meanwhile, like I say, we're reading about how we refused to do theatrics. We're like, what?! We're building this gigantic stage with hydraulics and everything, with a boxing ring that comes out from under the drum riser and all that. And we're reading interviews that we refused to do theatrics.

Anyway, when it came down to it, there we were being stranded without Alice, and then we had this gigantic show. We couldn't headline because Alice wasn't with us. And nobody would have us open for them. So it was a dark period. There was a dark period where I would sit in a dark room and kind of pout and be grouchy and everything. But you know, I had Cindy. Cindy would come in and kick me in the butt and tell me to snap out of it, you know, like **Moonstruck**: *"Snap out of it!"* (laughs). I was bitter about friendships. Shep and Alice, I thought, were my best friends—how could they do this? And I was bitter about the fans, kind of letting it just happen without saying much. In my opinion. And then nobody ever calling us to find out, to do an interview with us, and let us say, "What do you mean we don't want to do theatrics?" And then also the music business. Our record company bailed on us. So I was bitter about the music business too.

You know, and then seeing Alice from the crowd, it's typical for an entertainer in the audience to be thinking, I should be up there, you know? That's standard. But I'm not too bad that way. At first, say, Welcome to My Nightmare and stuff, it was kind of disturbing.

In fact I wrote a song about it. I wrote a song right after one of the first times I saw other people doing our thing, called "Friend." And basically it's about how, especially when Neal and I would be in the audience, seeing people in the audience, younger fans, who wouldn't even know who we were, right? You know, Alice's current touring band are all... they play the songs differently than we did; they do a good job, but they make it their own. I watch the show and of course, if I had a clipboard, I would be writing things down about... and I do this with any band that I watch. In my head I'm thinking about how I could make it better and how they should do *that* instead of that. There's a lot of that going on. But on the flipside of the coin, I'm thinking, we wrote those songs 50 years ago, and there is still a room—big giant arena full of people—that are singing along with it, you know? So in the end, I would also sit there and I would feel proud of what we did.

I started doing these monster conventions and stuff where they would have celebrities that would meet fans and sign things for them. And it seemed like when I first started doing them, which is maybe in the '80s, you would have parents bringing a kid to meet me, right? And the kid obviously looked like he had something better to do (laughs). And then it changed. It's like, ten years after that, all of a sudden because of "School's Out," they were brought there by their parents, and it's the parents who are looking at me like, "Oh boy, who is this guy?" you know? But that's the great thing. I mean, thank God for "School's Out" and "Eighteen" too, in the Midwest. There are little kids everywhere that on the last day of school, they hear our song.

Discography

Very simple discography for y'all. The original Alice Cooper band didn't even do a live album, with the only wrinkle being the emergence of a greatest hits album, which closes our story. I'm keeping this simple, because a lot of the trivia associated with these records is covered in the entries, right? But I also realize that given the structure of the book, what follows is necessary—or at least really, really handy—in terms of providing a tight roadmap of the records cranked out by the original band. As well, everything here gets a side 1/side 2 designation to reflect that all of these albums first came out long before there were CDs. In any event, here it is, the studio albums in order, with song titles, plus *Greatest Hits*.

Pretties for You
(June 1969)

Side 1:
1. Titanic Overture
2. 10 Minutes Before the Worm
3. Sing Low, Sweet Cherio
4. Today Mueller
5. Living
6. Fields of Regret

Side 2:
1. No Longer Umpire
2. Levity Ball
3. B.B. on Mars
4. Reflected
5. Apple Bush
6. Earwigs to Eternity
7. Changing Arranging

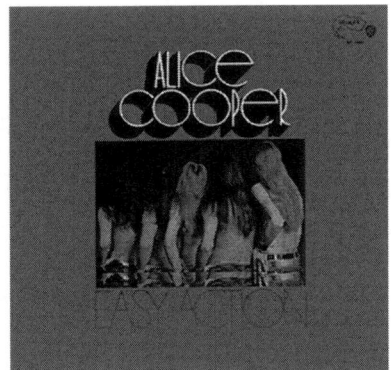

Easy Action
(March 1970)

Side 1:
1. Mr. & Misdemeanor
2. Shoe Salesman
3. Still No Air
4. Below Your Means

Side 2:
1. Return of the Spiders
2. Laughing at Me
3. Refrigerator Heaven
4. Beautiful Flyaway
5. Lay Down and Die, Goodbye

Love It to Death
(March 1971)

Side 1:
1. Caught in a Dream
2. I'm Eighteen
3. Long Way to Go
4. Black Juju

Side 2:
1. Is It My Body
2. Hallowed Be My Name
3. Second Coming
4. Ballad of Dwight Fry
5. Sun Arise

Discography

Killer
(November 1971)

Side 1:
1. Under My Wheels
2. Be My Lover
3. Halo of Flies
4. Desperado

Side 2:
1. You Drive Me Nervous
2. Yeah, Yeah, Yeah
3. Dead Babies
8. Killer

School's Out
(June 1972)

Side 1:
1. School's Out
2. Luney Tune
3. Gutter Cat vs. the Jets
4. Street Fight
5. Blue Turk

Side 2:
1. My Stars
2. Public Animal No.9
3. Alma Mater
4. Grande Finale

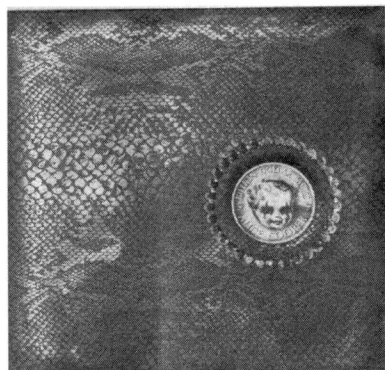

Billion Dollar Babies
(February 1973)

Side 1:
1. Hello Hooray
2. Raped and Freezin'
3. Elected
4. Billion Dollar Babies
5. Unfinished Sweet

Side 2:
1. No More Mr. Nice Guy
2. Generation Landslide
3. Sick Things
4. Mary Ann
5. I Love the Dead

Muscle of Love
(November 1973)

Side 1:
1. Big Apple Dreamin' (Hippo)
2. Never Been Sold Before
3. Hard Hearted Alice
4. Crazy Little Child

Side 2:
1. Working Up a Sweat
2. Muscle of Love
3. Man with the Golden Gun
4. Teenage Lament '74
5. Woman Machine

Discography

Greatest Hits
(August 1974)

Side 1:
1. I'm Eighteen
2. Is It My Body
3. Desperado
4. Under My Wheels
5. Be My Lover
6. School's Out

Side 2:
1. Hello Hooray
2. Elected
3. No More Mr. Nice Guy
4. Billion Dollar Babies
5. Teenage Lament '74
6. Muscle of Love

Sources

Most of the interview footage used in the compilation of this book, along with the follow-up, *Feed My Frankenstein: Alice Cooper, the Solo Years*, has come from my own archive of interviews with these guys. I've interviewed many of these folks multiple times, include of course Alice Cooper for most of the records over the past 25 years, plus Carmine Appice, Gavin Baddeley, Johnny Bee, Ernie Cefalu, Jimmy DeGrasso, Jack Douglas, Dennis Dunaway, Bob Ezrin, Dani Filth, Kim Fowley, Bob Gruen, Beau Hill, Steve Hunter, Damon Johnson, King Diamond, K.J. Knight, Bob Livingstone, Dee Long, Allan MacMillan, Dave Mustaine, John Nitzinger, Mike Pinera, Chris Poland, James Randi, Graham Shaw, Derek Sherinian, John Sinclair, Neal Smith, Cameron Strang, Drew Struzan, Jaan Uhelski, Michael Wagener and Dick Wagner.

Additional quotes also by kind permission from Sam Dunn, Tim Henderson (bravewords.com), Kevin Julie, Mitch Lafon (check out Mitch's Youtube channel, One on One with Mitch Lafon), Drew Masters, MetalRules.com (as usual, it's Marko Syrjala who is on the case—thanks Marko!), Steve Newton (EarofNewt.com), Brian Rademacher (rockeyez.com), Sydney Taylor (check out her awesome an' Alice-heavy Metal from the Inside podcast at metalfromtheinside.com) and Jeb Wright (classicrockrevisted.com).

I'd like to also acknowledge the excellent work of the SickthingsUK site, at sickthingsuk.co.uk for years at the top of the heap in terms of being a great info-packed fan site on any level, on anybody. Seriously, few sites on any band have ever been better. The timelines were a great reference as was the tour archive and press archive, although in terms of press directly referenced in this book, I stuck to my own stuff and the interviews of basically good buddies of mine, as cited above.

Finally, special thanks to Agustin Garcia de Paredes who applied his eagle eye to a copy edit of this book.

About the Author

At approximately 7900 (with over 7000 appearing in his books), Martin Popoff has unofficially written more record reviews than anybody in the history of music writing across all genres. Additionally, Martin has penned approximately 115 books on hard rock, heavy metal, progressive rock, punk, classic rock and record collecting. He was Editor-in-Chief of the now retired Brave Words & Bloody Knuckles, Canada's foremost heavy metal publication for 14 years, and has also contributed to Revolver, Guitar World, Goldmine, Record Collector, bravewords.com, lollipop.com and hardradio.com, with many record label band bios and liner notes to his credit as well. Additionally, Martin has been a regular contractor to Banger Films, having worked for two years as researcher on the award-winning documentary *Rush: Beyond the Lighted Stage*, on the writing and research team for the 11-episode Metal Evolution and on the ten-episode Rock Icons, both for VH1 Classic. Additionally, Martin is the writer of the original heavy metal genre chart used in *Metal: A Headbanger's Journey* and throughout the Metal Evolution episodes. He has solo-blabbed all over his own long-running audio podcast, History in Five Songs with Martin Popoff, for a number of years, and runs a Youtube channel with his buddy Marco D'Auria called The Contrarians. He is also a guest every Friday morning at 9:00 AM on Pete Pardo's Sea of Tranquility Youtube channel. Martin currently resides in Toronto and can be reached through martinp@inforamp.net or www.martinpopoff.com.

Martin Popoff – A Complete Bibliography

2022: Easy Action: The Original Alice Cooper Band, Lively Arts: The Damned Deconstructed, Yes: A Visual Biography II: 1982 – 2022, Bowie at 75, Dream Evil: Dio in the '80s, Judas Priest: A Visual Biography, UFO: A Visual Biography

2021: Hawkwind: A Visual Biography, Loud 'n' Proud: Fifty Years of Nazareth, Yes: A Visual Biography, Uriah Heep: A Visual Biography, Driven: Rush in the '90s and "In the End," Flaming Telepaths: Imaginos Expanded and Specified, Rebel Rouser: A Sweet User Manual

2020: The Fortune: On the Rocks with Angel, Van Halen: A Visual Biography, Limelight: Rush in the '80s, Thin Lizzy: A Visual Biography, Empire of the Clouds: Iron Maiden in the 2000s, Blue Öyster Cult: A Visual Biography, Anthem: Rush in the '70s, Denim and Leather: Saxon's First Ten Years, Black Funeral: Into the Coven with Mercyful Fate

2019: Satisfaction: 10 Albums That Changed My Life, Holy Smoke: Iron Maiden in the '90s, Sensitive to Light: The Rainbow Story, Where Eagles Dare: Iron Maiden in the '80s, Aces High: The Top 250 Heavy Metal Songs of the '80s, Judas Priest: Turbo 'til Now, Born Again! Black Sabbath in the Eighties and Nineties

2018: Riff Raff: The Top 250 Heavy Metal Songs of the '70s, Lettin' Go: UFO in the '80s and '90s, Queen: Album by Album, Unchained: A Van Halen User Manual, Iron Maiden: Album by Album, Sabotage! Black Sabbath in the Seventies, Welcome to My Nightmare: 50 Years of Alice Cooper, Judas Priest: Decade of Domination, Popoff Archive – 6: American Power Metal, Popoff Archive – 5: European Power Metal, The Clash: All the Albums, All the Songs

2017: Led Zeppelin: All the Albums, All the Songs, AC/DC: Album by Album, Lights Out: Surviving the '70s with UFO, Tornado of Souls: Thrash's Titanic Clash, Caught in a Mosh: The Golden Era of Thrash, Rush: Album by Album, Beer Drinkers and Hell Raisers: The Rise of Motörhead, Metal Collector: Gathered Tales from Headbangers, Hit the Lights: The Birth of Thrash, Popoff Archive – 4: Classic Rock, Popoff Archive – 3: Hair Metal

2016: Popoff Archive – 2: Progressive Rock, Popoff Archive – 1: Doom Metal, Rock the Nation: Montrose, Gamma and Ronnie Redefined, Punk Tees: The Punk Revolution in 125 T-Shirts, Metal Heart: Aiming High with Accept, Ramones at 40, Time and a Word: The Yes Story

2015: Kickstart My Heart: A Mötley Crüe Day-by-Day, This Means War: The Sunset Years of the NWOBHM, Wheels of Steel: The Explosive Early Years of the NWOBHM, Swords and Tequila: Riot's Classic First Decade, Who Invented Heavy Metal?, Sail Away: Whitesnake's Fantastic Voyage

2014: Live Magnetic Air: The Unlikely Saga of the Superlative Max Webster, Steal Away the Night: An Ozzy Osbourne Day-by-Day, The Big Book of Hair Metal, Sweating Bullets: The Deth and Rebirth of Megadeth, Smokin' Valves: A Headbanger's Guide to 900 NWOBHM Records

2013: The Art of Metal (co-edit with Malcolm Dome), 2 Minutes to Midnight: An Iron Maiden Day-by-Day, Metallica: The Complete Illustrated History, Rush: The Illustrated

History, Ye Olde Metal: 1979, Scorpions: Top of the Bill - updated and reissued as Wind of Change: The Scorpions Story in 2016

2012: Epic Ted Nugent, Fade To Black: Hard Rock Cover Art of the Vinyl Age, It's Getting Dangerous: Thin Lizzy 81-12, We Will Be Strong: Thin Lizzy 76-81, Fighting My Way Back: Thin Lizzy 69-76, The Deep Purple Royal Family: Chain of Events '80 – '11, The Deep Purple Royal Family: Chain of Events Through '79 - reissued as The Deep Purple Family Year by Year books

2011: Black Sabbath FAQ, The Collector's Guide to Heavy Metal: Volume 4: The '00s (co-authored with David Perri)

2010: Goldmine Standard Catalog of American Records 1948 – 1991, 7th Edition

2009: Goldmine Record Album Price Guide, 6th Edition, Goldmine 45 RPM Price Guide, 7th Edition, A Castle Full of Rascals: Deep Purple '83 – '09, Worlds Away: Voivod and the Art of Michel Langevin, Ye Olde Metal: 1978

2008: Gettin' Tighter: Deep Purple '68 – '76, All Access: The Art of the Backstage Pass, Ye Olde Metal: 1977, Ye Olde Metal: 1976

2007: Judas Priest: Heavy Metal Painkillers, Ye Olde Metal: 1973 to 1975, The Collector's Guide to Heavy Metal: Volume 3: The Nineties, Ye Olde Metal: 1968 to 1972

2006: Run for Cover: The Art of Derek Riggs, Black Sabbath: Doom Let Loose, Dio: Light Beyond the Black

2005: The Collector's Guide to Heavy Metal: Volume 2: The Eighties, Rainbow: English Castle Magic, UFO: Shoot Out the Lights, The New Wave of British Heavy Metal Singles

2004: Blue Öyster Cult: Secrets Revealed! – update and reissue 2009); updated and reissued as Agents of Fortune: The Blue Öyster Cult Story 2016, Contents Under Pressure: 30 Years of Rush at Home & Away, The Top 500 Heavy Metal Albums of All Time

2003: The Collector's Guide to Heavy Metal: Volume 1: The Seventies, The Top 500 Heavy Metal Songs of All Time

2001: Southern Rock Review

2000: Heavy Metal: 20th Century Rock and Roll, The Goldmine Price Guide to Heavy Metal Records

1997: The Collector's Guide to Heavy Metal

1993: Riff Kills Man! 25 Years of Recorded Hard Rock & Heavy Metal

See martinpopoff.com for complete details and ordering information.